IMAGES
Building English Vocabulary
Through Etymology
Introduction

Peter R. Beaven with Nikhil Deliwala

Images for Building English Vocabulary through Etymology
Introduction

Peter R. Beaven with Nikhil Deliwala

Editor: Christian Waters

Version 1.0 Revised: 22 August 2018

Published by
The Cheshire Press
an imprint of The Cheshire Group
Andover, MA 01810
www.cheshirepress.com

All rights reserved. No part of this book may be reproduced or transmitted in any form or by any means without the express written consent of the author, except for the inclusion of quotations in reviews.

Copyright ©2017 by Beaven & Associates

ISBN: 978-1-7327489-0-3

Library of Congress: 2016962689

Printed in the United States of America

Beaven & Associates
3 Dundee Park, #202 A
Andover, MA 01810
978 475-5487
www.beavenandassociates.com

Beaven, Peter R.; Deliwala, Nikhil
Images for Building English Vocabulary through Etymology
Introduction

IMAGES

When an object catches our eye, we want to know it and name it, and when we seek to know a word's meaning, we try to see it in our mind's eye. Whether first we see and then name, or vice versa, the image behind a word helps us learn vocabulary. An effective way to master a challenging word in English is to see the image of the word in its classical root, a three thousand year old picture that still speaks to us today, vibrant and simple in its original Latin family. Images takes the student back to the root's simple meaning, its home, its family and the multiple and varied members of the family. Through Images a student can watch his English vocabulary grow and realize that a picture is worth a thousand words.

The Building English Vocabulary series guides a student through classical prefixes and roots that underlie challenging vocabulary. While Images I through III take the student through the Roman past, and Images IV the Greek, Images, the Introduction, starts the journey with etymology from the Latin, the origins of that half of the English language that appeals to the intellect and sets a foundation for understanding great literature.

Images Introduction is part of the Series Building English Vocabulary with Etymology from Latin

From Abs to Ultra

From Acri to Mit

From Moneo to Volvo

Throughout Images, a student avails himself of time proven exercises to connect the prefixes and roots with the meanings of words. A student will discover that from just one root spring a variety of new words that in time yield an exponential growth in his knowledge of English. From cumulative review tests throughout the book, a student can gauge his success in mastering challenging vocabulary.

Etymology in Building English Vocabulary

The word "etymology" refers to tracing the origin and historical development of words in a language. How is a given word derived from an earlier word or words in a native or foreign language?

Just as we can "parse" or break up a sentence into parts of speech - noun, verb, adjective, adverb, etc. - so we can deconstruct a given word into its constituent meaning elements and trace their origins. For example, the word "etymology" consists of an original Greek root "etymon" - meaning "an earlier form of the same word" - and the Greek "logos" - meaning "word" or "speech", which took on the later form "-ology" - meaning "study of." So, there we have the etymology of the word "etymology."

Studying the etymology of vocabulary words reveals repeated word-formation patterns, so that we can dissect or guess the meanings of unfamiliar words based on their constituent prefixes and roots that we have encountered earlier. For example, by knowing that the prefix "pre-" means "before" or "ahead" and that "dict" is rooted in "speaking" or "saying," we can surmise that "predict" means to foretell or talk about something before it happens.

The English language is built primarily from the Anglo-Saxon (Germanic), Latin, and Greek languages. Historically, the Angles and Saxons drove out the original Celtic inhabitants and occupied Britain, and after a few brief occupations by the Roman legions, in 1066 the tribes were defeated by the Norman leader William the Conqueror, who spoke French - a language derived almost entirely from Latin. Over time, the Germanic and Latinate languages blended to become what we know as English.

Because Latin is such a fundamental basis of English and because Latin is built from a regular system of "reusable" prefixes and roots, studying these elements makes learning vocabulary more efficient. Instead of learning word meanings in isolation, by learning a standard set of Latin prefixes and common roots we can "mix and match" to learn several new words or variations. The study of etymology thus can accelerate the expansion of our vocabulary while helping us appreciate how meanings and usages have evolved.

For example, knowing that the root "gress" means "step" or "advance", and knowing a series of prefixes, we can deduce word meanings:

Prefix	Meaning	Example
"ad"	= to, toward	address ("g" in "gress" becomes a "d")
"co, con"	= together	congress (movement together)
"di"	= split	digress (move away from)
"e, ex"	= out of, from	egress (way out, exit)
"in"	= in, into	ingress (way in, entrance)
"pro"	= forward, for	progress (move forward)
"re"	= back	regress (move backward)
"trans"	= across, over	transgress (move across)

ETYMOLOGY IN BUILDING ENGLISH VOCABULARY

So many of the words in English that relate to the intellect, words that make us pause to think and study, come from the Greek. The Roman conquest of Greece and admiration for its culture led to the incorporation of many Greek terms into Latin. So we make a point of studying Greek roots and prefixes as well. For example, the Greek root "pathos" means "feeling" or "suffering", from which come such words as:

"a"	= not	apathy (not caring)
"anti"	= against	antipathy (dislike or hostility)
"em, en"	= into, in	empathy (sharing in another's feeling)
"sym"	= together, with	sympathy (feeling sorrow for another)

In addition, there are other English words based on the same root, such as "pathetic", "pathology", "pathos", and so on.

Consider the common prefixes and cross-connections of the words below:

telecommute	micron	automaton	extrasensory	intercede
telegraph	micrograph	autobiography	extravehicular	intercept
telephone	microphone	automobile	extraterrestrial	interrupt
telescope	microscope	autograph	extraordinary	interdict
television	micromanage	autonomy	extralegal	intervene

or the roots "duc" ("lead"), "fer" ("bear, bring"), "port" ("carry") and "vers" ("turn") as below:

aqueduct	confer	report	converse
conduct	defer	deport	diverse
deduce	refer	transport	reverse
duct	transfer	teleport	adverse
ductile	prefer	airport	perverse
educate	offer	purport	obverse
induce		export	averse
produce		import	inverse
seduce		comport	transverse
viaduct		support	controversy

In the series Building English Vocabulary, a student discovers that from just one Latin or Greek root springs an exponential growth in his vocabulary, sharpened tools to articulate the written or spoken word. A broader knowledge of English leads him to greater ties to the shared cognates of French, Spanish, Italian, and Greek. A stronger grasp of English brings a deeper understanding of the plays of Shakespeare, the novels of Dickens, the essays of Emerson, the poetry of Emily Dickinson, or the oratory of Lincoln and Churchill., who as national leaders, marshaled the English language — the former to invoke peace — the latter to evoke resolve for impending battles, the victories of which in the post bellum of the twentieth century helped thrust English into its role as the lingua franca of the modern world.

Contents

Lesson I	**Ab to Bi**	7
Lesson II	**Circus to Duo**	19
Lesson III	**Equi to Inter**	30
Lesson IV	**Magnus to Pre**	42
Lesson V	**Primus to Sub**	54
Lesson VI	**Acri to Apt**	66
Lesson VII	**Arm to Capt**	77
Lesson VIII	**Caput to Civis**	89
Lesson IX	**Clam to Cred**	101
Lesson X	**Cresc to Domus**	112
Lesson XI	**Dorm to Figur**	124
Lesson XII	**Firm to Gen**	136
Lesson XIII	**Grad to Junct**	147
Lesson XIV	**Labor to Ludus**	159
Lesson XV	**Manus to Mov, Mot**	171
Lesson XVI	**Mont to Nunc**	182
Lesson XVII	**Oculist to Ped**	194
Lesson XVIII	**Pet to Prehend**	206
Lesson XIX	**Press to Rot**	218
Lesson XX	**Sacra to Sens, Sent**	230
Lesson XXI	**Simil to Spect**	241
Lesson XXII	**Spir to Tempor**	252
Lesson XXIII	**Ten, Tain to Unda**	263
Lesson XXIV	**Urb to Vert**	275
Lesson XXV	**Via to Volv**	287
Answer Key (Answers for B Exercises begin on Page 311)		298
Index		320

Lesson I

Abduct

Fr. Enlever
It. Rapire
Port. Abduzir
Sp. Abducir

AB-, ABS-

from, away

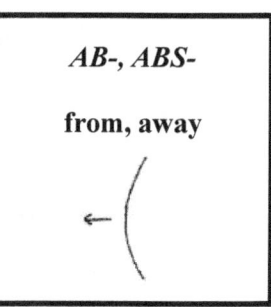

DUC-

to lead

Definition: **v.** to take away illegally by force or deception; to kidnap

Sentence: Paris <u>abducted</u> Helen from Sparta and fled with her to Troy

---

Abhor

Fr. Abhorrer (lit.)
It. Aborrire
Port. Aborrecer
Sp. Aborrecer

AB-, ABS-

from, away

HOR-

to shudder

Definition: **v.** to regard with loathing

Sentence: She became a vegetarian because she abhorred the slaughter of animals.

Abrasion

Fr. Abrasion
It. Abrasione
Port. Abrasão
Sp. Abrasión

AB-, ABS-

from, away

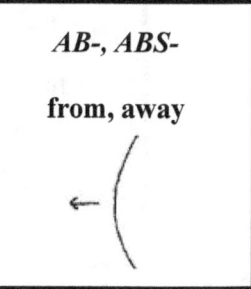

RAD-

to scrape, shave

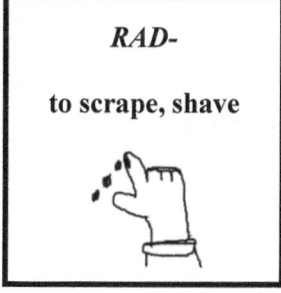

Definition: **n.** the action of, process of, or result of wearing away by friction and rubbing

Sentence: A slip on the asphalt caused the man to suffer a knee abrasion

Abrupt

Fr. Abrupte
It. Improvviso
Port. Abrupto
Sp. Abrupto

AB-, ABS-

from, away

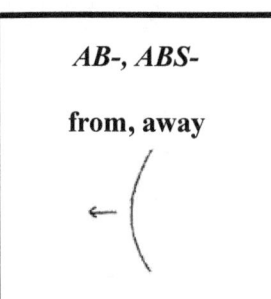

RUMP-, RUPT-

to break

Definition: **adj.** sudden and unexpected; brief to the point of rudeness

Sentence: Feeling suddenly ill, the diner abruptly left the table.

Absorb

Fr. Absorber
It. Assorbire
Port. Absorver
Sp. Absorber

AB-, ABS-

from, away

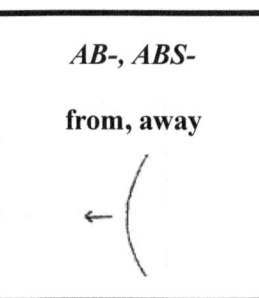

SORB-

to suck in

Definition: **v.** to soak up; to assimilate a lesser entity into a larger one

Sentence: Distracted by the music, the pupil did not absorb the lesson.

Accord

Fr. S'accorder (avec)
It. Accordare
Port. Acordar
Sp. Acordar

AC-, AD-

to, toward

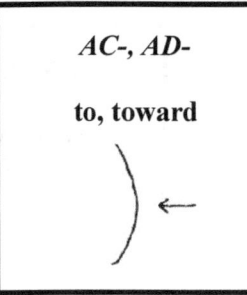

CORD-

heart, mind, spirit

Definition: **v.** to give or grant someone power or recognition
n. an official agreement or treaty; a meeting of the minds

Sentence: Hostilities ceased when the two sides reached a peace accord.

Adaptable

Fr. Capable (de), S'adapter (à)
It. Adattabile
Port. Adaptável
Sp. Adaptable

AC-, AD-
to, toward

APT-
to fit

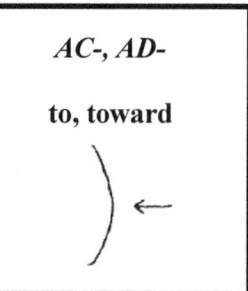

Definition: **adj.** able to adjust to new conditions

Sentence: Humans are adaptable to all kinds of climates.

Adhere

Fr. Adhérer
It. Aderire
Port. Aderir
Sp. Adherir

AC-, AD-
to, toward

HER- HES--
to stick

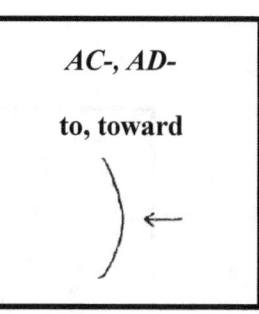

Definition: **v.** to stick fast to; to believe in and follow the practices of

Sentence: Orthodox Jews adhere to strict dietary laws.

Adjacent

Fr. Adjacent
It. Adiacente
Port. Adjacente
Sp. Adyacente

AC-, AD-
to, toward

JAC-, JEC-
to throw

Definition: **adj.** next to or adjoining something else; having a common vertex, side, or boundary

Sentence: Massachusetts is adjacent to five other states.

Adversary

Fr. Adversaire
It. Avversario
Port. Adversário
Sp. Adversario

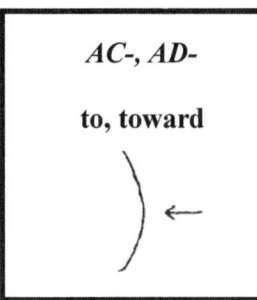

AC-, AD- — to, toward

VERT- — to turn

Definition: **n.** an opponent or enemy

Sentence: Barack Obama overcame his adversary, John McCain, to win the presidency in 2008.

Ambidextrous

Fr. Ambidextre
It. Ambidestro
Port. Ambidestro
Sp. Ambidiestro

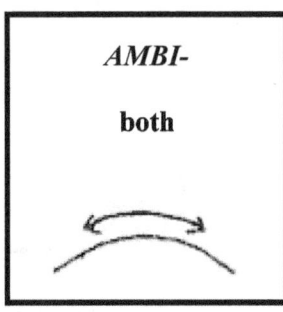

AMBI- — both

DEXTER- — right handed

Definition: **adj.** equally able to use the right and left hands

Sentence: Grover Cleveland, who was ambidextrous, could write with both hands simultaneously.

Ambiguous

Fr. Ambigu
It. Ambiguo
Port. Ambíguo
Sp. Ambiguo

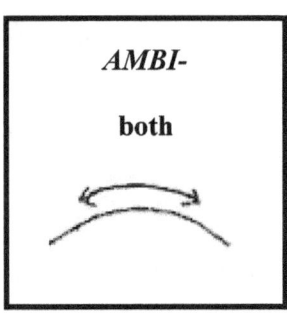

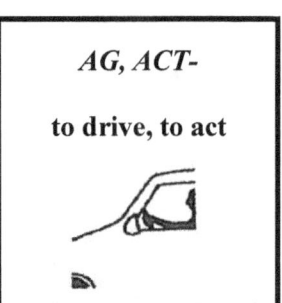

AMBI- — both

AG, ACT- — to drive, to act

Definition: **adj.** having more than one meaning, open to different interpretations

Sentence: The word 'sanction' is ambiguous as it has two opposite meanings.

Ante meridian

Fr. Du matin
It. Antimeridiano
Port. Ante meridiem
Sp. Ante meridiem

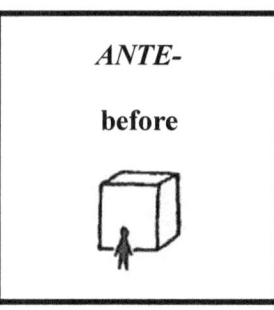

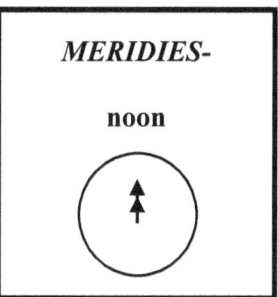

Definition: **adj.** of, relating to, or taking place in the morning; A.M

Sentence: Breakfast is normally an ante meridian meal.

Anticipate

Fr. Anticiper
It. Anticipare
Port. Antecipar
Sp. Anticipar

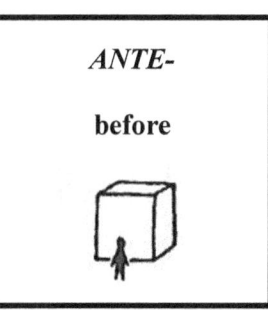

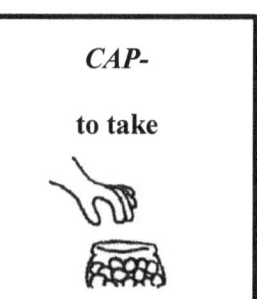

Definition: **v.** to be aware of in advance; to prepare for; to look forward to

Sentence: Hannibal was able to anticipate the Romans' moves and thwart them..

Benediction

Fr. Bénédition
It. Benedizione
Port. Bênção
Sp. Benedicción

Definition: **n.** the uttering or bestowing of a blessing

Sentence: The Sunday service closed with the minister's benediction.

Benefactor

Fr. Bienfaiteur/Bienfaitrice
It. Benefattore
Port. Benfeitor
Sp. Benefactor

BENE-	FAC-
good	to do, to make

Definition: **n.** a person who gives money or other help to a person or cause

Sentence: The benefactor gave money to charity anonymously.

Bicuspid

Fr. Bicuspide
It. Bicuspide
Port. Bicúspide
Sp. Bicúspide

BI-	CUSPIS-
two	sharp point

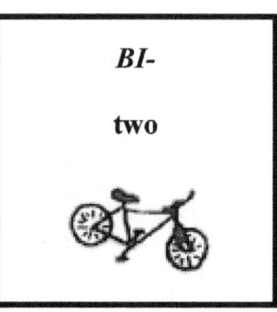

Definition: **adj.** having two cusps, or points
n. a tooth with two cusps, especially a human premolar tooth

Sentence: A crescent moon has a bicuspid form.
The dental hygienist noticed decay on the patient's upper right bicuspid.

Bilateral

Fr. Bilatéral
It. Bilaterale
Port. Bilateral
Sp. Bilateral

BI-	LATERAL-
two	side

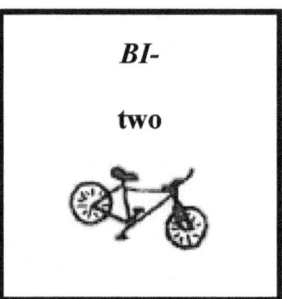 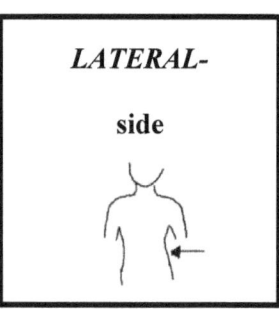

Definition: **adj.** having or relating to two sides (usually in mathematics or politics)

Sentence: Israel and Egypt are engaged in direct bilateral negotiations.

Bilingual

Fr. Bilingue
It. Bilingue
Port. Bilíngue
Sp. Bilingüe

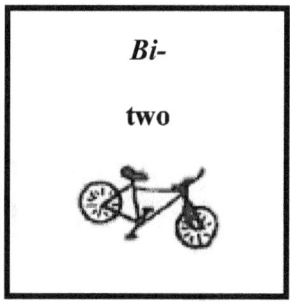

Definition: **adj.** speaking two languages fluently

Sentence: Most Swiss are at least bilingual, speaking German and French.

Bisect

Fr. Couper en deux
It. Bisecare
Port. Bissectar
Sp. Bisecar

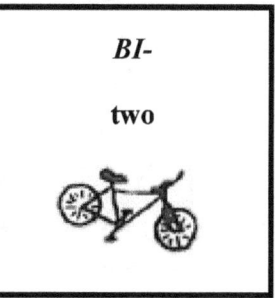 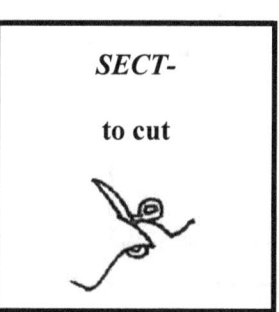

Definition: **v.** to divide into two parts, usually equal

Sentence: The Mississippi River roughly bisects the United States.

Exercise A

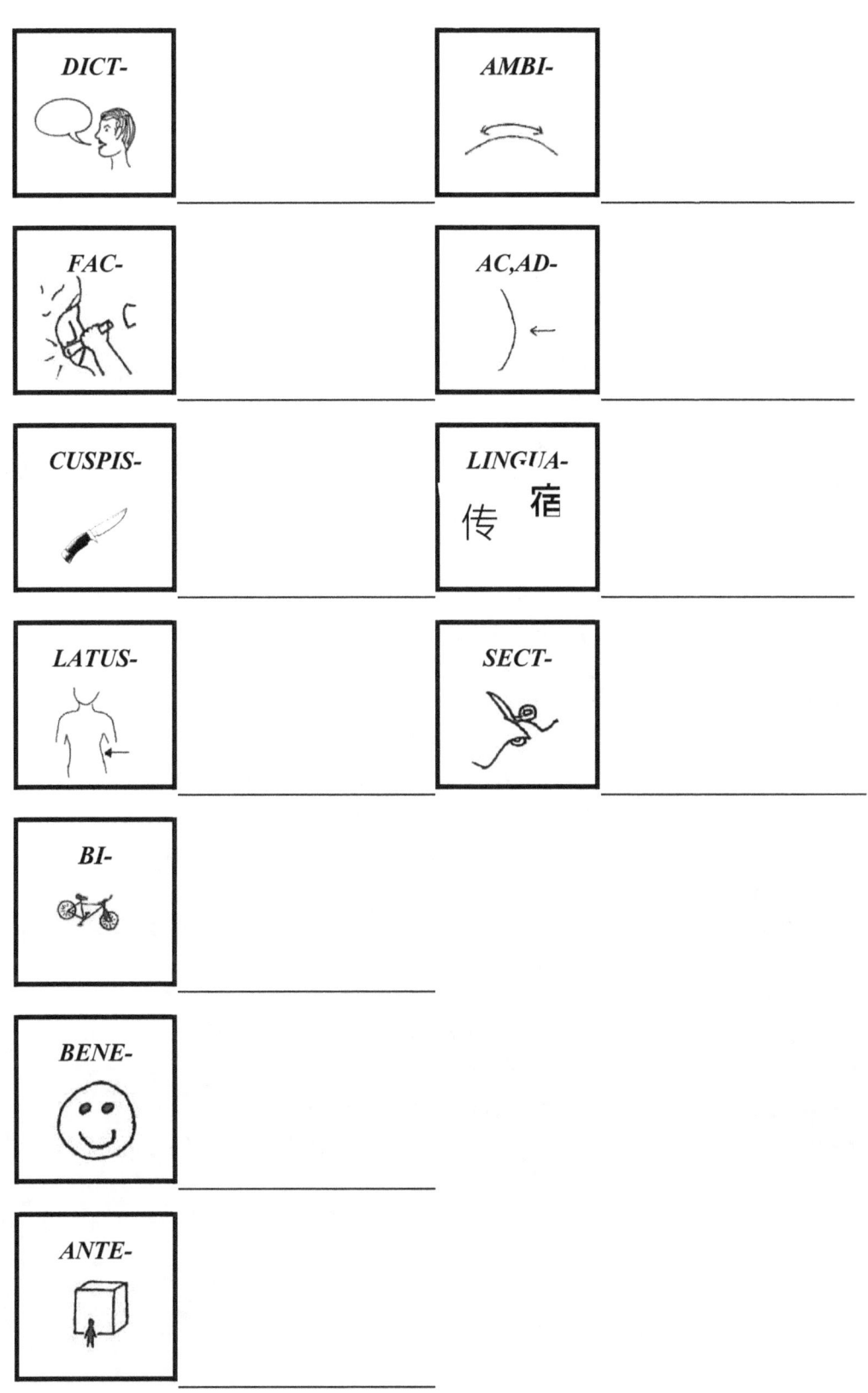

Answers for Exercise A begin on page 298

Exercise B

Match the word with the letter of its definition:

1. ____ abduct
2. ____ abhor
3. ____ abrasion
4. ____ abrupt
5. ____ absorb
6. ____ accord
7. ____ adaptable
8. ____ adhere
9. ____ adjacent
10. ____ adversary
11. ____ ambidextrous
12. ____ ambiguous
13. ____ ante meridian
14. ____ anticipate
15. ____ benediction
16. ____ benefactor
17. ____ bicuspid
18. ____ bilateral
19. ____ bilingual
20. ____ bisect

a) an opponent
b) to soak up
c) the result of wearing away
d) to detest
e) suddenly change in action or manner
f) to carry off unlawfully
g) an agreement
h) to stick
i) bordering
j) able to adjust to new situations
k) the ability to speak two languages
l) having more than one interpretation
m) to expect
n) the ability to use left and right hands equally
o) a blessing
p) a double pointed tooth
q) having two sides
r) before noon
s) to divide into two equal parts
t) a person who offers financial support

Answers for Exercise B begin on page 311

Exercise C

1. The ISIS terrorists lured the American journalist away from safety in order to _____ him.

2. Many Democrats _____ the practice of capital punishment.

3. The driver made an _____ evasive maneuver to avoid hitting a squirrel in the middle of the road.

4. When Karen spilled cranberry juice on the kitchen counter, she used a wad of paper towels to _____ the liquid.

5. The cement levee protecting the ocean-front cottage was crumbling after years of _____ from high tides and pounding waves.

6. After decades of fighting over Kashmir, India and Pakistan reached a tentative peace _____.

7. *Spiderman*, starring Toby McGuire as the web-slinger and Willem Dafoe as his _____, the Green Goblin, was so successful that it spawned a blockbuster sequel.

8. Though tempted to keep the paper bag full of money she'd found, Sarah _____ to her ethical principles and tracked down the rightful owner.

9. The SUV was too large for the parking space at Tan-O-Rama, so it ended up occupying half of an _____ space.

10. Since the rain jacket had a removable fleece lining for insulation, it was _____ for use in any climate or season.

11. Her boss's comments were so _____ that Sarah wasn't sure whether he was praising or blaming her.

12. Some _____ artists draw with one hand and write with another.

13. Seeing the puzzled look on Jessica's face, Nick explained that _____ was a term that meant "before noon".

14. Marco didn't _____ a holiday bonus, because he had begun working for Dynacorp just a few weeks earlier.

15. At the end of the interfaith service, the minister and rabbi pronounced the _____ together.

16. After losing all her baby teeth, Julia noticed that a _____ was beginning to grow next to her molars.

17. The dotted yellow line _____ the highway.

18. Ancient mathematicians found the _____ symmetry of the isosceles triangle so beautiful they included it in the architecture of their greatest buildings.

19. The Museum of Fine Arts in Boston, Massachusetts, recognizes its most generous _____ on a prominent plaque in the lobby.

20. Mr. Banderas grew up in a Spanish-speaking house, but went to an English-speaking school and became _____.

Answers for Exercise C begin on page 298

Exercise D

(l) indicates the answer is a Latin root

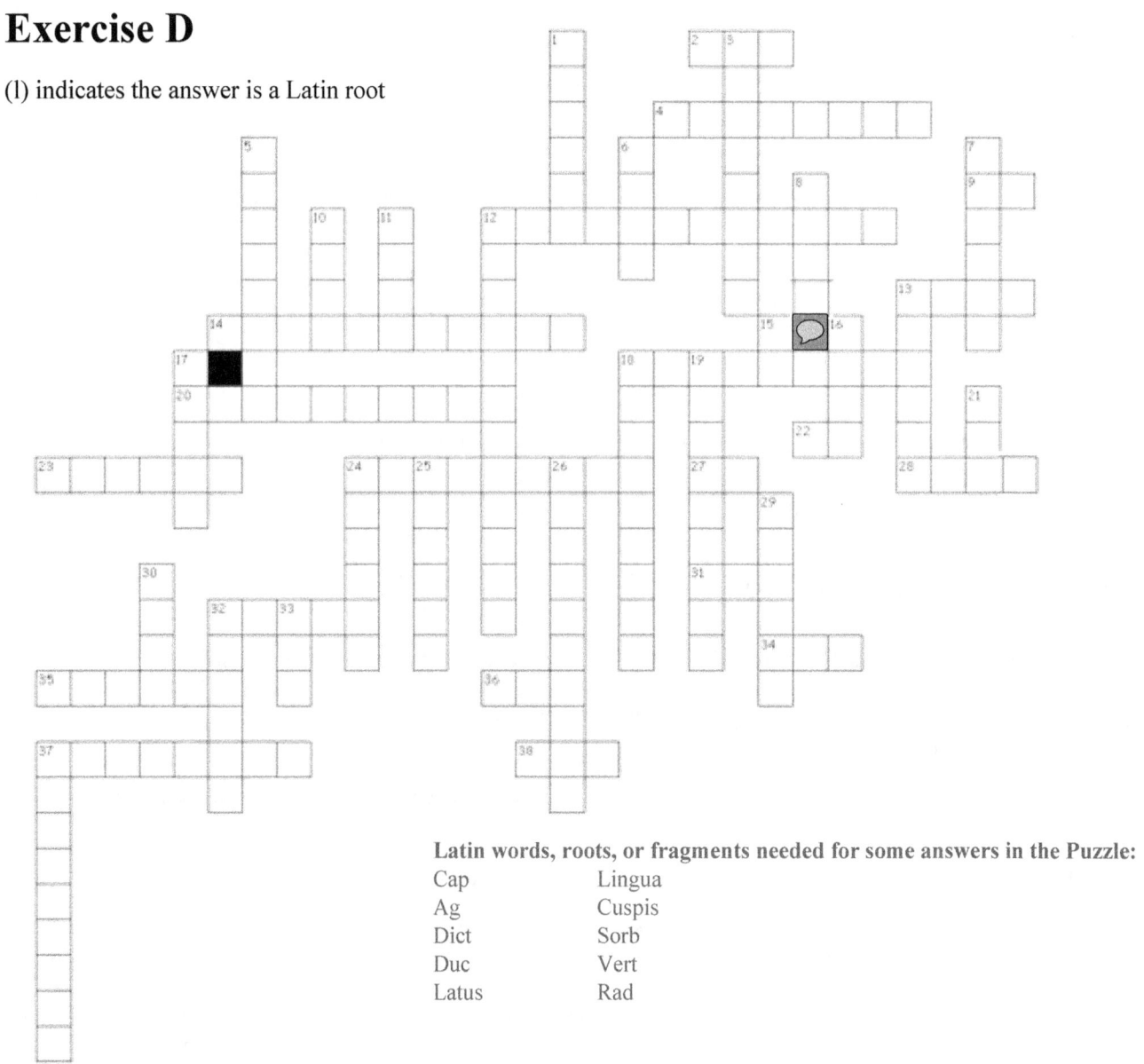

Latin words, roots, or fragments needed for some answers in the Puzzle:

Cap	Lingua
Ag	Cuspis
Dict	Sorb
Duc	Vert
Latus	Rad

Across
2. to make (l)
4. noon (l)
9. two
12. before noon
13. heart (l)
14. a blessing
18. more than one interpretation
20. to expect
22. from (l)
23. language (l)
24. able to adjust to new situations
27. to, toward
28. cut (l)
31. to scrape, shave (l)
32. to detest
34. to take (l)
35. right handed (l)
36. to throw (l)
37. a double pointed tooth
38. to shudder (l)

Down
1. to divide into two equal parts
3. the result of wearing away
5. bordering
6. to break (l)
7. to soak up
8. to say (l)
10. before (l)
11. both (l)
12. able to use left & right hand equally
13. sharp point (l)
15. to drive (l)
16. to suck (l)
17. side (l)
18. an opponent
19. having two sides
21. to lead (l)
24. to stick
25. an agreement
26. sponsor
29. to carry off unlawfully
30. to turn (l)
32. suddenly change in action or manner
33. to stick (l)
37. speaking two languages

Answers for Exercise D begin on page 298

Lesson II

Circulate

Fr. Circuler
It. Circolare
Port. Circular
Sp. Circular

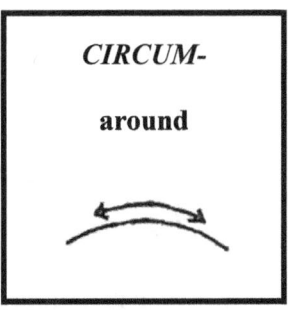

Definition: **v.** to move or cause to move around continuously or freely

Sentence: Harvey discovered that blood circulates throughout the body.

Circumscribe

Fr. Circonscrire
It. Circoscrivere
Port. Circunscrever
Sp. Circunscribir

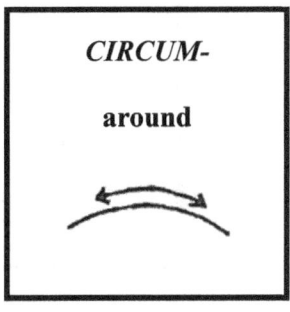 

Definition: **v.** to restrict or limit; to draw a circle around

Sentence: A bedridden hospital patient's mobility is circumscribed.

Circumstantial

Fr. Circonstancié
It. Circostanziale
Port. Circunstancial
Sp. Circunstancial

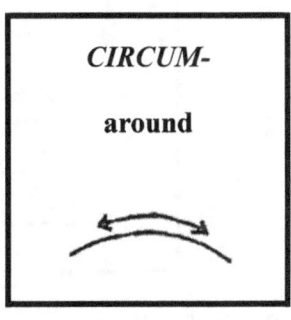 

Definition: **adj.** incidental; dependent on circumstances; suggestive, but not definitive

Sentence: No physical proofs linked him to the crime; all the evidence was circumstantial.

Collaborate

Fr. Collaborer
It. Collaborare
Port. Colaborar
Sp. Colaborar

CO-	LABOR-
together	to work

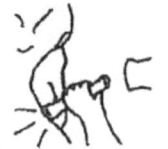

Definition: **v.** to work together on an activity or project

Sentence: I decided to collaborate with him, even though I am the better artist.

Collision

Fr. Collision
It. Collisione
Port. Colisão
Sp. Colisión

CO-	LAED-
together	to strike

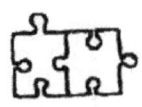 

Definition: **n.** the act or process of colliding; a crash or conflict

Sentence: A collision of views on immigration led to their disagreement.

Commiserate

Fr. Compatir (à)
It. Dolersi (per)
Port. Compadecer
Sp. Compadecer

CO-	MISERARI-
together	to pity, to lament

Definition: **v.** to express sympathy or pity

Sentence: The girls commiserated after they were ignored by the same fickle boy.

Condone

Fr. Tolérer
It. Ammettere
Port. Perdoar
Sp. Condonar

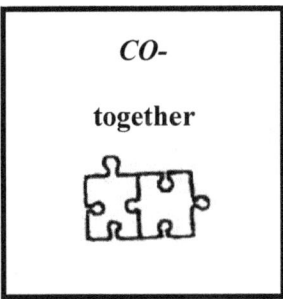

Definition:	**v.** to excuse or forgive; to allow to occur; to overlook or give implicit consent
Sentence:	The teacher did not condone cheating of any kind.

Contraband

Fr. De contrebande
It. Contrabbando
Port. Contrabando
Sp. Contrabando

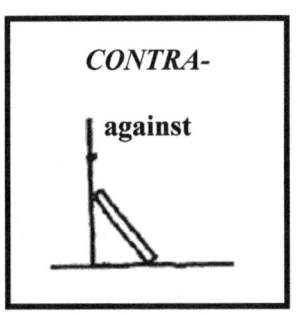 

Definition:	**n.** goods that have been imported or exported illegally **adj.** prohibited from being imported or exported
Sentence:	The Border Patrol's task is to seize contraband, such as cocaine The inmate smuggled a carton of contraband cigarettes into the prison.

Contradict

Fr. Contredire
It. Contraddire
Port. Contradizer
Sp. Contradecir

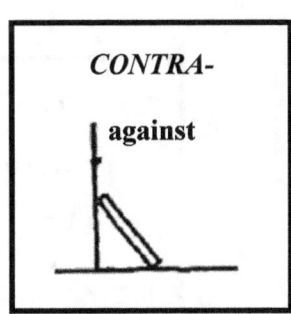 

Definition:	**v.** to deny a statement by asserting the opposite
Sentence:	The laboratory findings contradict the original diagnosis.

Contrast

Fr. n. Contraste, v. Contraster
It. n. Contrasto, v. Contrastare
Port. Contraste
Sp. Contraste

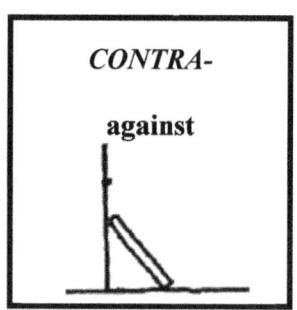

Definition:	**v.** to differ strikingly **n.** the state of being very different from something else; the degree of difference in colors or tones, especially in art or other visual display
Sentence:	Parents' and children's attitudes toward curfews usually contrast. The bright blue streaks were in striking contrast to the young woman's red hair.

Decadence

Fr. Décadence
It. Decadenza
Port. Decadência
Sp. Decadencia

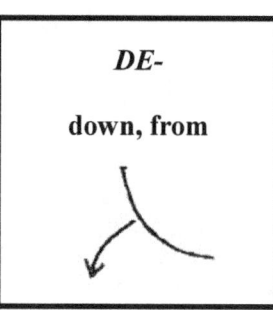

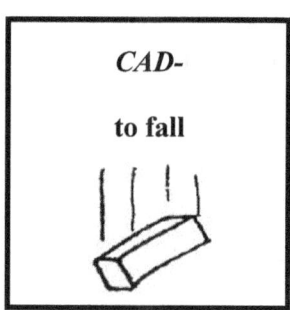

Definition:	**n.** the process or manifestation of moral, physical or cultural decline
Sentence:	Drunkenness, lewd behavior, and cursing are signs of his decadence.

Dedicate

Fr. Se consacrer, Dédier (à)
It. Dedicare
Port. Dedicar
Sp. Dedicar

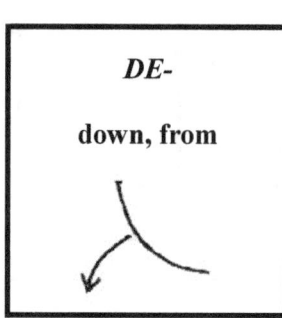

Definition:	**v.** to devote solely to a subject, task, or purpose; to address a book or composition
Sentence:	A professional musician dedicates most of his time to practice.

Demented

Fr. Dément
It. Demente
Port. Demente
Sp. Demente

DE-	MENTIS-
down, from	mind

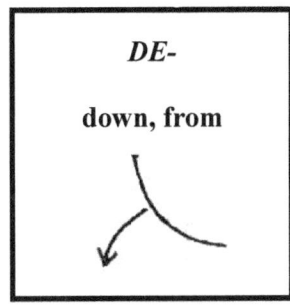

Definition: **adj.** insane; wild and irrational; suffering from dementia

Sentence: The patient believed he was rational, but he was clearly demented.

Demote

Fr. Rétrograder
It. Degradare, Retrocedere
Port. Degradar
Sp. Degradar

DE-	MOT-, MOV-
down, from	to move

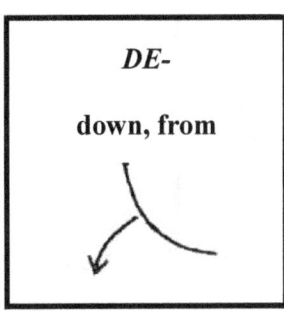 

Definition: **v.** to revoke a higher rank or senior position

Sentence: The disobedient corporal was demoted to the rank of private.

Deter

Fr. Dissuader
It. Dissuadere
Port. Deter
Sp. Disuadir

DE-	TERR-
down, from	to scare

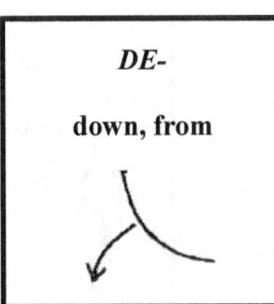 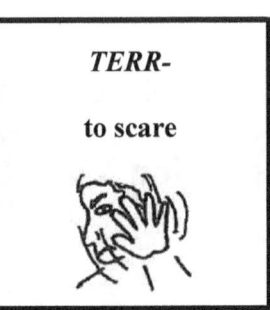

Definition: **v.** to discourage (someone) from doing something by instilling fear of the consequences

Sentence: The snowstorm deterred us from attending the party.

Devour

Fr. Dévorer
It. Divorare
Port. Devorar
Sp. Devorar

DE-	VOR-
down, from	to eat

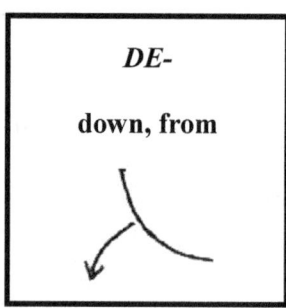

Definition: **v.** to consume voraciously or quickly

Sentence: "After going without food for three days, the rescued man devoured the soup."

Distinct

Fr. Distinct
It. Distinto
Port. Distinto
Sp. Distinto

DIS-	STINGU-
apart	mark off, separate

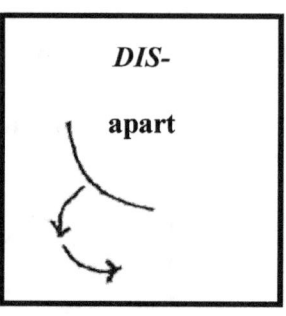

Definition: **adj.** dissimilar; different; clear; easily perceived

Sentence: To the afficionado, the most distinct pronunciation of Spanish is heard in Valladolid, the ancient seat of the Spanish kings.

Distortion

Fr. Distorsion, Deformation
It. Distorsione
Port. Distorsão
Sp. Distorsión

DIS-	TORT-
apart	to turn, to twist

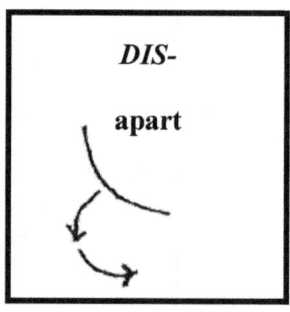 

Definition: **n.** the act of twisting (something) out of shape; an untruthful or unfair representation (of something)

Sentence: A funhouse mirror causes elongation and distortion of features.

Distract	Fr. Distraire It. Distrarre Port. Distrair Sp. Distraer	*DIS-* apart	*TRACT-* to pull

Definition: **v.** to prevent (someone) from concentrating on something

Sentence: I went to a movie to distract me from my sorrow.

Duet	Fr. Duo It. Duetto Port. Dueto Sp. Dueto	*DUO-* two

Definition: **n.** a performance by two singers, instrumentalists, or dancers

Sentence: In the opera, the hero and heroine sing a duet.

Duplicate	Fr. v. Reproduire, n. Copie It. Duplicare Port. Duplicar Sp. Duplicar	*DUO-* two	*PLIC-* to fold

Definition: **v.** to make an exact copy of; to do again unnecessarily
n. an exact copy
adj. exactly like something else; having two corresponding parts

Sentence: The boy duplicated his first-inning performance by hitting a second home run.
The painting appeared to be an exact duplicate of the original masterpiece.
Make several duplicate copies of this letter, please.

Exercise A

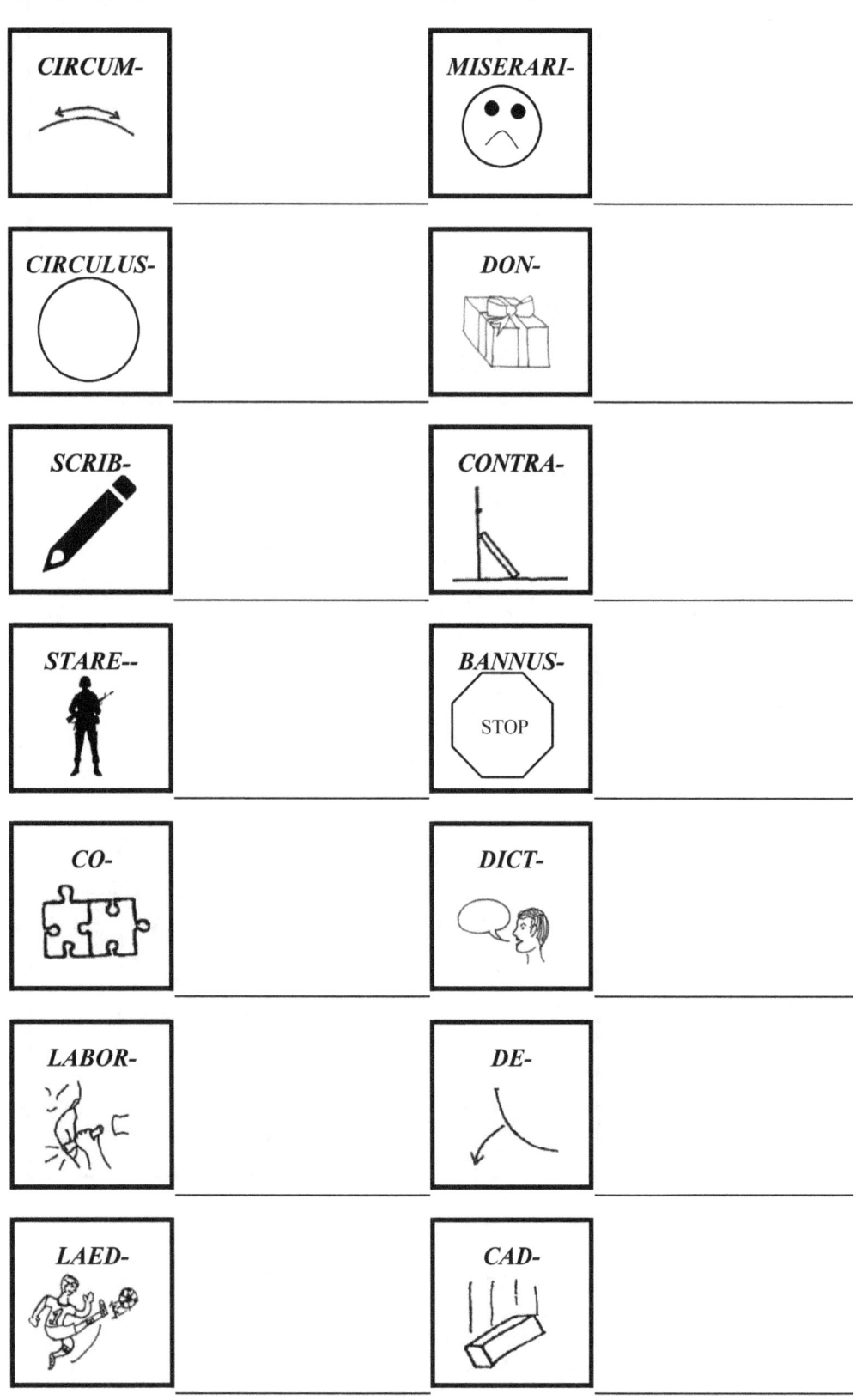

Exercise B

Match the word with the letter of its definition:

1. ____ circulate
2. ____ circumscribe
3. ____ circumstantial
4. ____ collaborate
5. ____ collision
6. ____ commiserate
7. ____ condone
8. ____ contraband
9. ____ contradict
10. ____ contrast
11. ____ decadence
12. ____ dedicate
13. ____ demented
14. ____ demote
15. ____ deter
16. ____ devour
17. ____ distortion
18. ____ distract
19. ____ duet
20. ____ duplicate
21. ____ distinct

a) to say the opposite of
b) striking difference in comparison
c) illegally imported or smuggled goods
d) incidental; dependent on circumstances
e) to move continuously or freely
f) to restrict
g) to excuse or forgive; to overlook
h) to work together on a project
i) to sympathize with the sorrow of another
j) a crash
k) to discourage or prevent from occurring
l) to lower in rank or grade
m) mentally ill; wild and irrational
n) to consume voraciously
o) the process of moral or cultural decline
p) to devote a creative work to a person
q) the action of twisting something out of shape
r) to make an exact copy
s) to draw attention away from
t) a performance by two entertainers
u) different from something else

Exercise C

1. Mike kept searching for the right color to _____ with the dark background of the painting.

2. To help prevent _____ drugs from entering our borders, we need to increase surveillance and security.

3. From all accounts, the accident was preventable, because the lifeguard had clearly _____ the swimming area with a rope.

4. The little girl had the unfortunate habit of _____ her parents' every instruction.

5. During the party, Sam and Paul _____ so they could meet as many new pledges as possible.

6. Mrs. Roberts decided the crumbs on her son's T-shirt provided sufficient _____ evidence of cookie theft.

7. Although they sympathized with their cause, few _____ the radical group's violent acts.

8. The _____ between the car and the pickup truck was so loud we could hear it a block away.

9. The widows _____ over the loss of their husbands during the war.

10. The artist and author _____ to create a children's book with exceptional prose and illustrations.

11. Brad was annoyed when he discovered that his gluttonous friends had _____ all of Jennifer's fabulous chocolate cake.

12. Helen wondered if Jack Nicholson was perhaps _____ himself after watching his stunning portrayals of madmen in *One Flew Over the Cuckoo's Nest* and *The Shining*.

13. Private O'Neill was once a major, but he was _____ after a case of liquor was found in his locker.

14. Supporters of capital punishment claim it _____ crime.

15. The _____ of the kingdom was most obvious at holiday celebrations, when the royals ate and drank to excess.

16. The graduating class _____ the yearbook to Mr. Bragdon, the retiring headmaster.

17. He mumbles when he's talking to himself, but when speaking to others, his words are _____ .

18. Mr. Thomson was embarrassed to learn that his cherished painting was only a _____ of an Old Master.

19. Salvador Dali's _____ of ordinary objects, such as melting watches, is a hallmark of his surrealist paintings.

20. The concert concluded with a _____ performed by the two famous violinists.

21. During the baseball game, the hometown fans tried to _____ the visiting pitcher.

Exercise D

Latin words, roots, or fragments needed for some answers in the Puzzle:
Tort
Bannus
Dict
Laed
Plic

Across
2. mentally ill; wild and irrational
5. to say (l)
9. to consume voraciously (l)
11. a crash
14. to say the opposite of
16. to say (l)
20. mind (l)
22. incidental
26. to work (l)
27. different from something else
28. two (l)
29. the process of moral or cultural decline
31. to pity; lament (l)
33. to turn, twist (l)
34. down from (l)
36. to devote a creative work to a person
38. to sympathize with the sorrow of another
39. to draw attention away from

Down
1. ban (l)
3. to move (l)
4. performance by two entertainers
6. around (l)
7. apart (l)
8. against (l)
10. to give (l)
12. to strike (l)
13. circle (l)
14. to move continuously or freely
15. to eat (l)
17. to work together on a project
18. to discourage or prevent from occurring
19. to fall (l)
22. together (l)
23. illegally imported or smuggled goods
24. to scare (l)
25. to fold (l)
27. to excuse or forgive; to overlook
30. striking difference in comparison
32. to stand (l)
35. to lower in rank or grade
37. to write (l)

Lesson III

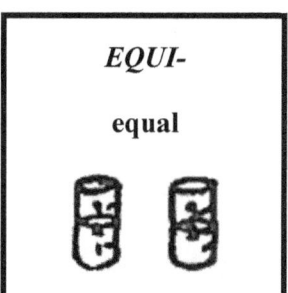

Equity

Fr. Fonds propres, Equity
It. Patrimonio netto, Equità
Port. Equidade
Sp. Equidad

Definition: **n.** fairness and impartiality; the value of shares issued by a company
n. value of a property or asset minus any debts against it

Sentence: The judge was known for his equity in commercial disputes.

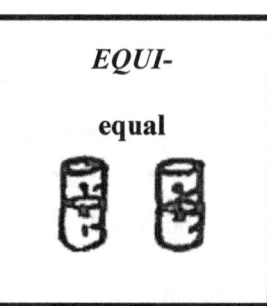

Equivalent

Fr. Équivalent
It. Equivalente
Port. Equivalente
Sp. Equivalente

Definition: **adj.** equal or nearly equal in value, amount, function, or meaning

Sentence: 100 degrees Celsius and 212 degrees Fahrenheit are equivalent.

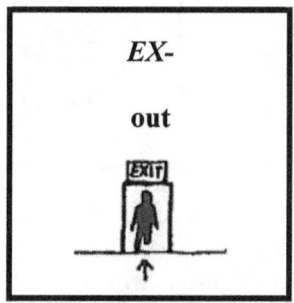 

Emigrate

Fr. Émigrer
It. Emigrare
Port. Emigrar
Sp. Emigrar

Definition: **v.** to leave one's native country to reside in another

Sentence: The Irish emigrated from their homeland to escape the potato famine.

Eradicate

Fr. Éradiquer
It. Debellare
Port. Erradicar
Sp. Erradicar

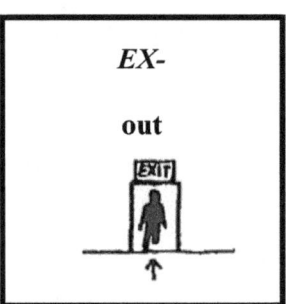

Definition: **v.** to remove or destroy completely

Sentence: Smallpox was eradicated in the U.S. several decades ago.

Evoke

Fr. Évoquer
It. Rievocare
Port. Evocar
Sp. Evocar

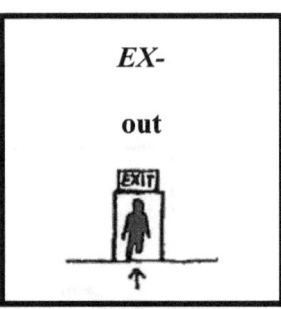 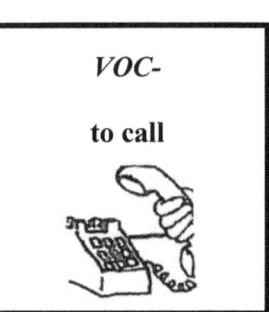

Definition: **v.** to recall to the conscious mind; to bring out

Sentence: A small cake dipped in tea evoked a torrent of memory in Proust.

Extrovert

Fr. Extraverti
It. Estroverso
Port. Extroversão
Sp. Extroversión

 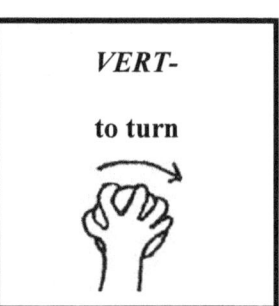

Definition: **n.** an outgoing, socially confident person

Sentence: Cheerleaders typically are extroverts.

Illuminate

Fr. Illuminer
It. Illuminare
Port. Iluminar
Sp. Iluminar

IL-, IM-, IN-
in, not

LUMIN-
to light up

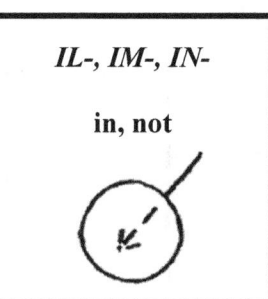

Definition: **v.** to light up

Sentence: Large windows illuminated the upper floors, while the finished basement had recessed lighting.

Implicate

Fr. Impliquer
It. Implicare
Port. Implicar
Sp. Implicar

IL-, IM-, IN-
in, not

PLIC-
to fold

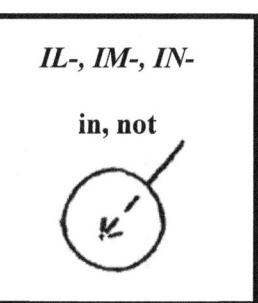 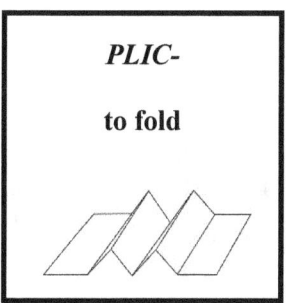

Definition: **v.** to show to be involved in a crime or mishap; to incriminate

Sentence: A faulty tile was implicated in the failure of the space shuttle.

Inclusive

Fr. Ouvert
It. Inclusivo
Port. Inclusivo
Sp. Inclusivo

IL-, IM-, IN-
in, not

CLAUS-
to close, to shut

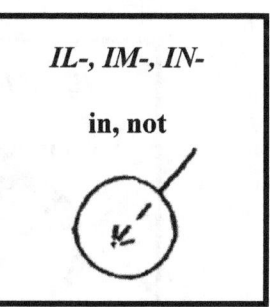 

Definition: **adj.** including the limits specified; containing as part of the whole

Sentence: The school aims to be inclusive, admitting Muslims, Jews, and Christians.

Inscription

Fr. Inscription/Dédicace
It. Iscrizione/Dedica
Port. Insprição
Sp. Inscripción

IL-, IM-, IN-
in, not

SCRIB-
to write

Definition: **n.** words written, as on a monument or in a book

Sentence: The famous inscription on the Rosetta Stone is in three languages.

Illegible

Fr. Illisible
It. Illeggibile
Port. Ilegível
Sp. Ilegible

IL-, IM-, IN-
in, not
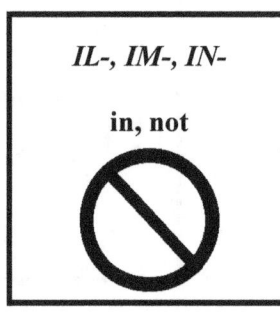

LEG-
to read

Definition: **adj.** not clear enough to be read

Sentence: You must print the information on the form; your handwriting is illegible.

Illiterate

Fr. Illettré
It. Illetterato
Port. Iletrado
Sp. Iletrado

IL-, IM-, IN-
in, not
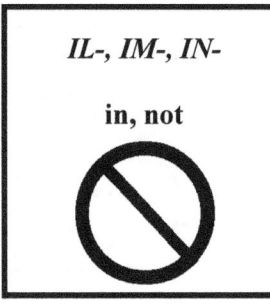

LITTERA-
letter, books

Definition: **adj.** unable to read or write

Sentence: Uniformly illiterate, pharaohs relied on scribes to read and write.

Incessant

Fr. Incessant
It. Incessante
Port. Incessante
Sp. Incesante

IL-, IM-, IN-
in, not

CESS-
to cease

Definition: **adj.** continuing without pause or interruption (often unpleasantly)

Sentence: A beehive is an incessant buzz of activity.

Irrelevant

Fr. Hors de propos
It. Irrilevante
Port. Irrelevante
Sp. Irrelevante

IR-
in, not

RELEV-
to raise up, to elevate

Definition: **adj.** not closely connected to (something); not mattering; unimportant

Sentence: Since all work was done indoors, the weather was irrelevant.

Interjection

Fr. Interjection
It. Interiezione
Port. Interjeição
Sp. Interjección

INTER-
between

JAC-
to throw

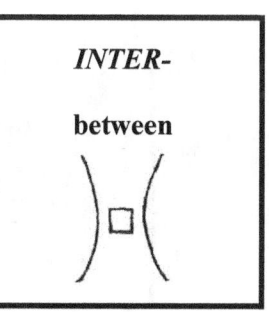
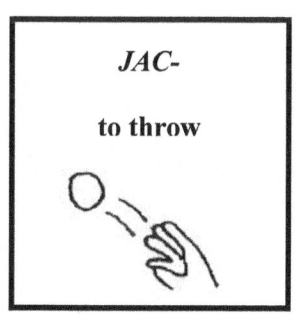

Definition: **n.** a remark inserted when someone else is speaking; an exclamation

Sentence: 'Ach!' is an interjection in both Scottish and German.

Interlude

Fr. Intervalle, Interlude
It. Intervallo, Interludio
Port. Interlúdio
Sp. Interludio

INTER- between	LUD-, LUS- to play, game
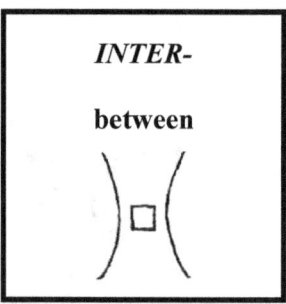	

Definition: **n.** a dissimilar event or period between two others; an intermission

Sentence: The Great Depression occurred during the interlude between world wars.

Intersect

Fr. Se couper
It. Intersecarsi
Port. Intersectar
Sp. Intersecar

INTER- between	SECT- to cut
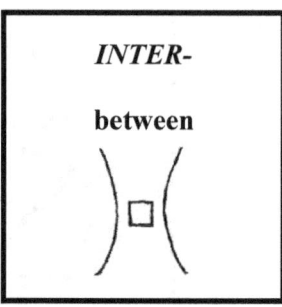	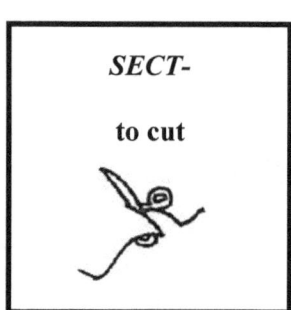

Definition: **v.** to divide across or through; to cross; to meet at a point

Sentence: The road near my house intersects a state highway.

Intervene

Fr. Intervenir
It. Intervenire
Port. Intervir
Sp. Intervenir

INTER- between	VENI- to come
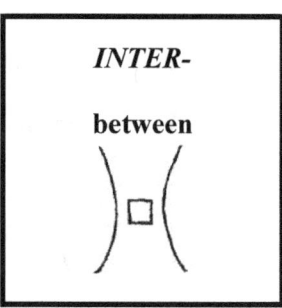	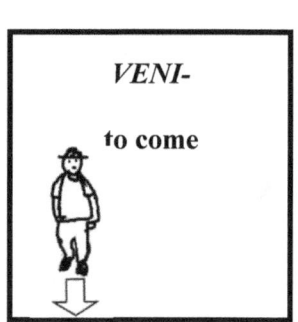

Definition: **v.** to come between; to occur as an unplanned circumstance

Sentence: The policeman intervened to end the fistfight.

Intravenous

Fr. Intraveineux
It. Endovenoso
Port. Intravenoso
Sp. Intravenoso

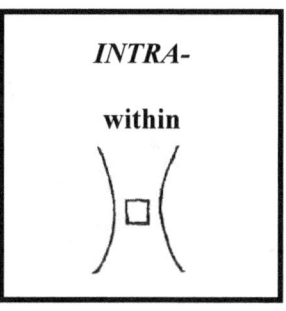

Definition: **adj.** within or into a vein or veins

Sentence: Medicines administered by needle are intravenous.

Introvert

Fr. Introverti
It. Introverso
Port. Introvertido
Sp. Introvertido

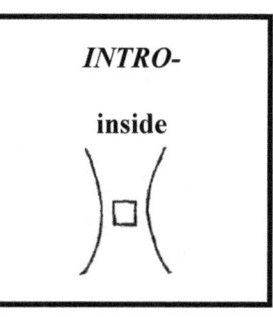 

Definition: **n.** a shy, reticent person (opposite of extrovert)

Sentence: An introvert, he greatly preferred reading at home to going out.

Exercise A

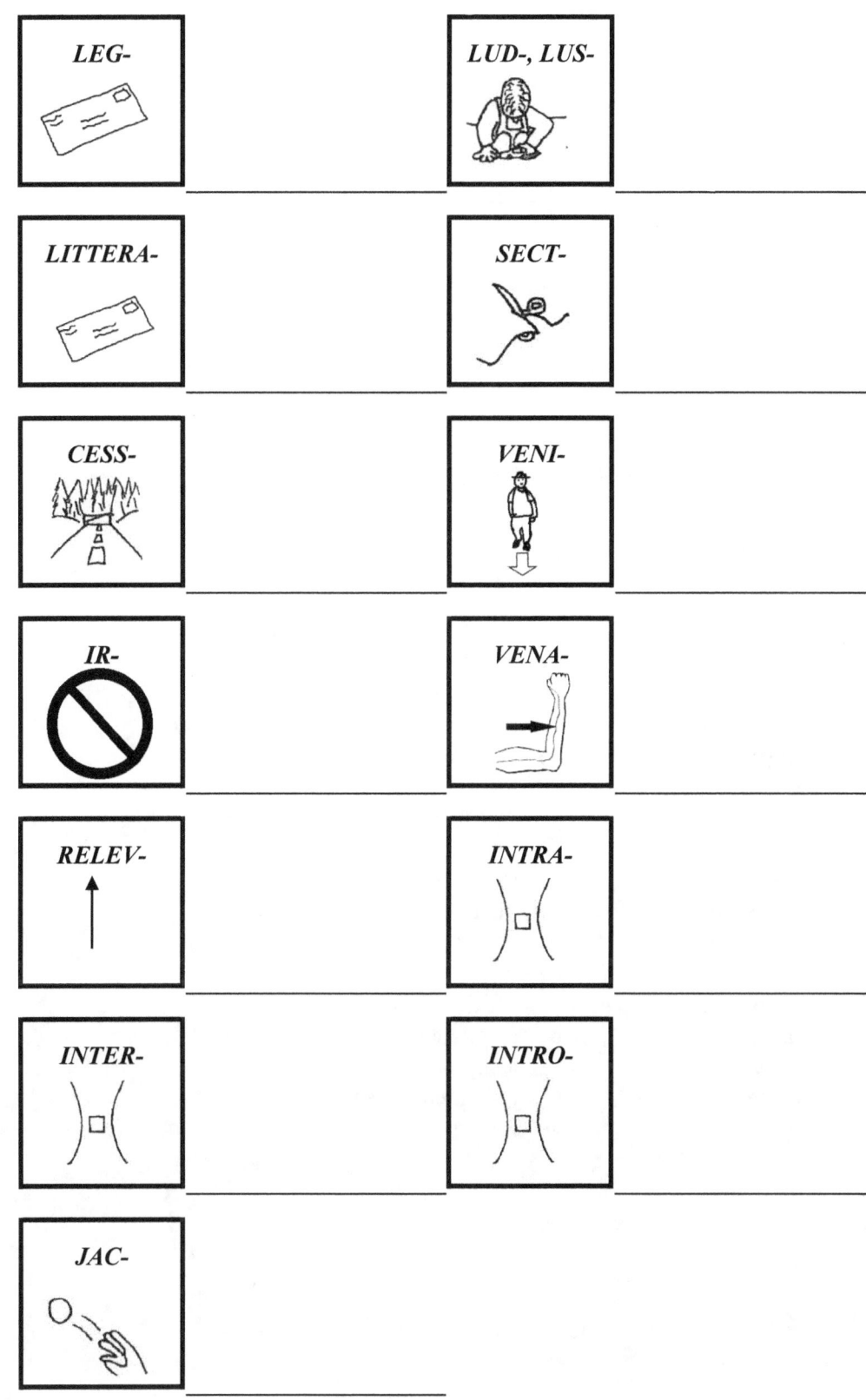

Exercise B
Match the word with the letter of its definition:

1. _____ equity
2. _____ equivalent
3. _____ emigrate
4. _____ eradicate
5. _____ evoke
6. _____ extrovert
7. _____ illuminate
8. _____ implicate
9. _____ inclusive
10. _____ inscription
11. _____ illegible
12. _____ illiterate
13. _____ incessant
14. _____ irrelevant
15. _____ interjection
16. _____ interlude
17. _____ intersect
18. _____ intervene
19. _____ intravenous
20. _____ introvert

a) to get rid of entirely
b) equal in all respects
c) to call forth
d) to leave one's country for another
e) an outgoing person
f) value of property after debts
g) to show to be involved in a crime
h) to light up; to shed light on
i) including the limits specified
j) words written on a monument
k) the time between two events
l) to cut across or through
m) difficult or impossible to read
n) continuing without interruption
o) unable to read or write
p) off the subject
q) an exclamation
r) a shy person
s) to come between
t) into vein(s)

Exercise C

1. When two formulas express the same value, they are _____.

2. Lo-Han's parents _____ from China while in their teens.

3. Although Yellow Fever has been _____ in the United States, it still exists in countries unable to properly vaccinate against it.

4. Carrot Top could not _____ laughter from an audience, even if he were to run around in clown shoes with his pants on fire.

5. The value of a company's _____ usually exceeds the value of the bonds it issues.

6. You would think that all professional actors are _____ by nature, but in fact many of them are quite reserved off camera.

7. Adding a floodlight will better _____ the front door and steps.

8. The witness could not testify without _____ herself in the crime.

9. The club was very _____; anyone interested in coin collecting could join.

10. The book is very valuable because an _____ inside the front cover shows it was a gift from the author to his mistress.

11. Doctors are required to sign so many documents each day that their signatures rapidly become _____ strings of loops and lines.

12. He claims that gender is _____ in the workplace, but I notice that he only promotes men to the top jobs, even when there are qualified women candidates.

13. Creating stable and well-balanced economies in third-world countries is a momentous task, because in many nations most workers are _____ and therefore ill-equipped to handle jobs that require reading or writing.

14. The _____ call of the raven in Edgar Allen Poe's poem drives the narrator to madness.

15. New York City is far easier to navigate than Boston, because the streets of New York _____ at right angles, while roads in Boston cross at arbitrary angles.

16. During the intermission, the Boston Pops played a brief _____.

17. _____ drugs affect the patient more rapidly than those taken orally because they enter the bloodstream immediately.

18. Although he exudes confidence and charm on camera, Toby McGuire describes himself as an _____.

19. The crossing guard tried to _____ in the fight, but got only a bloody nose for his efforts.

20. Stephen exclaimed "Holy cow!" when he saw the shooting star, but his _____ failed to stop the argument between his parents.

Exercise D

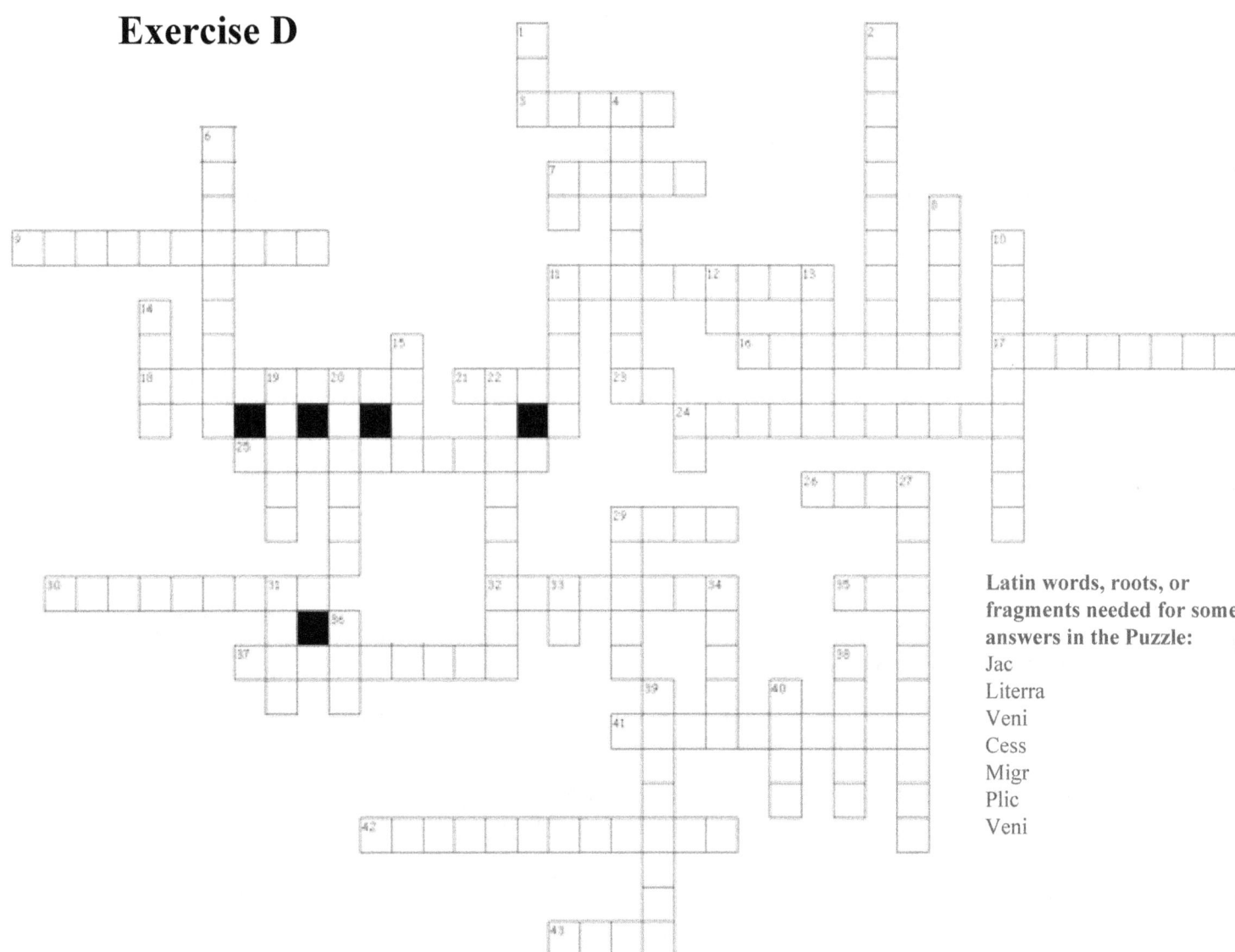

Latin words, roots, or fragments needed for some answers in the Puzzle:
Jac
Literra
Veni
Cess
Migr
Plic
Veni

Across
3. to light up (l)
7. between (l)
9. equal in all respects
11. difficult or impossible to read
16. letter, books (l)
17. an outgoing person
18. to come between
21. to move (l)
23. out (l)
24. into vein(s)
25. to light up; to shed light on
26. equal (l)
29. to cut (l)
30. including the limits specified
32. to leave one's country for another
35. to throw (l)
37. continuing without interruption
41. off the subject
42. an exclamation
43. to turn (l)

Down
1. strong (l)
2. unable to read or write
4. the time between two events
6. to show to be involved in a crime
7. in, not (l)
8. within (l)
10. to cut across or through
11. inside (l)
12. in, not (l)
13. outside (l)
14. to fold (l)
15. to come (l)
19. to raise up, to elevate (l)
20. value of property after debts
22. a shy person
24. in, not (l)
27. words written on a monument
29. to write (l)
31. vein (l)
33. in, not (l)
34. to call forth
36. to read (l)
38. to close, to shut (l)
39. to get rid of entirely
40. to cease (l)

Lesson IV

Magnificent

Fr. Magnifique
It. Magnifico
Port. Magnífico
Sp. Magnífico

Definition:	**adj.** very beautiful, elaborate, or impressive
Sentence:	The Great Pyramid of Gaza is a magnificent tribute to King Khufu.

Magnitude

Fr. Magnitude
It. Magnitudine
Port. Magnitude
Sp. Magnitud

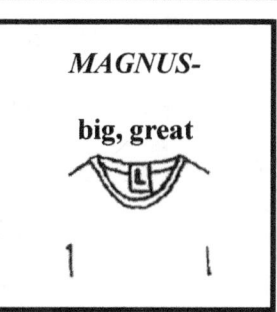

Definition:	**n.** size, extent, or importance
Sentence:	Matt realized the magnitude of his ignorance after he failed the test.

Major

Fr. Majeur
It. Maggiore
Port. Major
Sp. Mayor

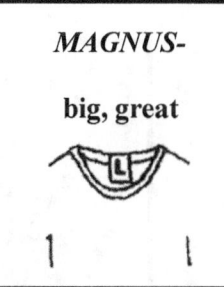

Definition:	**adj.** important, serious, or significant; great or large (in size) **n.** a military or police rank; a student's principal course of study
Sentence:	George Soros was a major contributor to Obama's presidential campaign. After taking an introductory course, she decided to major in electrical engineering.

Majority

Fr. Majorité
It. Maggioranza
Port. Maioria
Sp. Mayoría

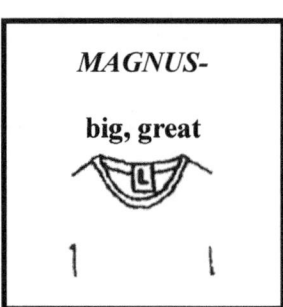

MAGNUS- big, great

Definition: **n.** more than half; most

Sentence: A presidential candidate in the United States must win a majority of votes in the Electoral College – but not a majority of the popular vote – to be elected.

Malicious

Fr. Malveillant
It. Malizioso
Port. Malicioso
Sp. Malicioso

MALIGNUS- evil

Definition: **adj.** intending harm or intended to do harm

Sentence: Sticking pins in a voodoo doll shows malicious intent.

Multilateral

Fr. Multilatéral
It. Multilaterale
Port. Multilateral
Sp. Multilateral

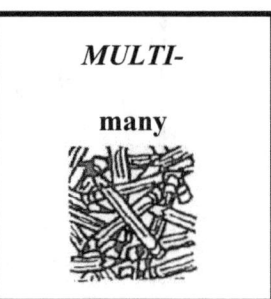

MULTI- many

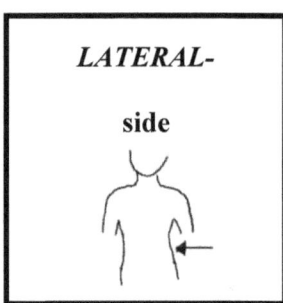

LATERAL- side

Definition: **adj.** agreed upon or done by three or more political parties or nations

Sentence: Japan, the United States, Russia, and China have joined North and South Korea in multilateral talks over the northern state's nuclear weapons program.

Multitude

Fr. Multitude
It. Moltitudine
Port. Multidão
Sp. Multitud

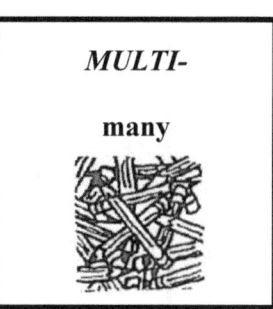

Definition: **n.** a large number of people or things; the mass of ordinary people

Sentence: A multitude of locusts blackened the sky, then alit in the cornfields.

Obligation

Fr. Obligation
It. Obbligo
Port. Obligação
Sp. Obligación

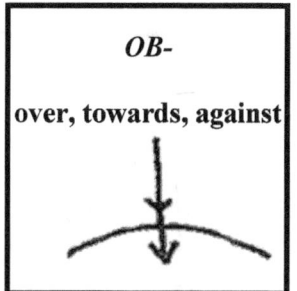 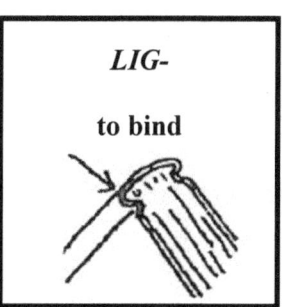

Definition: **n.** an act or course of action to which a person is legally or morally bound

Sentence: It once was an obligation for all men to serve in the military.

Obliterate

Fr. Oblitérer
It. Obliterare
Port. Obliterar
Sp. Obliterar

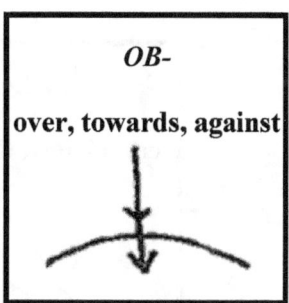 

Definition: **v.** to destroy utterly; to wipe out; to erase

Sentence: After she broke his heart, he tried to obliterate all reminders of her.

		OB-	**SID-, SED-, SESS-**
Obsess	Fr. Obséder It. Ossessionare Port. Obsedar Sp. Obsesionar	toward 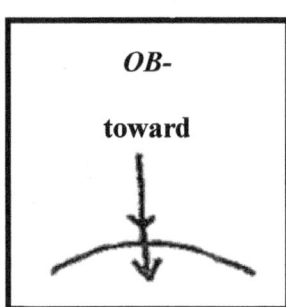	sit, stay, besiege

Definition:	**v.** to be continually preoccupied with, or intensely focused on (something or someone)
Sentence:	Ahab was so obsessed with capturing Moby Dick that he endangered the lives of his crew

		OMNI-	**VOR-**
Omnivorous	Fr. Omnivore It. Onnivoro Port. Omnívoro Sp. Omnívoro	all 	to eat

Definition:	**adj.** eating food of both plant and animal origin
Sentence:	Humans are omnivorous, which allows them to adapt to a wide variety of climates.

		PER-	**FOR-**
Perforate	Fr. Perforer It. Perforare Port. Perfurar Sp. Perforar	completely, through 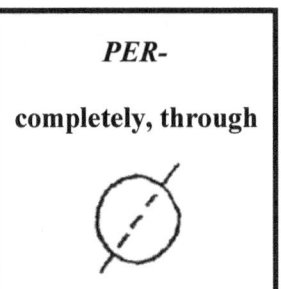	to pierce 

Definition:	**v.** to pierce and make a hole or holes in
Sentence:	Band-Aids are perforated with tiny holes to allow air flow.

		PER-	*SEVERUS-*
Persevere	Fr. Persévérer It. Perseverare Port. Perseverar Sp. Perseverar	completely, through	severe

Definition: **v.** to continue a course of action despite difficulty or low odds of success

Sentence: Because the tortoise persevered, he beat the hare.

		PER-	*SPECT-, SPIC-*
Perspective	Fr. Perspective It. Prospettiva Port. Perspectiva Sp. Perspectiva	completely, through	to look

Definition: **n.** (1) an artistic technique for representing distance and three-dimensional objects on a flat surface; a view or prospect
n. (2) a point of view

Sentence: The use of perspective in Renaissance drawing gave an appearance of depth and dimension.
The war seems very different when analyzing it from Iraq's perspective.

		POST-
Posterity	Fr. Postérité It. Posterità Port. Posteridade Sp. Posteridad	after, behind

Definition: **n.** future generations; all the descendants of one person

Sentence: Public libraries were Franklin's gift to posterity.

Postpone

Fr. Reporter, Postposer (Belgian)
It. Postporre
Port. Pospor
Sp. Posponer

POST- — after, behind

PON- — to place

Definition: **v.** to put off until later (something scheduled or due)

Sentence: The cross-examination was postponed after the witness fell ill.

Postscript

Fr. Post-scriptum
It. Post scriptum
Port. Postscriptum
Sp. Posdata

POST- — after

SCRIB- — to write

Definition: **n.** an additional remark at the end of a letter; a brief sequel

Sentence: A postscript added after the signature at the bottom of a letter is abbreviated 'P.S.'

Preclude

Fr. Empêcher
It. Impedire
Port. Impedir
Sp. Impedir

PRE-, PRAE- — before

CLAUS- — to close, to shut

Definition: **v.** to prevent (someone from doing something); to prevent (something) from happening

Sentence: Her infirmities preclude her from living a normal life.

Prediction

Fr. Prédiction
It. Previsione
Port. Previsão
Sp. Predicción

Definition:	**n.** a forecast
Sentence:	The Oracle of Delphi issued strange predictions, which were interpreted and written down by priests.

Presume

Fr. Présumer
It. Presumere
Port. Presumir
Sp. Presumir

 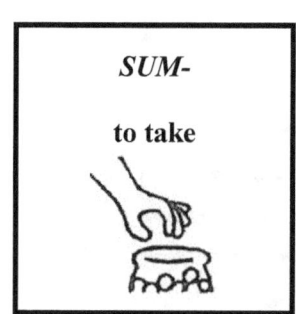

Definition:	**v.** to suppose (something) is true or take it for granted; to venture (to do something)
Sentence:	Dewey was the presumed victor, but in the end Truman won.

Exercise A

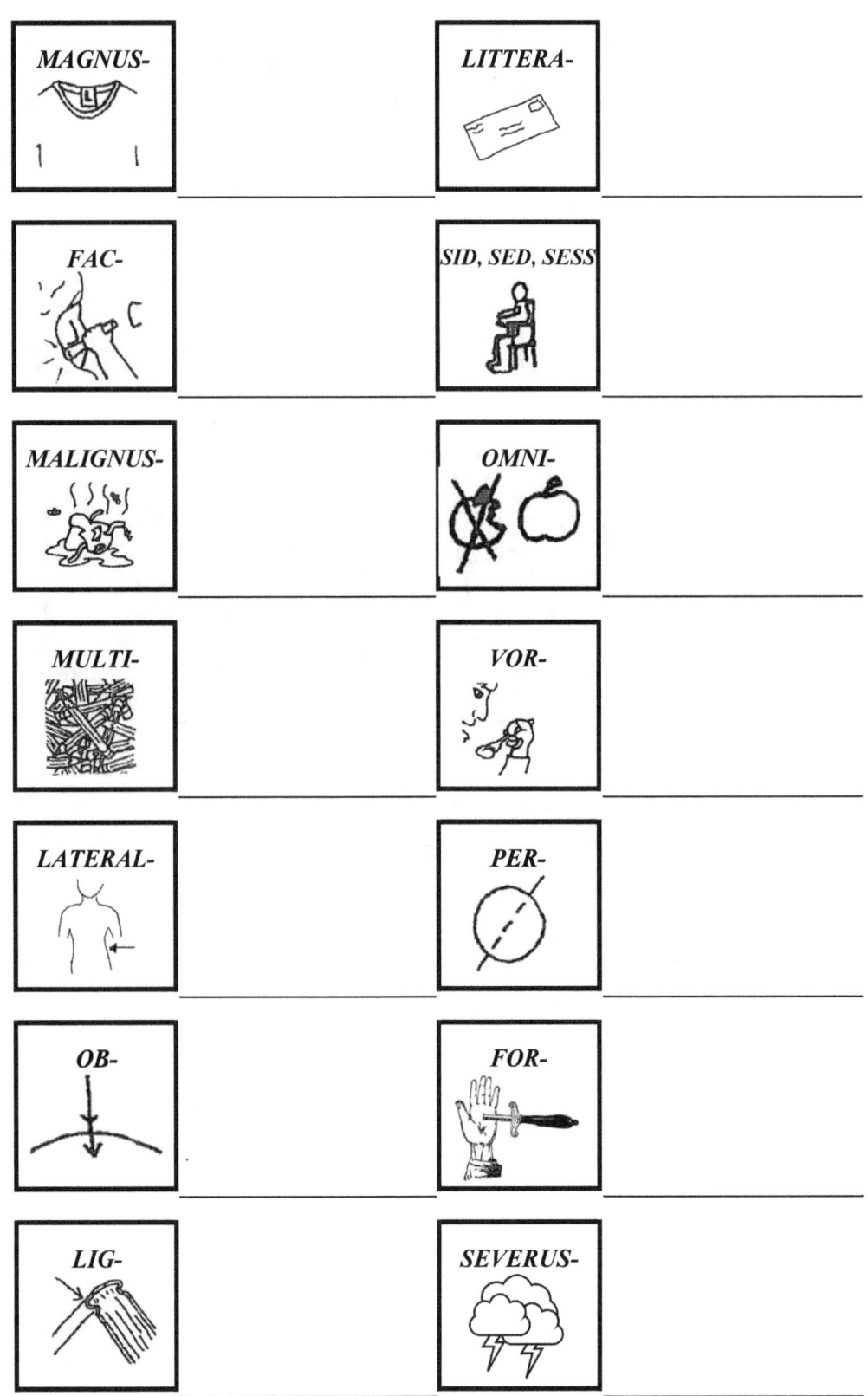

Exercise B
Match the word with the letter of its definition:

1. ____ magnificent
2. ____ magnitude
3. ____ major
4. ____ majority
5. ____ malicious
6. ____ multilateral
7. ____ multitude
8. ____ obligation
9. ____ obliterate
10. ____ obsess
11. ____ omnivorous
12. ____ perforate
13. ____ persevere
14. ____ perspective
15. ____ posterity
16. ____ postpone
17. ____ post script
18. ____ preclude
19. ____ prediction
20. ____ presume

a) a great throng of people or things
b) a rank in the army
c) involving three or more parties
d) more than half of a group
e) spectacular; exceptional
f) scope or importance
g) intending to do harm
h) a duty
i) to utterly destroy
j) to think about constantly
k) to remain devoted to a difficult task
l) to make a hole in; to pierce
m) a point of view
n) feeding on both plants and animals
o) to put off to a later time
p) future generations
q) to make an assumption
r) a claim about future events
s) to make impossible; to prevent
t) an added note at the end of a letter

Exercise C

1. The view outside Rachel's apartment window, of the setting sun casting a purple glow on the snowy mountains, was _____.

2. The _____ agreement among the western European nations will promote trade.

3. Harold did not know whether to declare physics or chemistry as his _____ at MIT.

4. He was clearly a _____ person, always hoping that others would be thwarted or humiliated.

5. The ferocity of the tropical storm caught the deep sea fishing vessel by surprise; the crew was not expecting a tempest of such _____.

6. In a democratic nation, the _____ vote usually determines who will be elected.

7. After scoring the winning goal for Spain in the World Cup, Cristiano Ronaldo smiled at the _____ of ecstatic fans before collapsing from exhaustion.

8. Fish and Game divers and volunteers worked to _____ milfoil, an invasive weed that crowds out native plants and harms fish populations, from the lake.

9. Derek spent his vacation in Spain _____ over his upcoming exams, instead of enjoying the attractions and museums.

10. He didn't want to serve on the budget committee, but felt it was an _____ he couldn't sidestep.

11. A marathon is a test of an athlete's willingness to _____ through pain and exhaustion.

12. The hole punch _____ the construction paper so it could be put in the binder.

13. From Steve's _____, the ball appeared to land in bounds, but the line judge declared it out.

14. Though Susan simply meant that John was not a vegetarian, everyone found it funny that she called him _____, because he seemed to eat everything in sight.

15. Although it had begun to drizzle, the fans had already arrived, so the referee was reluctant to _____ the game.

16. Mike's _____ that *Chicago* would not win anything at the Academy Awards appeared foolish when the movie won seven Oscars, including "Best Picture."

17. Starring in *The Lord of the Rings* trilogy _____ actor Elijah Wood from accepting any other roles for the entire, three-year production period.

18. With no physical description or photo to go by, Hank could only _____ that the woman sitting alone at a table was his blind date, Elizabeth.

19. Indiana Jones was able to decipher the cryptic letter when he realized that the seemingly innocuous _____, "P.S. Don't forget to feed the cat," was actually a coded message referring to the Nazis on his trail.

20. We need to pay down the national debt so that it is manageable for _____.

Exercise D

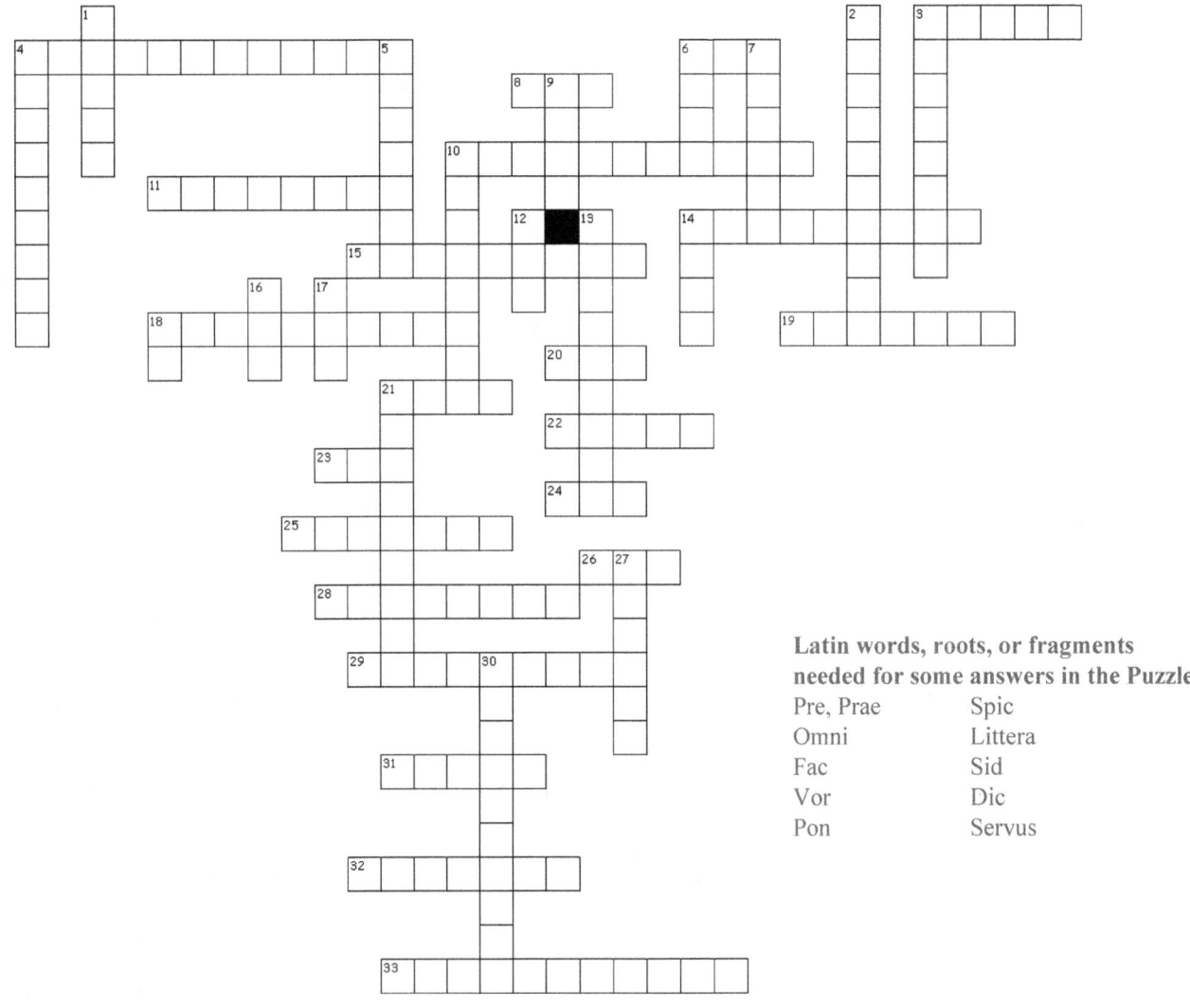

Latin words, roots, or fragments needed for some answers in the Puzzle:
Pre, Prae   Spic
Omni   Littera
Fac   Sid
Vor   Dic
Pon   Servus

Across
3. a rank in the army
4. involving three or more parties
6. to take (l)
8. to pierce (l)
10. spectacular; exceptional
11. to put off to a later time
14. future generations
15. intending to do harm
18. a duty
19. to make an assumption
20. to say (l)
21. after, behind (l)
22. many (l)
23. to eat (l)
24. completely, through (l)
25. side (l)
26. to place (l)
28. to make impossible; to prevent
29. to make a hole in; to pierce
31. to write (l)
32. severe (l)
33. a point of view

Down
1. to close, to shut (l)
2. to utterly destroy
3. more than half of a group
4. scope or importance
5. letter, books (l)
6. to look (l)
7. big, great (l)
9. all (l)
10. evil (l)
12. to bind (l)
13. a great throng of people or things
14. before (l)
16. sit, stay, besiege (l)
17. to do, to make (l)
18. over, towards, against (l)
21. to remain devoted to a difficult task
27. to think about constantly
30. feeding on both plants and animals

53

Lesson V

Primary

Fr. Premier
It. Primario
Port. Primário
Sp. Primario

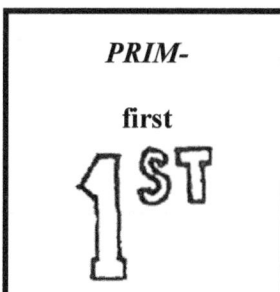

Definition: **adj.** of chief importance, principal; earliest in time or order; an election within a party to determine its candidates for the general election (U.S.)

Sentence: His job was the family's primary means of support.

Primate

Fr. Primate
It. Primate
Port. Primata
Sp. Primate

Definition: **n.** a mammal of the order including humans, monkeys and gorillas; an archbishop or bishop who is more important than others in a region

Sentence: Unlike our close primate relatives, we humans walk upright.

Procession/

Proceed

Fr. Procession/Procéder
It. Processione/Procedere
Port. Procissão/Proceder
Sp. Procesión/Proceder

 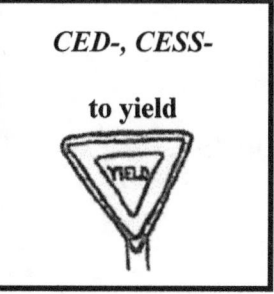

Definition: **n.** a number of people or vehicles moving forward in an orderly fashion; a parade; **v.** go forward or onward, continue without interruption

Sentence: The procession of job seekers continued throughout the day.
On an icy road, one should proceed with caution.

Profit

Fr. v. Profiter, n. Profit
It. v. Beneficiare, n. Profitto
Port. Proveito
Sp. Provecho

PRO- forward

FAC- to do, to make

Definition: **v.** to benefit from
n. a financial gain; proceeds; an advantage or benefit;

Sentence: When he retired, he lived off the profit from his investments.

Provoke

Fr. Provoquer
It. Provocare
Port. Provocar
Sp. Provocar

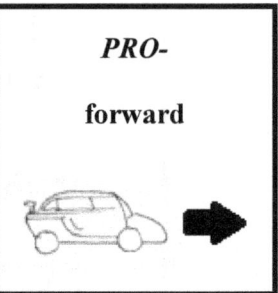 

PRO- forward

VOC- to call

Definition: **v.** to cause something to happen; to annoy

Sentence: Exposure to poison oak may provoke a rash.

Recite

Fr. Réciter
It. Recitare
Port. Recitar
Sp. Recitar

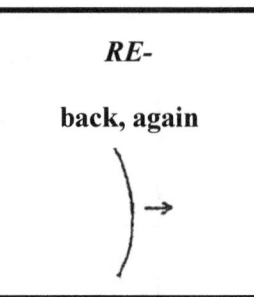 

RE- back, again

CIT- read out, summon

Definition: **v.** to repeat aloud from memory; to state in order

Sentence: Children are often required to recite poems in school.

Recline

Fr. Incliner
It. Reclinare
Port. Reclinar
Sp. Reclinar

RE-	CLIN-
back, again	to lean

Definition: **v.** to lean against or lie back in a relaxed manner

Sentence: He reclined on the bench, smoking and studying her insolently.

Reiterate

Fr. Réitérer
It. Reiterare
Port. Reitar
Sp. Reiterar

RE-	ITERARE-
back, again	to repeat

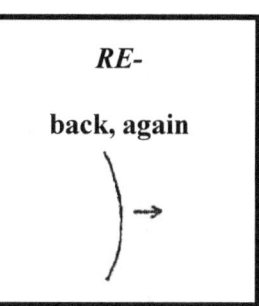

Definition: **v.** to say something again; to restate

Sentence: I said it before and I'll reiterate: No new taxes!

Retrospect

Fr. Recul
It. Retrospettiva
Port. Retrspecto
Sp. Retrospección

RETRO-	SPECT-, SPIC-
backward	to look

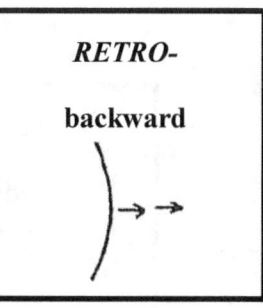 

Definition: **n.** a survey or review of a past course of events

Sentence: At the time, it seemed like a good idea. In retrospect, I see that it wasn't.

Seclude

Fr. Isoler
It. Isolare
Port. Isolar
Sp. Aislar

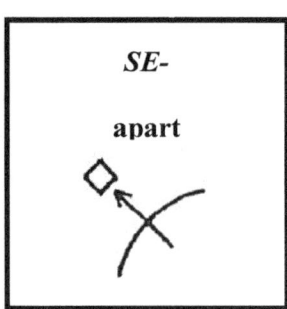
SE- apart

CLAUS- to shut

Definition: **v.** to shut someone away from other people

Sentence: J. D. Salinger refused interview requests and lived a secluded life.

Secure

Fr. Attacher
It. Assicurare
Port. Seguro
Sp. Seguro

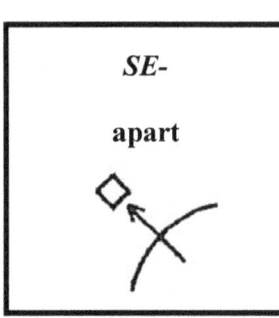
SE- apart

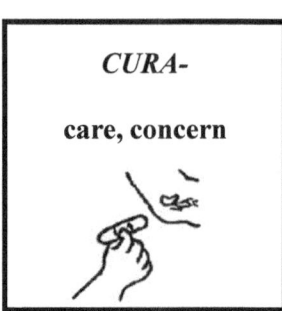
CURA- care, concern

Definition: **v.** to obtain; to fasten; to protect against threats
adj. fixed or fastened so as not to give way, become loose, or be lost;

Sentence: The Harvard Law grad secured a job as a Supreme Court clerk.
The wounded soldier had to be moved to a secure area before he could be given medical attention.

Subscribe

Fr. Souscrire
It. Sottoscrivere
Port. Suscrever
Sp. Suscribir

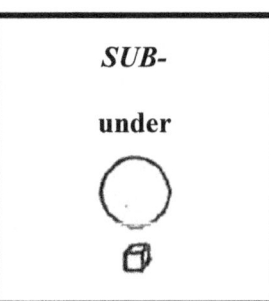
SUB- under

SCRIB- to write

Definition: **v.** to arrange to receive something (such as a periodical); to agree with

Sentence: I don't subscribe to the Republican economic agenda.

Suffocate	Fr. Suffoquer It. Soffocare Port. Suficar Sp. Sofocar	*SUB-* below 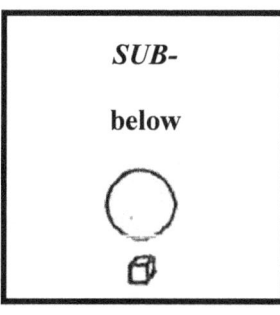	*FAUCES-* throat 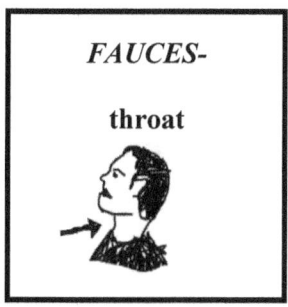

Definition: **v.** to be unable to breathe; to stop someone from breathing; to die from lack of air

Sentence: Putting dirt or sand on a campfire will suffocate the flames.

Suggest	Fr. Suggérer It. Suggerire Port. Sugerir Sp. Sugerir	*SUB-* below 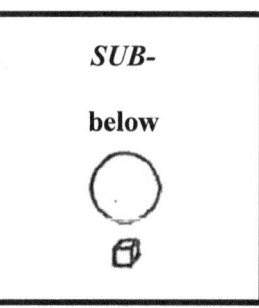	*GER-* to carry, to manage 

Definition: **v.** to put forward for consideration; to hint at

Sentence: His muddy boots suggested it was raining outside.

Supervise	Fr. Superviser It. Supervisionare Port. Superisionar Sp. Supervisar	*SUPER-* over 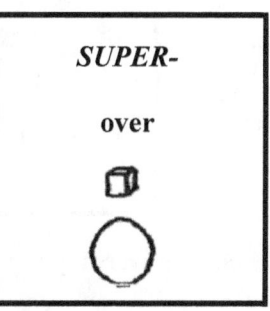	*VID-, VIS-* to see 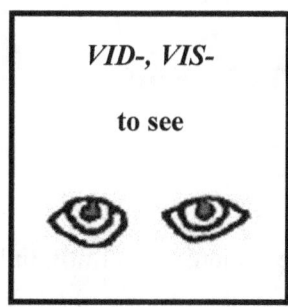

Definition: **v.** to oversee and direct the execution of a task or activity

Sentence: A foreman supervises the workers and is responsible for quality.

Translucent

Fr. Translucide
It. Traslucido
Port. Translúcido
Sp. Translúcido

TRANS-	LUC-
across	to shine
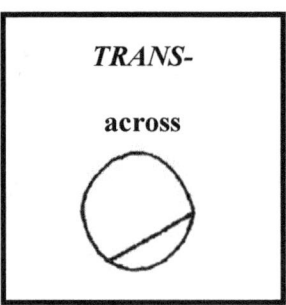	

Definition: **adj.** allowing some light to pass through; semi-transparent

Sentence: Stained glass is translucent, while clear glass is transparent.

Transparent

Fr. Transparent
It. Trasparente
Port. Transparente
Sp. Transparente

TRANS-	PARERE-
across	to show
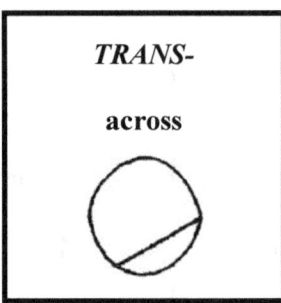	

Definition: **adj.** (of a substance) allowing light to pass through so that objects behind; can be distinctly seen; (of someone) easy to see through

Sentence: His true motives were transparent to everyone but his adoring wife.

Unanimous

Fr. Unanime
It. Unanime
Port. Unânime
Sp. Unánime

UNI-	ANIM-
one	spirit, mind, life
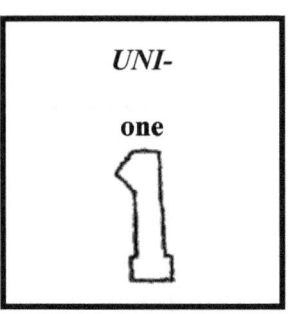	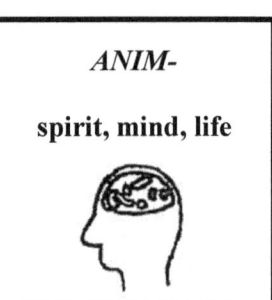

Definition: **adj.** fully in agreement; universally in accord

Sentence: The court's decision was unanimous, surprising those who had expected Justice Scalia to dissent.

Unity

Fr. Unité
It. Unità
Port. Unidade
Sp. Unidad

Definition: **n.** the state of being united; forming a complex whole

Sentence: After the terrorist attacks of Sept. 11, 2001, American politicians displayed a rare unity in the face of the nation's enemies.

Exercise A

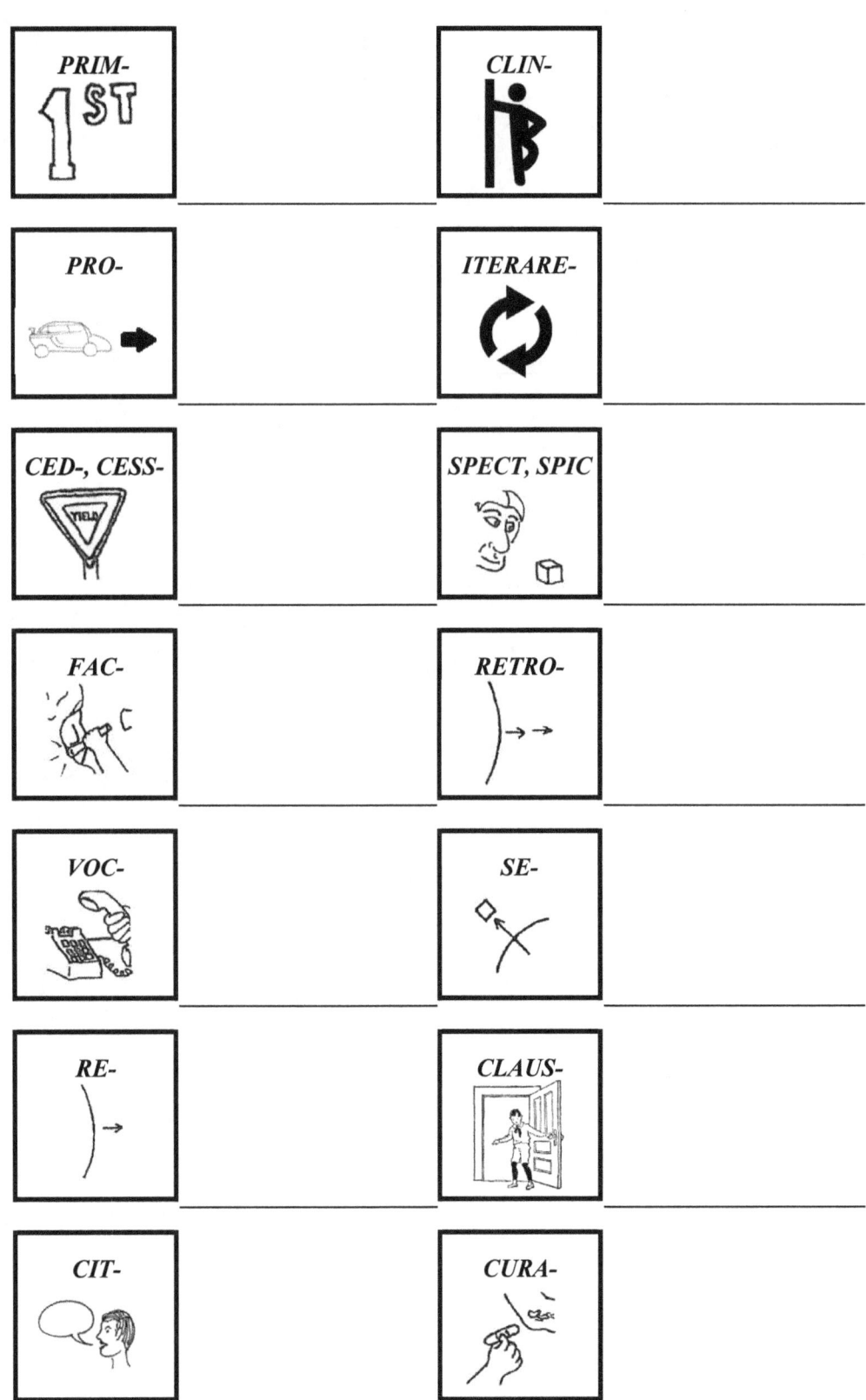

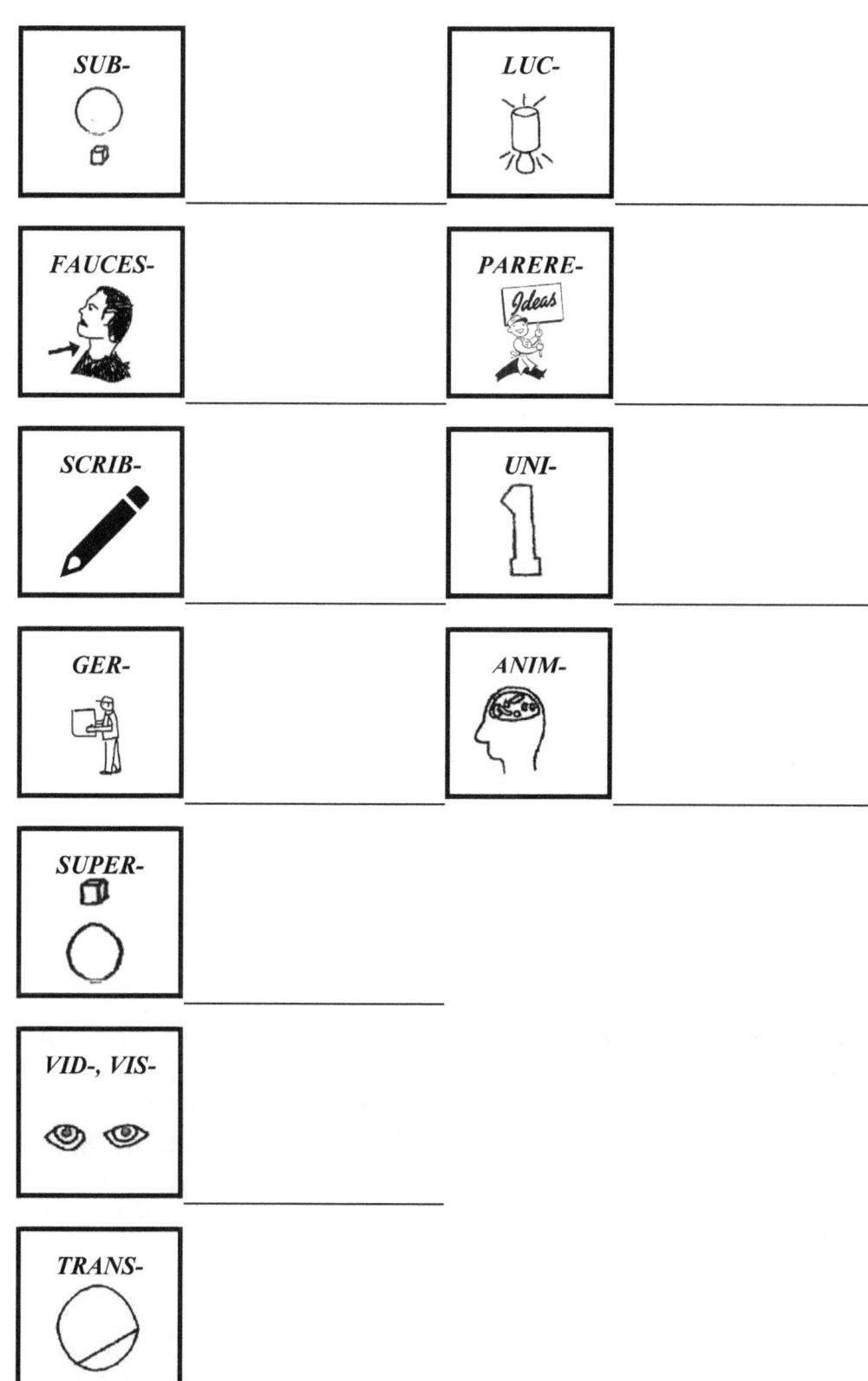

Exercise B
Match the word with the letter of its definition:

1. ____ primary
2. ____ primate
3. ____ proceed
4. ____ procession
5. ____ profit
6. ____ provoke
7. ____ recite
8. ____ recline
9. ____ reiterate
10. ____ retrospect
11. ____ seclude
12. ____ secure
13. ____ supervise
14. ____ subscribe
15. ____ suffocate
16. ____ suggest
17. ____ translucent
18. ____ transparent
19. ____ unanimous
20. ____ unity

a) humans, gorillas, and monkeys
b) a parade
c) to benefit financially
d) first in rank or importance
e) to begin a course of action
f) to deliberately annoy or anger
g) to say again
h) a review of past events
i) to repeat by memory
j) to lean back or lie down
k) to protect against threats
l) to put forward for consideration
m) to oversee
n) to remove from social interaction; to isolate
o) make unable to breathe
p) to arrange to receive periodically
q) oneness
r) allowing light to pass through partially
s) see-through
t) completely in agreement

Exercise C

1. Every four years, New Hampshire hosts the nation's first presidential _____, but prospective candidates start visiting the state a year earlier to see if they can drum up support.

2. When Suzy the chimp escaped the zoo, it took the animal control officer weeks to locate the resourceful _____, who slept in trees and scavenged from garbage cans.

3. After the plane landed, the airline steward announced that we should _____ to the baggage claim.

4. Oftentimes during a funeral, a black hearse will lead a _____ of cars, which by law no vehicle other than an emergency vehicle may interrupt.

5. All during school, Mike _____ Susan by grabbing her ponytail and yanking it.

6. Since its founding, the company has increased its _____ by 10% annually.

7. To qualify for the summer trip around the country, each student had to memorize and _____ the Gettysburg Address.

8. After the Red Sox committed three errors in the ninth inning to lose the game, the manager _____ the importance of defense.

9. In _____, we might have been able to move in earlier, if we had not taken our vacation before I transferred to the new job.

10. Chairs that _____ are far more comfortable than ones that do not.

11. Betsey sought out a bench in a _____ spot where she could be alone with her thoughts.

12. The Secret Service tried to find a _____ location for the president on Martha's Vineyard, in case of a terrorist attack during his summer vacation.

13. Peter _____ the project, while Amanda and Mike implemented it.

14. Members of the acting class _____ numerous possibilities for the school musical before agreeing on *Oklahoma!*

15. She felt as if she would _____ if she didn't escape from the vile fumes as quickly as possible.

16. I read the same newspaper all of the time, but I _____ to a different magazine each year.

17. The outcome was _____; the entire class voted to go on a whale watch at the end of the year.

18. The new _____ curtains made the room appear lighter and brighter.

19. Our team's _____ helped us win the championship; the other team had some better players, but they were *prima donnas*.

20. Glass greenhouses remain _____ for decades, while clear plastics, although more durable, can become scratched and cloudy quickly.

Exercise D

Latin words, roots, or fragments needed for some answers in the Puzzle:
Clin
Ced
Scrib
Vis
Luc
Anim
Ger
Cit

Across
1. apart (l)
6. to say again
7. one (l)
8. to do, to make (l)
11. back, again (l)
12. forward (l)
14. over (l)
15. to lean back or lie down
17. to call (l)
20. throat (l)
22. to benefit financially
23. see-through
25. to begin a course of action
26. to put forward for consideration
27. spirit, mind, life (l)
28. to carry (l)
29. a parade
31. to deliberately annoy or anger
32. completely in agreement
34. to lean (l)
35. oneness
36. to arrange to receive periodically
38. a review of past events
39. read out, summon (l)

Down
1. to make unable to breathe
2. backward (l)
3. first in rank or importance
4. across (l)
5. to shine (l)
9. to repeat (l)
10. humans, gorillas, and monkeys
13. to protect against threats
15. to repeat by memory
16. to yield (l)
18. to close, to shut (l)
19. to see (l)
21. to oversee
24. allowing light to pass through partially
26. to look (l)
30. to remove social interaction; to isolate
31. first (l)
33. under
37. to write (l)

65

Quiz 1

Quiz answers begin on page 318

> *magnificent, postpone, provoke, obliterate, evoke, retrospect, bilingual, anticipated, emigrate, demote, unity, eradicate, condone, abhor, secluded, multitude, interjection, demote, irrelevant, intersection, unity*

1. She _____ her upcoming wedding with a mixture of excitement and dread.

2. In _____, the coach should have called a time out, but he hoped the players would rally and remember how to run an effective defense.

3. Even though they do not _____ violence, the police may, at times, be forced to resort to violent behavior themselves.

4. "And above all things, have fervent charity among yourselves: for charity shall cover the _____ of sins." Peter 4:8

5. He tried to _____ a reaction by clowning around, but the other kids ignored him.

6. After Rome conquered Egypt, the authorities tried to _____ all hieroglyphs in order to _____ all remnants of the Egyptians' culture and language.

7. Most coaches try to promote _____ by emphasizing teamwork and not comparing the abilities of individual players.

8. The counselors _____ the trip to the water park because of _____ thunderstorms.

9. Some teams in the NBA are so atrocious that the commissioner may _____ them to a developmental league.

10. In poetry, authors use symbolism and metaphors to _____ emotion in the reader.

11. Red Sox fans are known to _____ the Yankees, and vice-versa.

12. The mansion was _____, but the family chose not to buy the home because it was too _____ and isolated.

13. After the Polish family _____ to the United States, the children quickly became _____ because they spoke English in school all day long.

14. The rude student continuously made unnecessary _____ and _____ remarks.

15. The _____ of Chestnut and Main streets can be very dangerous because many drivers speed through the crosswalk without stopping.

Lesson VI

Acrid

Fr. Âcre
It. Acre
Port. Acre
Sp. Acre

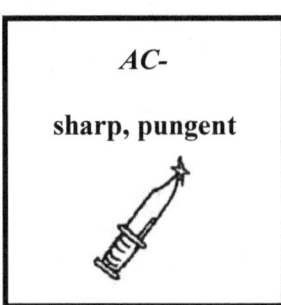

AC-

sharp, pungent

Definition: **adj.** unpleasantly bitter or pungent; biting or bitter (remarks)

Sentence: The acrid smoke made our eyes water and our throats burn.

Acute

Fr. Aigu
It. Acuto
Port. Agudo
Sp. Agudo

AC-

sharp, pungent

Definition: **adj.** perceptive, finely honed; (of a situation) dire, severe; (of a disease) of sudden onset and short duration

Sentence: Migratory birds need an acute sense of direction.

Agility

Fr. Agilité
It. Agilità
Port. Agilidade
Sp. Agilidad

AG-

to drive, to urge

Definition: **n.** the state or quality of being nimble

Sentence: An Olympic gymnast's routines require great agility.

Agitate

Fr. Agiter
It. Agitare
Port. Agitar
Sp. Agitar

AG-
to drive, to urge

Definition: **v.** to upset (someone) or make them nervous; to arouse public opinion for a cause; to shake vigorously

Sentence: Although he knew the music annoyed Matt, Steve made it louder simply to agitate him.

Agriculture

Fr. Agriculture
It. Agricoltura
Port. Agricultura
Sp. Agricultura

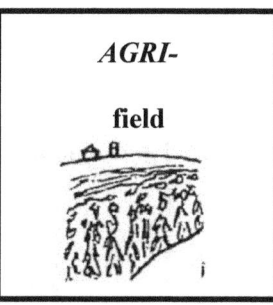

AGRI- field

CULTURA- growing

Definition: **n.** the science or practice of farming

Sentence: Agriculture in the U.S. has shifted from small family farms to large, corporate agribusinesses.

Alias

Fr. Alias
It. Alias
Port. Aliás
Sp. Alias

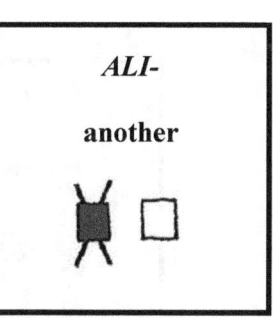

ALI- another

Definition: **n.** a false or assumed identity; an alternative name or label

Sentence: William Bonney was better known by his alias, Billy the Kid.

Alien

Fr. Alien
It. Alieno
Port. Alienígena
Sp. Alienígena

ALI-

another

Definition:	**adj.** belonging to a foreign country; unfamiliar and distasteful **n.** a foreigner; a being from another world
Sentence:	He found his surroundings alien when he first emigrated. About 20 percent of Americans believe space aliens exist and visit our planet.

Alienate

Fr. S'aliéner
It. Alienare
Port. Alienar
Sp. Alienar

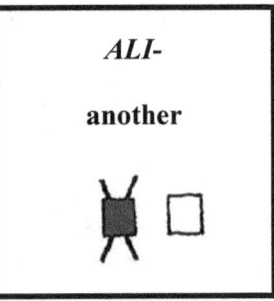

ALI-

another

Definition:	**v.** to cause to feel isolated; to estrange
Sentence:	His nasty gossip alienated his friend and ended their relationship.

Alter

Fr. Altérer
It. Alterare,
Port. Alterar
Sp. Alterar

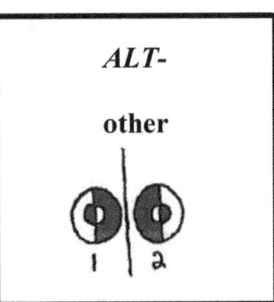

ALT-

other

Definition:	**v.** to change in character, appearance, or composition; to adjust clothing for a better fit; to spay a domestic animal
Sentence:	Global warming threatens to alter the climate for the worse.

Altitude

Fr. Altitude
It. Altitudine
Port. Altitude
Sp. Altitud

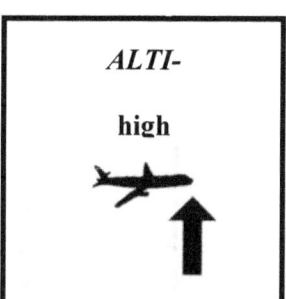

Definition: **n.** the height of an object or point in relation to sea level or ground level

Sentence: As altitude climbs from sea level to mountaintop, the air thins.

Amateur

Fr. Amateur
It. Amatore, Dilettante
Port. Amador
Sp. Amateur

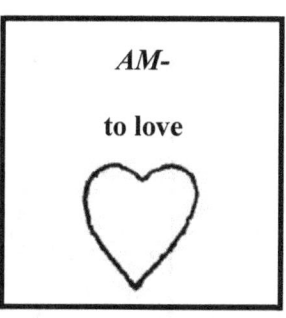

Definition: **n.** a person who does an activity for love, not money; a person considered inept at a particular activity
adj. non-professional; inept, unskillful

Sentence: The tennis pro handily defeated most amateurs, even the most devoted players.
The amateur skateboarder loved to learn new tricks.

Amiable

Fr. Aimable
It. Amabile
Port. Amável
Sp. Amable

Definition: **adj.** friendly and pleasant in manner

Sentence: I warmed to my new acquaintance quickly for he was an amiable fellow.

Ambulatory

Fr. Ambulatoire
It. Ambulatory
Port. Ambulatório
Sp. Ambulatorio

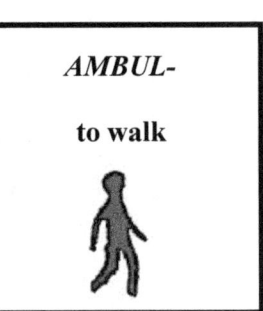

AMBUL-

to walk

Definition: **adj.** walking or able to walk; movable, mobile

Sentence: After the motorcycle accident, she was no longer ambulatory without a wheelchair.

Animate

Fr. v. Animer, n. Animé
It. v. Animare, n. Animato
Port. Animado
Sp. Animado

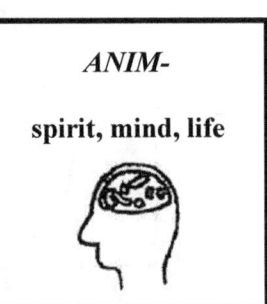

ANIM-

spirit, mind, life

Definition: **v.** to give life or vigor to; to give the appearance of movement
adj. alive or having life

Sentence: Dr. Frankenstein animated a dead body, creating a semi-human monster.
He manipulated the marionettes so skillfully they seemed animate.

Animosity

Fr. Animosité
It. Animosità
Port. Animosidade
Sp. Animosidad

ANIM-

spirit. mind. life

Definition: **n.** strong hostility

Sentence: Dogs display animosity by baring their teeth and growling.

Annual	Fr. Annuel It. Annuale Port. Anual Sp. Anual	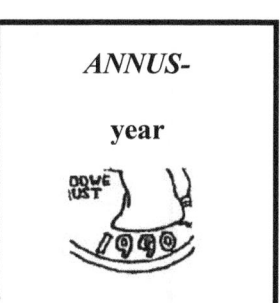 *ANNUS-* year

Definition: **adj.** occurring once every year; calculated over or covering a year; (of a plant) dying after one season (contrast with perennial)
n. a book or magazine of a series published once a year; an annual plant

Sentence: He stopped holding the annual company Christmas party after his wife died.
She bought some annuals at the garden store.

Annuity	Fr. Viager It. Annualità Port. Anuidade Sp. Anualidad	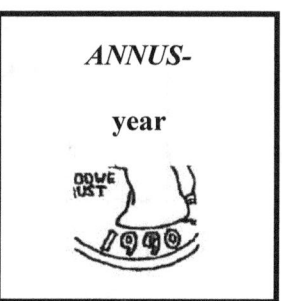 *ANNUS-* year

Definition: **n.** a fixed sum of money paid to someone each year, typically for the rest of their lives; an investment that yields such an income

Sentence: A sizable annuity allowed him to travel the world after he retired.

Aperture	Fr. Overture It. Apertura Port. Abertura Sp. Apertura	 *APER-* to open

Definition: **n.** an opening, hole, or gap

Sentence: A camera's aperture is the lens opening that allows light to enter.

Aptitude

Fr. Aptitude
It. Attitudine
Port. Aptidão
Sp. Aptitud

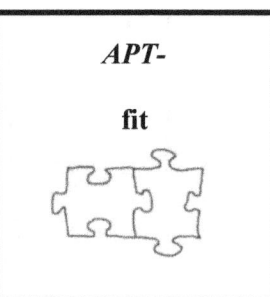

APT-
fit

Definition: **n.** a natural ability or propensity

Sentence: Unlike her brother, the girl showed a strong aptitude for mathematics.

Inept

Fr. Inepte
It. Inetto
Port. Inepto
Sp. Inepto

IL-, IM-, IN-
in, not

APT-
fit

Definition: **adj.** incompetent; awkward or clumsy

Sentence: The new kid proved inept as a catcher.

Exercise A

Exercise B

Match the word with the letter of its definition:

1. ____ acrid
2. ____ acute
3. ____ agility
4. ____ agitate
5. ____ agriculture
6. ____ alias
7. ____ alien
8. ____ alienate
9. ____ alter
10. ____ altitude
11. ____ amateur
12. ____ amiable
13. ____ ambulatory
14. ____ animate
15. ____ animosity
16. ____ annual
17. ____ annuity
18. ____ aperture
19. ____ aptitude
20. ____ inept

a) yearly
b) nimbleness
c) foreign
d) to change
e) height from the ground or sea level
f) to bring to life; to inspire
g) pungent and bitter
h) farming
i) incompetent
j) a strong hostility
k) able to walk; mobile
l) very perceptive
m) an opening
n) to disturb
o) a false label or name
p) to estrange
q) a non-professional
r) a yearly payment of money
s) a natural ability
t) friendly

Exercise C

1. Her _____ comments made him redden with embarrassment and anger.

2. Superman's _____ is Clark Kent.

3. Nastia Liukin's _____, strength, and grace won her the gold medal in gymnastics in the 2008 Olympics.

4. The pilot said the airplane's cruising _____ was 30,000 feet.

5. Nick had an _____ sense of smell: He could tell from a block away when Grandma Lachey was making his favorite strawberry-rhubarb pie.

6. We did not mean to _____ the ants, but when we accidentally stepped on the anthill, they began to swarm around the opening.

7. Because the English teacher was known for giving extra assignments for misbehavior or a poor attitude, her students tried hard not to _____ her.

8. When her metabolism began to slow down, Suzanne Somers had to _____ her diet to maintain her svelte physique.

9. Foreigners who enter the United States without legal permission are called illegal _____.

10. _____ accounts for a dwindling share of the U.S. economy, although small organic farms are on the rise.

11. Theodora's _____ income tripled in one year as a result of increased sales.

12. The first construction crew was so _____ that the entire addition had to be torn down and rebuilt by a more competent contractor.

13. When they shared the stage at the Video Music Awards, one could sense the _____ between the feuding divas.

14. The museum requested that the tour guides _____ their presentations to attract more visitors.

15. Miriam was a complete _____ and never should have been hired for the highly skilled position.

16. Mozart had an innate _____ for music: He displayed dazzling talent at an extraordinarily young age.

17. By adjusting the size of the camera _____, a photographer can control the amount of light that enters the lens when she releases the shutter.

18. Since my $10,000 _____ has a yield of 6 percent, I get a check for $600 each year.

19. His _____ disposition and charisma contributed to Tony Blair's success in establishing good relationships with other politicians.

20. The late Christopher Reeve, the star of the movie *Superman*, who became paralyzed from the neck down, vowed to become fully _____ again.

Exercise D

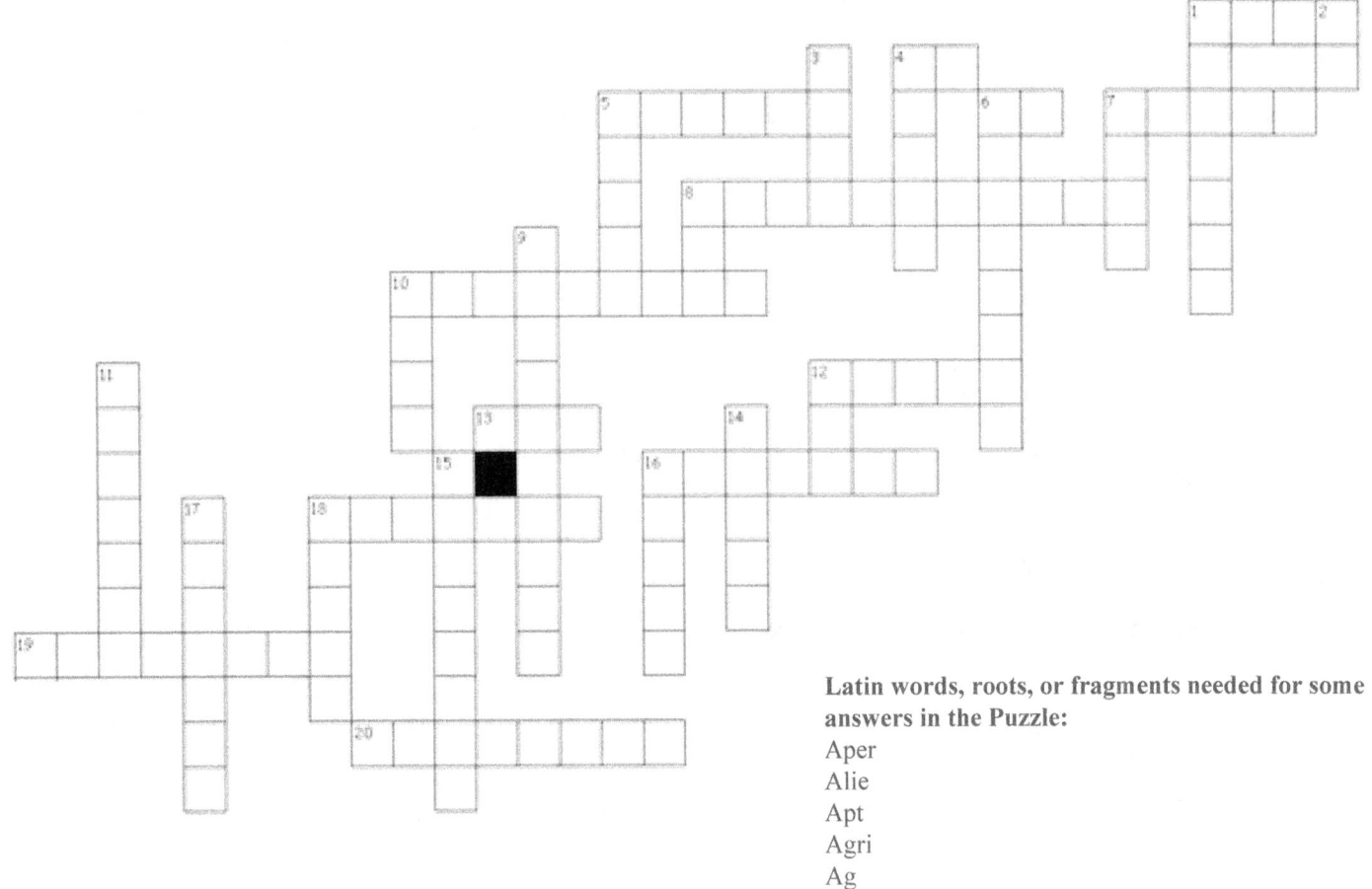

Latin words, roots, or fragments needed for some answers in the Puzzle:
Aper
Alie
Apt
Agri
Ag

Across
1. field (l)
4. love (l)
5. yearly
6. to drive, to urge (l)
7. a false label or name
8. farming
10. a strong hostility
12. pungent and bitter
13. other (l)
16. a yearly payment of money
18. nimbleness
19. an opening
20. height from the ground or sea level

Down
1. friendly
2. in, not (l)
3. high (l)
4. to walk (l)
5. year (l)
6. a natural ability
7. to open (l)
8. to fit (l)
9. able to walk; mobile
10. spirit, mind, life (l)
11. to bring to life; to inspire
12. another (l)
14. incompetent
15. to estrange
16. to change
17. growing (l)
18. foreign

Lesson VII

Army

Fr. Armée
It. Esercito
Port. Exército
Sp. Ejército

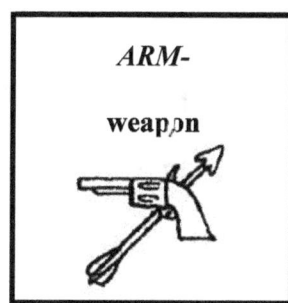

Definition: **n.** an organized military force; a large number of similar people or things

Sentence: The highly unpopular politician faced an army of critics.

Artifact

Fr. Objet ancien
It. Manufatto
Port. Artefacto
Sp. Artefacto

Definition: **n.** an object made by a human being

Sentence: Archaeological sites in Egypt yielded artifacts showing a high degree of skill among ancient artisans.

Artificial

Fr. Artificiel
It. Artificiale
Port. Artificial
Sp. Artificial

Definition: **adj.** not natural; man-made; untruthful

Sentence: Artificial flowers may deceive initially, but not on closer inspection.

Audible

Fr. Audible
It. Udibile
Port. Audível
Sp. Audible

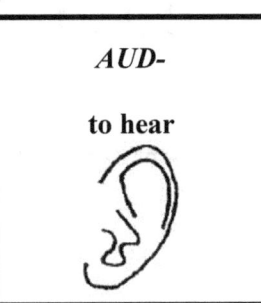

Definition: **adj.** able to be heard

Sentence: The music was audible from across the lawn.

Audience

Fr. Audience
It. Audience
Port. Audiência
Sp. Audiencia

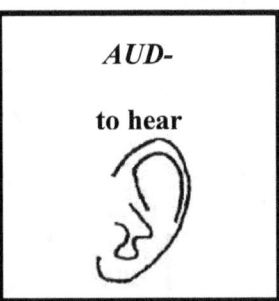

Definition: **n.** the assembled spectators or listeners at an event; the readership of a book, magazine, or newspaper; a formal interview with a person in authority

Sentence: The Pope rarely grants an audience to ordinary churchgoers.

Auditorium

Fr. Auditorium
It. Auditorium
Port. Auditório
Sp. Auditorio

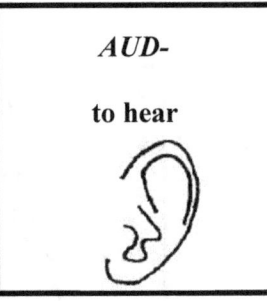

Definition: **n.** the part of a theater or hall in which an audience sits

Sentence: The crowd milled about the auditorium while the musicians tuned up.

Avuncular

Fr. Avunculaire
It. Come uno zio, Avuncolare
Port. Avuncular
Sp. Avuncular

AVUNCULUS-

uncle

Definition: **adj.** like an uncle in being kind and friendly toward a younger or less experienced person

Sentence: Santa Claus is portrayed as a rosy-cheeked, avuncular figure.

Battery

Fr. Batterie
It. Batteria
Port. Bateria
Sp. Bateria

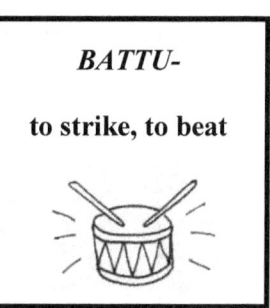

BATTU-

to strike, to beat

Definition: **n.** a container consisting of one or more cells in which chemical energy is converted into electricity to be used as a source of power; any large group of things; striking of one person by another; two or more pieces of artillery

Sentence: He was charged with assault and battery after he smashed a cream pie into the newspaper owner's face.

Beatitude

Fr. Béatitude
It. Beatitudine
Port. Beatitude
Sp. Beatitud

BEATUS-

blessed

Definition: **n.** supreme blessedness or happiness; Jesus' proclamations of blessedness in the "Sermon on the Mount"

Sentence: One of the Beatitudes from the Gospel of Matthew is 'Blessed are the peacemakers, for they shall be called children of God.

Rebellious

Fr. Rebelle
It. Ribelle
Port. Revbelde
Sp. Rebelde

RE-

back, again

BELLUM-

war

Definition:	**adj.** showing a desire to rebel; resisting control, unruly
Sentence:	A mutiny is a rebellious uprising to wrest command from a ship's captain.

Imbibe

Fr. Absorber
It. Assorbire
Port. Embeber
Sp. Embeber

IL-, IM-, IN-

in, not

BIB-

to drink

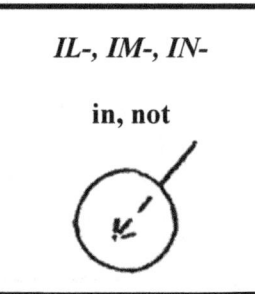

Definition:	**v.** to drink (usually alcohol); to absorb (knowledge, ideas, etc.)
Sentence:	Seventh Day Adventists do not imbibe alcoholic drinks of any kind.

Abbreviation

Fr. Abbréviation
It. Abbreviazione
Port. Abreviação
Sp. Abreviación

BREVE-

brief, short

Definition:	**n.** the act or product of shortening; a shortened form of a word
Sentence:	Etc. is an abbreviation for the Latin words 'et cetera,' meaning 'and so on.

Brevity

Fr. Brièveté
It. Brevità
Port. Brevidade
Sp. Brevedad

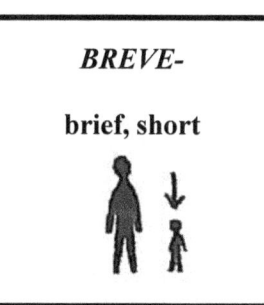

BREVE-
brief, short

Definition: **n.** concise and exact use of words; the quality of being brief

Sentence: The Gettysburg Address, which lasted only a few minutes, was a marvel of brevity.

Casualty

Fr. Victime, Mort
It. Vittima, Morto, Ferito
Port. Baixa
Sp. Baja

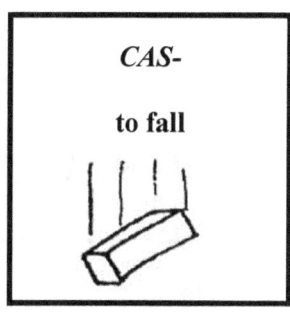

CAS-
to fall

Definition: **n.** a person killed or injured in a war or accident

Sentence: It is said that in war the first casualty is the truth.

Recalcitrant

Fr. Récalcitrant
It. Recalcitrante
Port. Recalcitrante
Sp. Recalcitrante

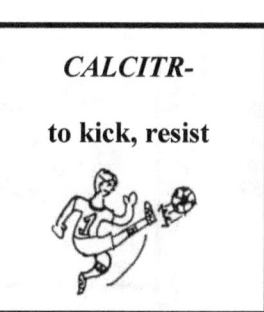

CALCITR-
to kick, resist

Definition: **adj.** obstinately uncooperative

Sentence: The recalcitrant child stubbornly refused to obey the rules.

Candid

Fr. Sincère
It. Sincero
Port. Sincero
Sp. Sincero

CANDIDUS-
transparent, white, glow

Definition: **adj.** truthful and straightforward; frank

Sentence: Let's be candid, instead of beating around the bush.

Candidate

Fr. Candidat
It. Candidato
Port. Candidato
Sp. Candidato

CANDIDUS-
transparent, white, glow

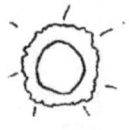

Definition: **n.** a person who applies for a job or is nominated for election; a person or thing suitable for or likely to receive a particular fate, treatment, or position

Sentence: A scholar with strong social and leadership skills, he was a perfect candidate for university president.

Incantation

Fr. Incantation
It. Incantesimo
Port. Encantação
Sp. Encantación

CANT-
to sing

Definition: **n.** a series of words said as a magic spell or in a ritual

Sentence: 'Abracadabra' is the stage magician's standard incantation.

Capture

Fr. Capturer
It. Catturare
Port. Capturar
Sp. Capturar

Definition: **v.** to take possession of or to control; to seize by force; to arrest

Sentence: The blurry photograph failed to capture her true beauty.

Participate

Fr. Participer
It. Partecipare
Port. Participar
Sp. Participar

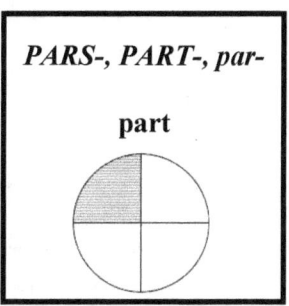 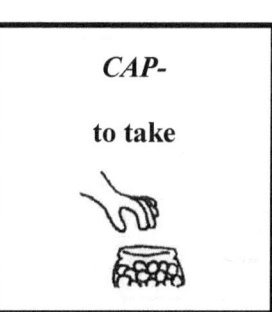

Definition: **v.** to share; to take part in

Sentence: Patriots dressed as Indians participated in the Boston Tea Party.

Exercise A

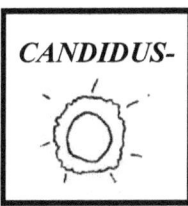 CANDIDUS- _____

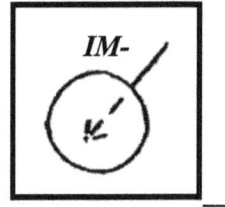 IM- _____

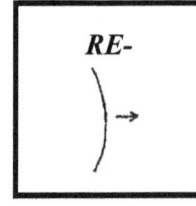 RE- _____

 CANT- _____

 CAP- _____

Exercise B

Match the word with the letter of its definition:

1. ____ abbreviation
2. ____ army
3. ____ artifact
4. ____ artificial
5. ____ audible
6. ____ audience
7. ____ auditorium
8. ____ avuncular
9. ____ battery
10. ____ beatitude
11. ____ brevity
12. ____ casualty
13. ____ candid
14. ____ candidate
15. ____ capture
16. ____ imbibe
17. ____ incantation
18. ____ participate
19. ____ rebellious
20. ____ recalcitrant

a) a man-made object
b) honest and frank
c) a theater or hall
d) the quality of being concise
e) injury purposefully inflicted on someone else
f) to take, seize
g) a shortened form of a word
h) to take part in
i) able to be heard
j) a magic spell
k) supreme blessedness or happiness
l) to drink
m) an organized military force
n) a person or thing killed or injured, usually in war
o) spectators
p) unruly
q) kindly, like an uncle
r) obstinate
s) a job applicant or nominated official
t) unnatural

Exercise C

1. The Buddhist monk radiated the _____ of one who has attained liberation from desire, pain and suffering.

2. The radio requires either a _____ or an AC adapter for power.

3. The substitute teacher's pleas for order were barely _____ over the students' chatter.

4. The American _____ uses a combination of infantry, armored vehicles, and tactical weapons during combat.

5. The Dave Matthews Band performed before an enthusiastic _____ on Saturday.

6. Pottery and arrowheads were some of the most valuable _____ found at the prehistoric village.

7. The silk flowers in the arrangement, although _____, are still attractive.

8. Joan's uncle Herb, her guardian since her father had died, met with Joan before her wedding to dispense a bit of _____ advice.

9. The school raised enough money to build a new _____ for plays and concerts.

10. Although a soldier may not be a _____ of war in the traditional sense, the psychological damage he suffers may cause life-long hardship.

11. The _____ for the United States of America is simply U.S.A.

12. A _____ photo is one that is natural, not posed.

13. Helen Keller was extremely _____ as a young child; it took the genius of Annie Sullivan to understand that Helen was protesting her inability to comprehend the world around her and communicate with others.

14. Jessica surprised the audience with the _____ of her song, which lasted only thirty seconds.

15. Choosing a _____ for each party is the purpose of the primary elections.

16. As Gandalf spoke the _____, the wind swirled and the earth shook menacingly.

17. It is illegal for people under 21 to _____ alcoholic beverages in most states.

18. In *The Catcher in the Rye*, Holden Caulfield is portrayed as a depressed and _____ teenager.

19. The Greeks were able to _____ Troy by withdrawing most of their forces, but leaving an apparent gift outside the city gates: a huge wooden horse containing soldiers, who opened the city gates after the Trojans dragged the horse inside.

20. In high school, Britney Spears _____ in varsity basketball and other sports.

Exercise D

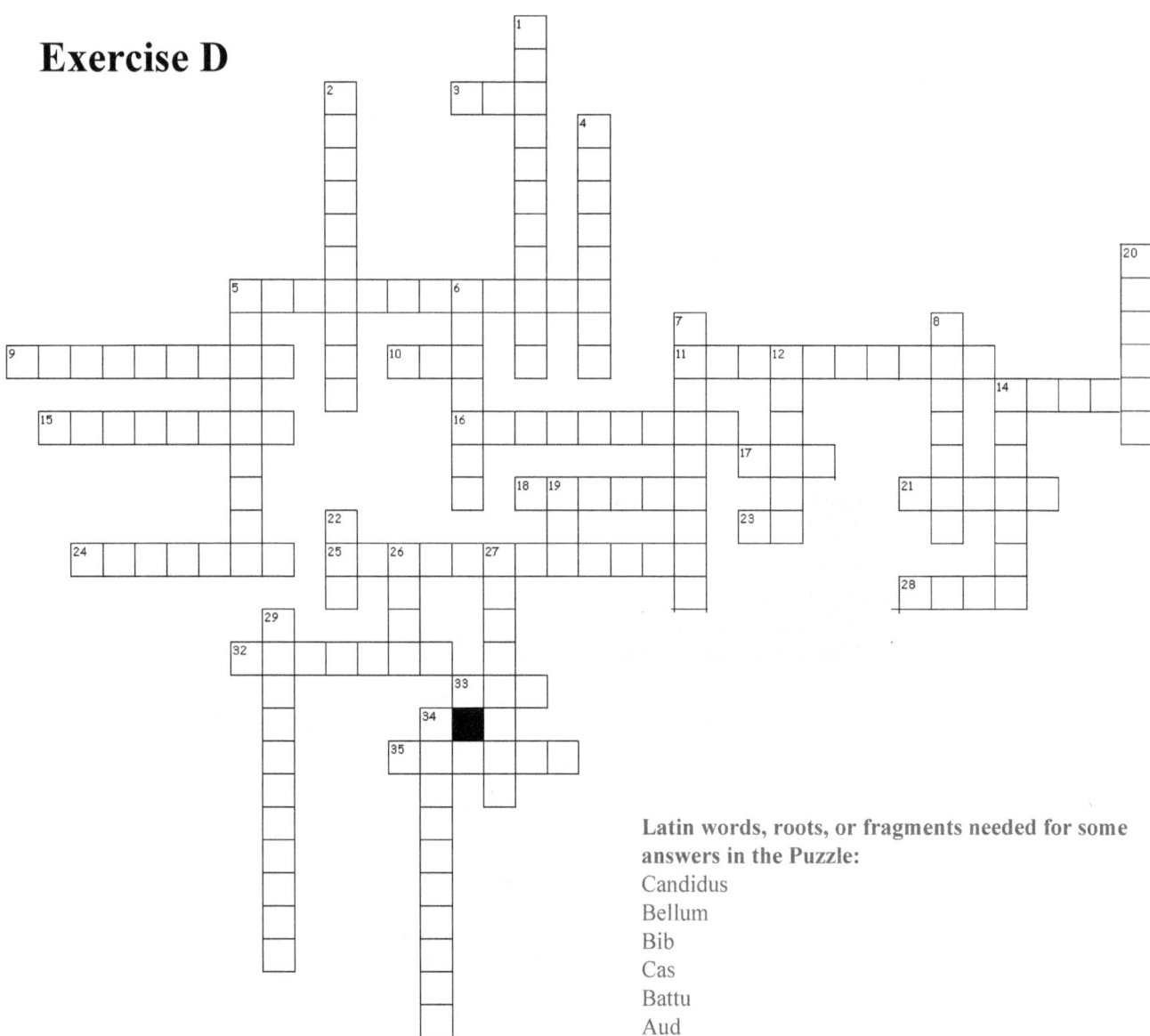

Latin words, roots, or fragments needed for some answers in the Puzzle:
Candidus
Bellum
Bib
Cas
Battu
Aud

Across
3. to do, to make (l)
5. a shortened form of a word
9. uncle (l)
10. to hear (l)
11. unnatural
14. to strike, to beat (l)
15. a man-made object
16. supreme blessedness or happiness
17. to drink (l)
18. honest and frank
21. brief, short (l)
23. back, again (l)
24. to control by force
25. obstinate
28. an organized military force
32. to kick, resist (l)
33. to fall (l)
35. blessed (l)

Down
1. a magic spell
2. a theater or hall
4. spectators
5. kindly, like an uncle
6. able to be heard
7. job applicant or nominated official
8. injury purposely inflicted on someone else
12. to drink
14. the quality of being concise
19. skill, craft (l)
20. war (l)
22. weapon (l)
26. to sing (l)
27. a person or thing killed or injured, usually in war
29. to take part in
34. unmanageable

Lesson VIII

Decapitate

Fr. Décapiter
It. Decapitare
Port. Decapitar
Sp. Decapitar

DE- — down, from

CAPUT- — head

Definition: **v.** to cut off the head

Sentence: The guillotine decapitated scores of aristocrats – as well as its inventor.

Carnivorous

Fr. Carnivore
It. Carnivoro
Port. Carnívoro
Sp. Carnívoro

CARN- — flesh, meat

VOR- — to eat

Definition: **adj.** of an animal feeding on meat or other animal life

Sentence: Unlike the brachiosaurus, whose diet consisted entirely of plants, the tyrannosaurus rex was carnivorous.

Castigate

Fr. Châtier, Blâmer
It. Castigare
Port. Castigar
Sp. Castigar

CASTIG- — to punish

Definition: **v.** to reprimand or punish severely

Sentence: Horrible machines of torture castigated medieval prisoners.

Cerebral	Fr. Cérébral It. Cerebrale Port. Cerebral Sp. Cerebral	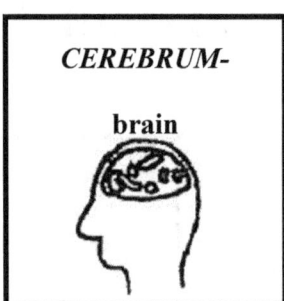 CEREBRUM- brain

Definition: **adj.** of the brain; intellectual rather than physical or emotional

Sentence: A scholar's work is cerebral rather than physical.

Discernment	Fr. Discernement It. Discernimento Port. Discernimento Sp. Discernimiento	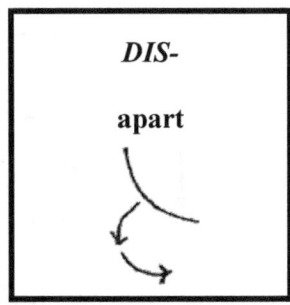 DIS- apart	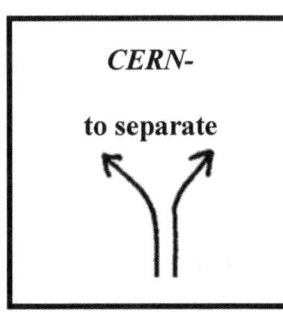 CERN- to separate

Definition: **n.** the ability to see something that tends to blend into its surroundings; the ability to understand despite obfuscation or confusion

Sentence: Thanks to his powers of discernment, he is able to diagnose psychiatric patients quickly, even when they are uncooperative or difficult.

Access	Fr. n. Accès/v. Accéder It. n. Accesso/v. Accedere Port. Acesso Sp. Acceso	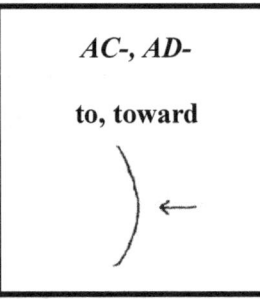 AC-, AD- to, toward	 CED-, CESS- to yield

Definition: **n.** the means or opportunity to approach or enter a place
v. to approach or enter (a place); to retrieve information stored in a computer

Sentence: Only men and male animals get access to Mt. Athos monastery.
Joe was able to access the stairway because the door was not locked.

Accessory

Fr. Accessoire
It. Accessorio
Port. Acessório
Sp. Accesorio

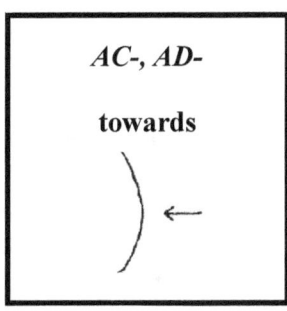

AC-, AD- towards

CED-, CESS- to yield

Definition: **n.** A supplement or object which can be added to something else, making it more useful, versatile, or attractive; a person who helps a criminal
adj. subsidiary or supplementary

Sentence: Chris thought the dress very plain, but the sales clerk showed her how a couple of accessories, such as a jazzy handbag and belt, could dress it up.
That application is accessory to the payroll software, but you don't need it.

Accelerate

Fr. Accélérer
It. Accelerare
Port. Acelerar
Sp. Acelerar

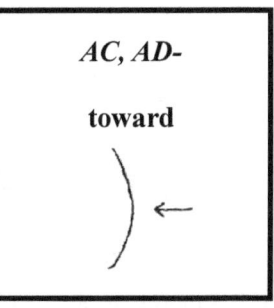

AC, AD- toward

CELER- fast

Definition: **v.** to speed up

Sentence: The spread of a fire can be accelerated with gasoline.

Decelerate

Fr. Décélérer
It. Decelerare
Port. Desacelerar
Sp. Decelerar

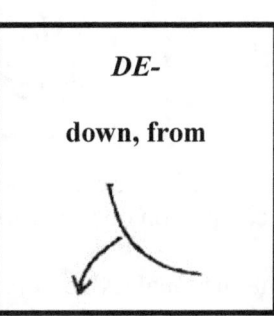

DE- down, from

CELER- fast

Definition: **v.** to slow down

Sentence: Brakes decelerate a moving vehicle and bring it to a stop.

Censor	Fr. n. Censeur, v. Censurer It. n. Censore, v. Censurare Port. Censor Sp. Censor	*CENS-* **to assess** 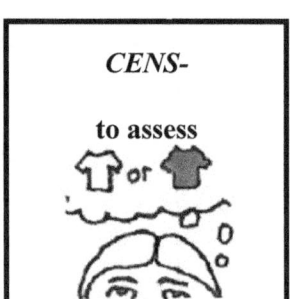

Definition: **n.** an official who examines material before publication in order to suppress parts deemed offensive or a threat to security
v. to examine (a book, film, etc.) and suppress portions of it

Sentence: The censor must do his job right in order to protect the public from vulgar language. In the United States, the government may not censor news stories before publication unless it can persuade a judge that a story poses an extreme and immediate threat to life.

Census	Fr. Recensement It. Censimento Port. Censo Sp. Censo	*CENS-* **to assess** 

Definition: **n.** an official count or survey of a population

Sentence: The U.S. Constitution mandates a census every decade to ensure that each congressional district represents about the same number of people.

Centennial	Fr. Centenaire It. Centenario Port. Centenário Sp. Centenario	*CENT-* **One hundred** 

Definition: **n.** a century; the completion or celebration of a 100-year period
adj. marking the completion of 100 years

Sentence: The Centennial International Exhibition, the first official world's fair, was held in Philadelphia in 1876 to mark the hundredth anniversary of the signing of the Declaration of Independence.
The centennial celebration of Custer's last stand occurred in 1976, when the United States was celebrating its bicentennial as a nation.

Century

Fr. Siècle
It. Secolo
Port. Século
Sp. Siglo

CENT-

one hundred

Definition: **n.** a period of one hundred years

Sentence: The century plant blooms roughly every hundred years.

Concise

Fr. Concis
It. Conciso
Port. Conciso
Sp. Conciso

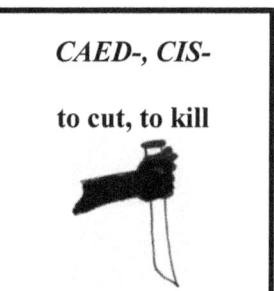

Definition: **adj.** giving information clearly and in a few words

Sentence: A concise history of the flea: 'Adam had 'em.'

Incision

Fr. Incision
It. Incisione
Port. Incisão
Sp. Incisión

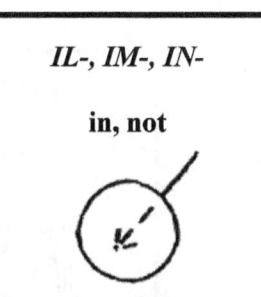

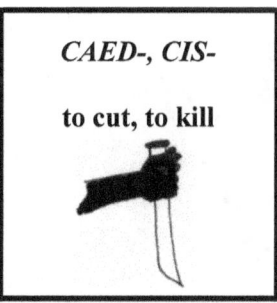

Definition: **n.** a surgical cut

Sentence: The surgeon was nervous about making the incision, for she knew if her cut was even a centimeter off, she risked the patient's life.

Excite	Fr. Enthousiasmer It. Entusiasmare Port. Excitar Sp. Excitar	*EX-* out 	*CIT-* to start. call

Definition: **v.** to cause to feel enthusiastic and eager; to awaken or arouse

Sentence: She tried to excite his interest, but he was so tired he couldn't focus on what she was saying.

Incite	Fr. Inciter It. Incitare Port. Incitar Sp. Incitar	*IL-, IM-, IN-* in, not 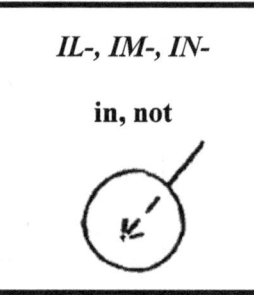	*CIT-* to start. call 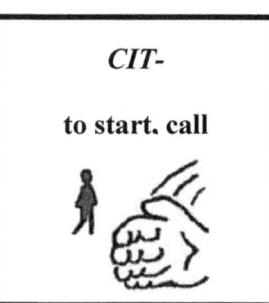

Definition: **v.** to encourage or stir up

Sentence: Revere, Prescott, and Dawes incited the colonists to take up arms.

Civil	Fr. Civil It. Civile Port. Civil Sp. Civil	*CIVIS-* citizen 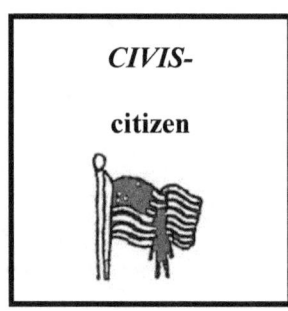

Definition: **adj.** relating to ordinary citizens, as distinct from military, religious, or criminal matters; courteous and polite

Sentence: Civil courts decide lawsuits between businesses or individuals; criminal courts hear cases involving crimes.

Civilian

Fr. Civil
It. Civile, Cittadino
Port. Civil
Sp. Civil

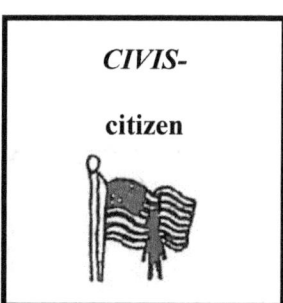

Definition: **n.** a person not in the armed services or the police force
adj. relating to citizens

Sentence: The army general was happy to retire and live as a civilian again.
When on leave at home, soldiers are required to wear civilian clothes, or 'civvies,' instead of their uniforms.

Civilization

Fr. Civilisation
It. Civilizzazione
Port. Civilização
Sp. Civilización

Definition: **n.** an advanced stage or system of human social development; a particular culture or society

Sentence: Ancient Greek civilization is credited with advancing the arts, sciences, philosophy, and mathematics.

Exercise A

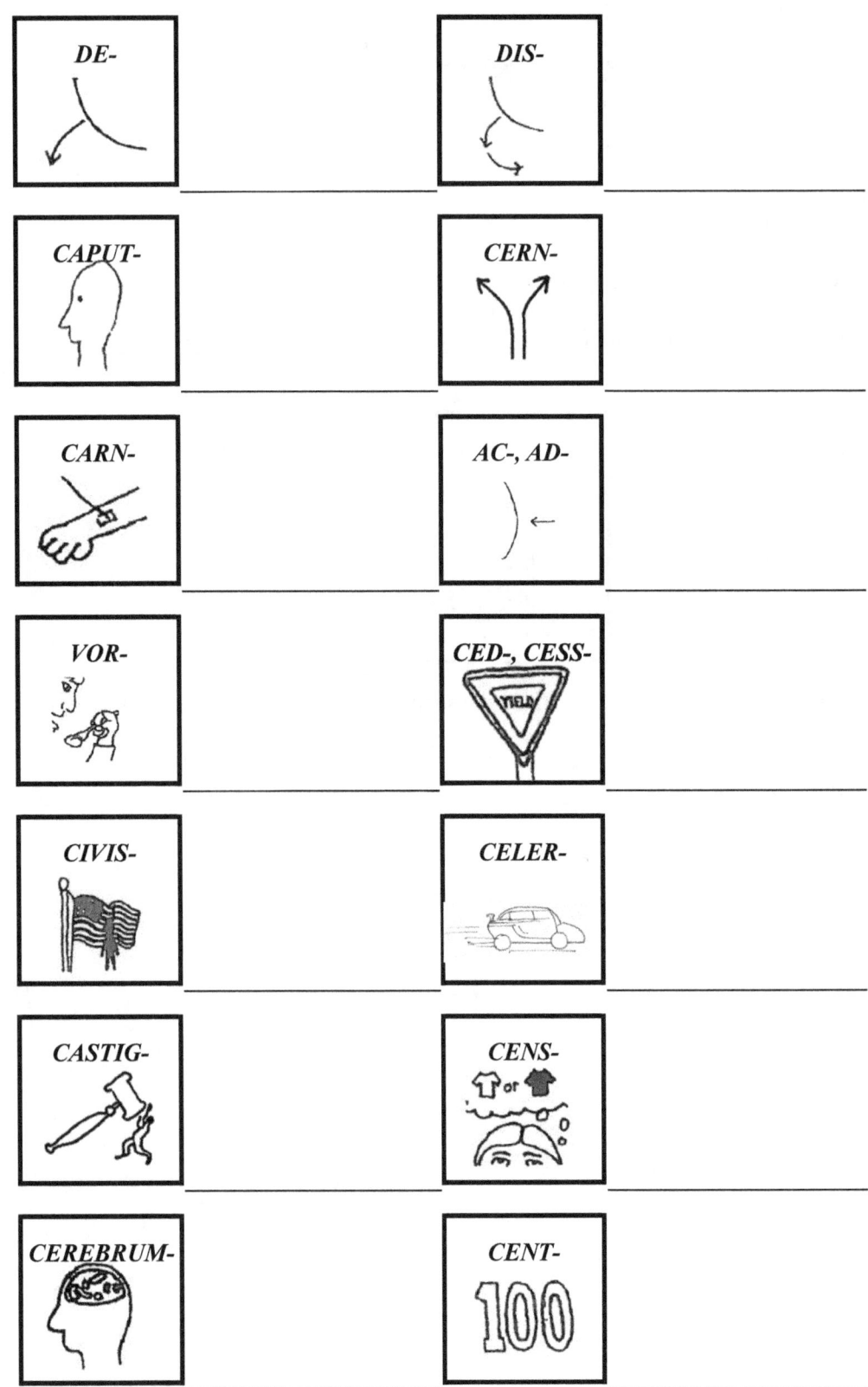

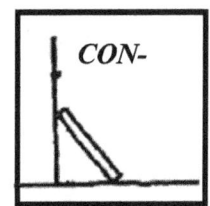 CON- _____

 CAED-, CIS- _____

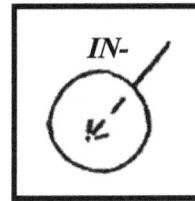 IN- _____

 EX- _____

 CIT- _____

Exercise B
Match the word with the letter of its definition:

1. ____ access
2. ____ accessory
3. ____ accelerate
4. ____ carnivorous
5. ____ castigate
6. ____ censor
7. ____ census
8. ____ cerebral
9. ____ centennial
10. ____ century
11. ____ civil
12. ____ civilian
13. ____ civilization
14. ____ concise
15. ____ decapitate
16. ____ decelerate
17. ____ discernment
18. ____ excite
19. ____ incision
20. ____ incite

a) eating only meat
b) someone who monitors and suppresses unacceptable speech
c) one-hundredth anniversary
d) relating to ordinary citizens
e) an advanced system of human development
f) to approach or enter
g) the ability to make fine distinctions
h) a surgical cut
i) to reprimand severely
j) a supplementary item
k) to stir up or cause to act
l) of the brain; intellectual
m) a period of one hundred years
n) to cut off the head
o) someone not in the military
p) to speed up
q) an official count of population
r) to slow down
s) expressed clearly and in a few words
t) to arouse; to awaken

Exercise C

1. Although all dogs are _____ by nature, real meat is still a treat for most pets.

2. The detective's _____ helped him sort out the important clues from the mass of witness statements, forensic evidence, and crime scene photographs.

3. Abominable extremists have been known to _____ their hostages.

4. Her father _____ Susan for going to the movies the night before her math test, instead of studying.

5. The world's tallest man grew to a height of 8'4" because of slight _____ damage he suffered during brain surgery.

6. Only highly trusted employees have _____ to casino vaults.

7. The town conducted an annual _____ using property and tax records to determine whether its population was growing or shrinking.

8. Although computers have become less expensive, the prices of optional _____ have remained the same or gone up.

9. A fully loaded tractor-trailer can maintain its speed on a slight incline, but _____ when climbing steeper hills.

10. In China, the government tries to _____ any discussion of opposing political views, but cell phones and the internet have made it difficult to stifle all dissent.

11. To get through the intersection before the light turned red, the sports car had to _____.

12. The doctors made a small _____ in Daniel's abdomen to extract the bullet from his spleen.

13. The fifth _____ A.D. saw the fall of the Roman Empire, one of the greatest civilizations on Earth.

14. The Yankee fan's verbal abuse of the Red Sox player _____ a riot in the bleachers.

15. The attacks of Sept. 11, 2001, caused more _____ casualties than any previous terrorist attack against the United States.

16. Her brief, _____ speech was well received by the audience, which was weary of long-winded politicians.

17. A 1997 book celebrates the _____ of Queen Victoria's Silver Jubilee in 1897, which included ceremonies intended to demonstrate the British Empire's power.

18. Chinese _____ was flourishing when Europe, ravaged by the bubonic plague, entered the Dark Ages.

19. Merely the thought of the upcoming basketball season was enough to _____ Tom Nicholson, a die-hard Lakers fan.

20. The U.S. Supreme Court has the responsibility of protecting the _____ rights of all citizens, including criminals.

Exercise D

Latin words, roots, or fragments needed for some answers in the Puzzle:

Cent   Civis
Cit   Cern
Cens   Castig
Carn   Vor
Celer

Across
1. against (l)
4. a supplementary item
6. down, from (l)
10. someone who monitors and suppresses unacceptable speech
11. to, toward (l)
13. expressed clearly and in few words
14. brain (l)
15. to assess (l)
19. the ability to make fine distinctions
21. to cut off the head
23. to punish (l)
27. in, not (l)
29. to arouse; to awaken
30. eating only meat
31. out (l)
32. to approach or enter
34. to slow down
35. a surgical cut

Down
1. a period of one hundred years
2. to separate (l)
3. flesh, meat (l)
5. to reprimand severely
7. someone not in the military
8. to speed up
9. an official count of population
12. of the brain; intellectual
14. to start, call (l)
16. citizen (l)
17. head (l)
18. one hundred (l)
20. relating to ordinary citizens (not military)
22. an advanced system of human development
24. fast (l)
25. one hundredth anniversary
26. to eat (l)
28. apart (l)
30. to cut, to kill (l)
33. to yield (l)

100

Lesson IX

Acclaim

Fr. v. Reconnaître, n. Éloges
It. v. Acclamare, n. Lodi
Port. Aclamação
Sp. Aclamación

AC-, AD- — to, toward

CLAM- — to shout

Definition: **v.** to praise enthusiastically and publicly
n. widespread public praise

Sentence: Lindberg was acclaimed for his solo Atlantic flight.
Steven Spielberg's films have garnered critical and popular acclaim.

Clarity

Fr. Clarté
It. Chiarezza
Port. Claridade
Sp. Claridad

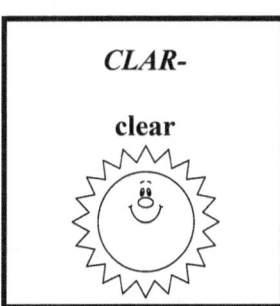

CLAR- — clear

Definition: **n.** the state or quality of being clear, distinct, and easily perceived or understood; transparency

Sentence: Even at age 90, the scholar showed great clarity of mind.

Clarify

Fr. v. Clarifier, n. Clarté
It. v. Chiarificare, n. Chiarezza
Port. Clarficar
Sp. Clarificar

CLAR- — clear

Definition: **v.** to make more comprehensible; to separate out impurities

Sentence: Butter is clarified by heating it and skimming off the milk solids.

Cloister

Fr. v. Cloîtrer, n. Cloître
It. Chiostro
Port. Claustro
Sp. Clausstro

Definition: **n.** a covered, and typically colonnaded, passage round an open court in a convent, monastery, college, or cathedral
v. to seclude or shut up in a convent, monastery or other secluded place

Sentence: A medieval woman's choice was marriage or the cloister.
He cloistered himself in a solitary cabin while he completed his novel.

Closure

Fr. Clôture
It. Chiusura
Port. Clausura
Sp. Clausura

Definition: **n.** the act or process of closing; a feeling that turmoil from a troubling experience has been resolved

Sentence: The divorce decree signaled closure for their marriage, but not their relationship as parents.

Enclosure

Fr. Enclos
It. Recinto, Allegato
Port. Cercado
Sp. Cercado

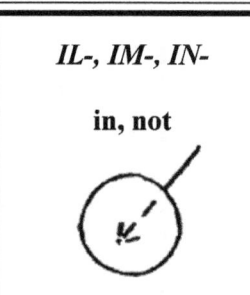 

Definition: **n.** an area that is sealed off by a barrier; a document or object placed in an envelope together with a letter

Sentence: Although they were refugees, the government held them in a barbed wire enclosure so they would not mix with the local population and settle there.

		RE-	*CLAUS-*
		back, again	to close, to shut
Recluse	Fr. Reclus It. Eremita/Recluso Port. Recluso Sp. Recluso	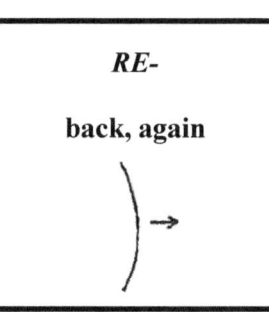	

Definition: **n.** a person who avoids others and lives a solitary life; a hermit

Sentence: A hermit disdains company and lives as a recluse.

		DE-	*CLIN-*
		down, from	to lean
Decline	Fr. v. Décliner, n. Déclin It. v. Declinare, n. Declino Port. Declinar Sp. Declinar	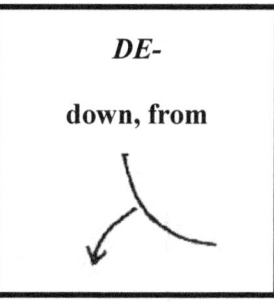	

Definition: **v.** to become smaller, fewer, or less; to decrease; to say no to
n. a continuous loss of strength, numbers, or value; a downward slope

Sentence: They declined the invitation because they were ill.
After a steady decline in sales, the store had to lay off some employees.

		IL-, IM-, IN-	*CLIN-*
		in, not	to lean
Inclined	Fr. Enclin (à) It. Incline (a) Port. Inclinado Sp. Inclinado	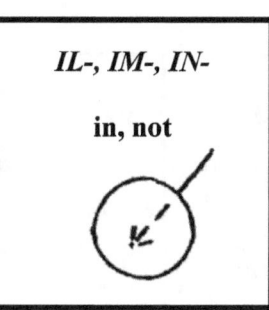	

Definition: **v.** to be favorably disposed toward or willing to do; sloping or leaning

Sentence: I was not inclined to agree with his radical viewpoint.

Cognition

Fr. Cognition
It. Cognizione
Port. Cognição
Sp. Cognción

Definition: **n.** the mental action or process of acquiring knowledge through thought, experience, and the senses

Sentence: His cognition was impaired after he suffered a concussion.

Incognito

Fr. Incognito
It. Incognito
Port. Incógnito
Sp. Incógnito

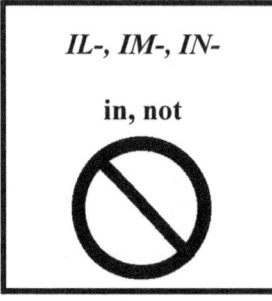 

Definition: **adj. & adv.** with one's true identity concealed
n. an assumed or false identity

Sentence: To escape their fans, Hollywood stars often travel incognito.
Once the secret agent's incognito was uncovered, he had to change his appearance and alias.

Accolade

Fr. Accolade, Récompense
It. Onorificenza
Port. Elogio
Sp. Elogio

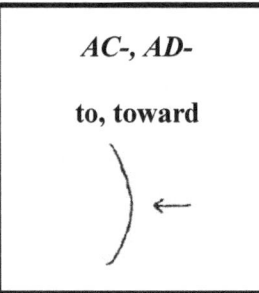 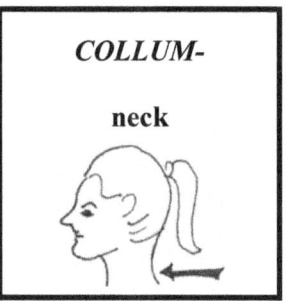

Definition: **n.** something granted as a special honor or in recognition of merit; applause; a touch on the shoulder with a sword that is part of the knighthood ceremony

Sentence: The Nobel Prize for Literature is the highest literary accolade.

Complement

Fr. Complément
It. Complemento
Port. Complemento
Sp. Complemento

COMPL-

to fill

Definition: **v.** to add something that enhances or improves (something else)
n. a thing that adds to and completes something else; the opposite of something else (in a positive sense)

Sentence: Her vision and his business ability complemented each other nicely.
In Chinese philosophy, Yin is the complement to Yang.

Comply

Fr. Conformer
It. Conformarsi
Port. Cumprir
Sp. Cumplir

COMPL-

to fill

Definition: **v.** to act in accordance with a wish or command; to meet specified standards

Sentence: Even the president must comply with the law.

Copious

Fr. Copieux
It. Copioso
Port. Copioso
Sp. Copioso

COPIA-

plenty

Definition: **adj.** abundant in quantity or supply

Sentence: He is a diligent student who takes copious notes in class.

Cordial

Fr. Cordial
It. Cordiale
Port. Cordial
Sp. Cordial

CORD-

heart, mind, spirit

Definition: **adj.** warm and friendly; strongly felt
n. a post-dinner liqueur

Sentence: The diplomat extended a cordial welcome to her guests.
Many Italian restaurants serve cordials after dinner.

Corpse

Fr. Corps, Cadavre
It. Cadavere
Port. Corpo
Sp. Cuerpo

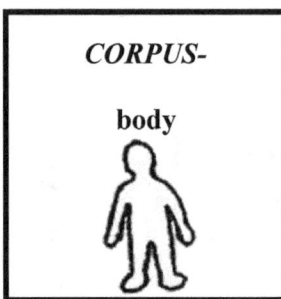

CORPUS-

body

Definition: **n.** a dead body, especially human

Sentence: While hiking in the backcountry, he stumbled across a decaying corpse.

Incorporate

Fr. Incorporer
It. Incorporare
Port. Incorporar
Sp. Incorporar

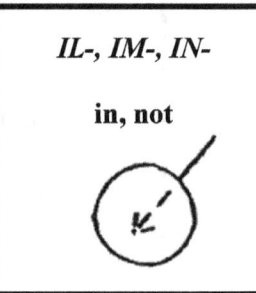 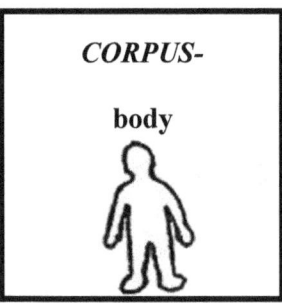

IL-, IM-, IN-   *CORPUS-*

in, not   **body**

Definition: **v.** to take in or include as part of a whole; to constitute as a legal corporation

Sentence: The two Andovers decided to incorporate as a single town.

Creditable

Fr. Estimable
It. Lodevole
Port. Acreditável
Sp. Creible

Definition: **adj.** competent, but not necessarily outstanding

Sentence: The applicant had a creditable but undistinguished work history.

Creed

Fr. Crédo, Croyance
It. Credo
Port. Credo
Sp. Credo

Definition: **n.** a system of belief; a religious doctrine

Sentence: The creed of the jungle is kill or be killed.

Exercise A

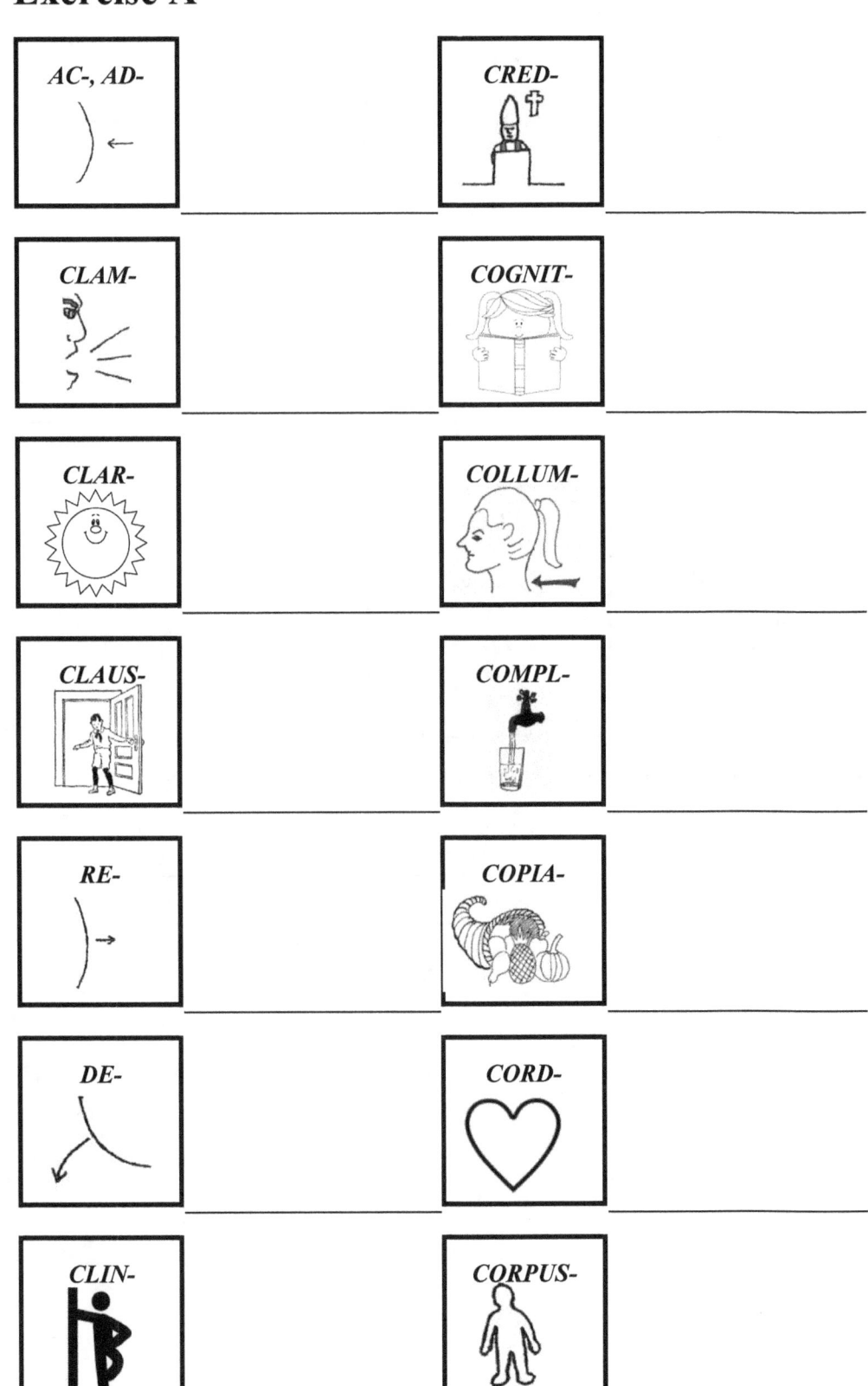

Exercise B
Match the word with the letter of its definition:

1. ____ acclaim
2. ____ accolade
3. ____ clarify
4. ____ clarity
5. ____ cloister
6. ____ closure
7. ____ cognition
8. ____ complement
9. ____ comply
10. ____ copious
11. ____ cordial
12. ____ corpse
13. ____ creditable
14. ____ creed
15. ____ decline
16. ____ enclosure
17. ____ inclined
18. ____ incognito
19. ____ incorporate
20. ____ recluse

a) to decrease; to refuse
b) articles of faith
c) warm and friendly
d) to meet specified standards
e) a covered walkway; to seclude in an abbey or monastery
f) anonymously
g) to separate out the impurities; to clear up
h) the process of thinking
i) a dead body
j) praise
k) transparency
l) to fit well with something else
m) competent, but not outstanding
n) a high honor
o) to take in; to include
p) a feeling of resolution
q) a hermit
r) abundant
s) leaning toward (something)
t) something placed in an envelope with a letter

Exercise C

1. The _____ protected the monks from rain and snow as they walked between the chapel and the dining hall, offices, and cells.

2. He asked his teacher to _____ several points so he could understand the theory.

3. After adjusting the microscope carefully, Peter could see the parasite with great _____.

4. Her Carnegie Hall premiere was greeted with critical _____.

5. Years after her son's sudden death, she dedicated a playground in his memory, which helped her achieve a sense of _____.

6. During the winter, the sheep exercised in an _____ near the barn.

7. She was initially _____ to vote for Hillary Clinton in the Democratic primary, but changed her mind at the last minute and cast her ballot for Barack Obama.

8. Lindsay wished she could _____ the invitation, but her publicist said she could start rehabilitating her image by going to the party and staying sober.

9. The United States was asked to _____ with the Geneva Conventions on human rights during the invasion and occupation of Iraq.

10. He drank _____ amounts of water, but it did nothing to abate his hunger.

11. After a sterling performance, Jerome received the highest _____: first prize and the opportunity to perform his concerto with the Boston Symphony Orchestra.

12. Illustrations should _____ the author's text.

13. Research on _____ has helped psychologists devise more effective strategies for helping patients with phobias, obsessive thinking, and depression.

14. James Bond, even though he is a spy, operates openly and rarely goes _____.

15. Although he is publicly _____ to the former Green Party presidential candidate, privately Al Gore feels nothing but bitterness toward Ralph Nader.

16. To capture the attention of the class, the math teacher sought to _____ rap music into his multimedia presentation of integrals.

17. "Practice makes perfect" is the personal _____ of Jerry Rice, perhaps the greatest football player ever to grace the gridiron.

18. The Egyptians were able to preserve the _____ of their pharaohs by mummifying their remains.

19. Her proposal was thorough and _____, but not particularly original or inspired.

20. After his wife's death, he declined all invitations to golf or dinner, had his groceries delivered, stopped answering his phone, and became a _____.

Exercise D

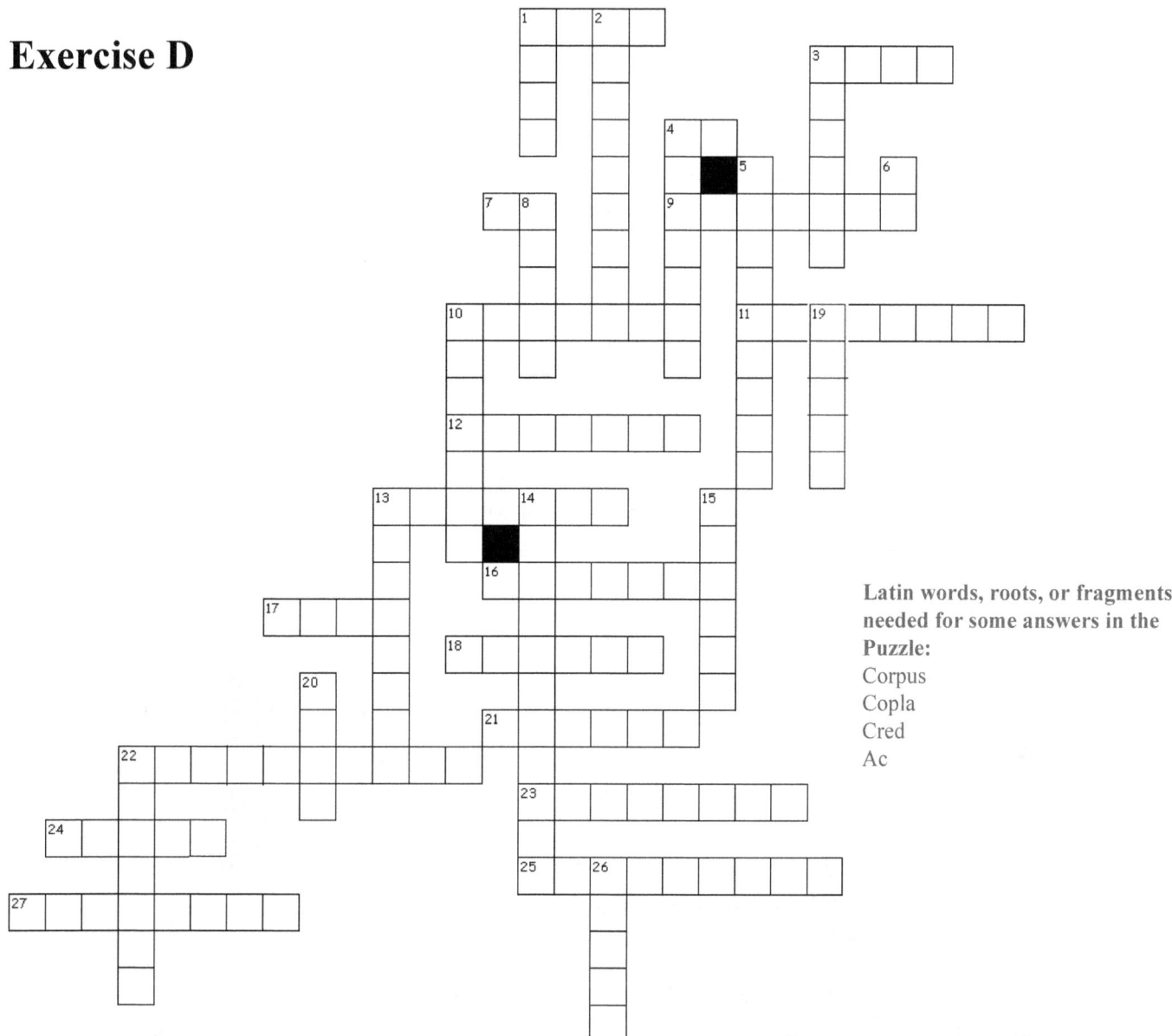

Latin words, roots, or fragments needed for some answers in the Puzzle:
Corpus
Copla
Cred
Ac

Across
1. to lean (l)
3. clear (l)
4. back, again (l)
7. to, toward (l)
9. a feeling of resolution
10. abundant
11. leaning toward (something)
12. to decrease; to refuse
13. transparency
16. praise
17. heart, mind, spirit (l)
18. a dead body
21. to learn (l)
22. to fit well with something else
23. a high honor
24. to close, to shut (l)
25. something placed in an envelope with a letter
27. a covered walkway; to seclude in an abbey or monastery

Down
1. to shout (l)
2. anonymously
3. body (l)
4. a hermit
5. the process of thinking
6. down, from (l)
8. to fill (l)
10. warm and friendly
13. competent, but not outstanding
14. to take in; to include
15. to meet specified standards
19. plenty (l)
20. to believe (l)
22. to separate out the impurities; to clear up
26. articles of faith

111

Lesson X

Crescendo

Fr. Crescendo
It. Crescendo
Port. Crescendo
Sp. Crescendo

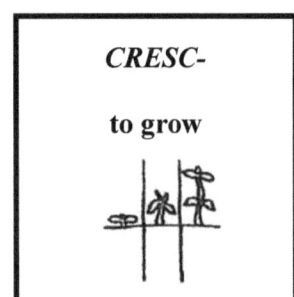

Definition: **n.** a gradual increase in volume in a piece of music; the peak of such loudness

Sentence: *The 1812 Overture* ends with a crescendo of cannons and bells.

Accrue

Fr. S'accumuler
It. Accrescere
Port. Acumular
Sp. Acumular

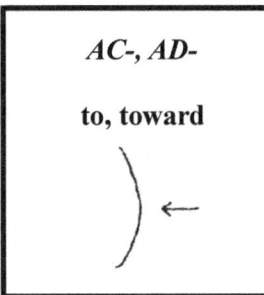 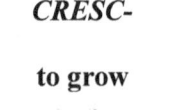

Definition: **v.** (of a benefit or sum of money) to grow through regular increases or additions

Sentence: Over the years, a savings bond accrues annual interest.

Cruciform

Fr. Cruciforme
It. Cruciforme
Port. Cruciforme
Sp. Cruciforme

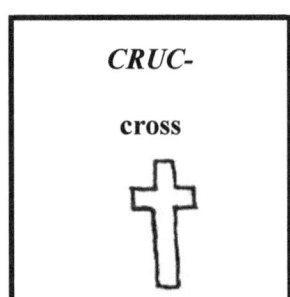 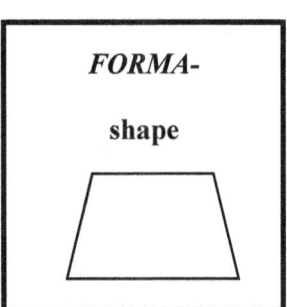

Definition: **adj.** having the shape of a cross

Sentence: The ankh is a looped, cruciform symbol of life dating from ancient Egypt.

Incumbent

Fr. Titulaire
It. Titolare
Port. Incumbência
Sp. Incumbencia

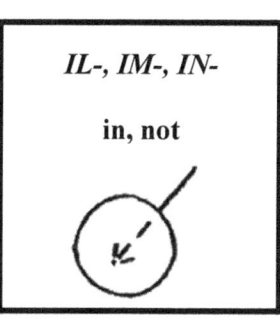
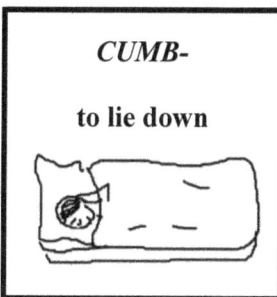

Definition: **adj.** required of (someone) as a duty or responsibility
n. the current holder of a post or elective office

Sentence: It is incumbent upon a soldier to obey the orders of his superior.
Donald Trump is the incumbent president.

Succumb

Fr. Succomber (à)
It. Soccombere (a)
Port. Sucumbir
Sp. Sucumbir

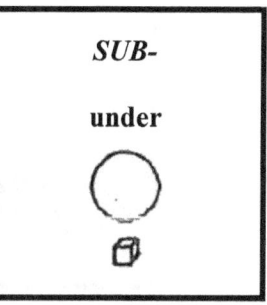

Definition: **v.** to fail to resist (pleasure, temptation, etc.); to die from the effect of a disease or injury; to yield or to give in

Sentence: Eve succumbed to the serpent's suggestion that she eat the forbidden fruit.

Culpable

Fr. Coupable
It. Responsabile, Colposo
Port. Culpável
Sp. Culpable

Definition: **adj.** deserving blame; guilty

Sentence: Pamela Smart was culpable in her husband's murder, even though she wasn't present when her teenage lover shot him.

Cupidity

Fr. Cupidité
It. Cupidigia
Port. Cupidez
Sp. Codicia

Definition: **n.** greed for money or possessions

Sentence: King Midas's name is synonymous with cupidity.

Concur

Fr. Concorder
It. Concordare
Port. Concordar
Sp. Concordar

Definition: **v.** to agree; to happen at the same time

Sentence: We can't begin until all parties concur on the plan.

Curriculum

Fr. Cv, Programme de base
It. Curriculum
Port. Curriculum
Sp. Curriculum

Definition: **n.** the subjects comprising a course of study in a school or college

Sentence: The pre-med curriculum is very challenging.

Data

Fr. Données
It. Dati
Port. Dados
Sp. Datos

DO-, DA-, DAT-

to give

Definition:	**n.** facts, statistics, and other items of information
Sentence:	His experiment did not yield enough data to draw meaningful conclusions.

Mandate

Fr. Mandat
It. Mandato
Port. Mandato
Sp. Mandato

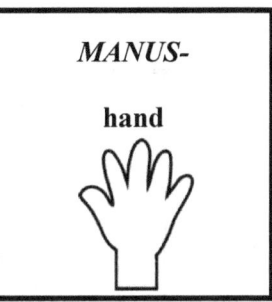

MANUS-

hand

DO-, DA-, DAT-

to give

Definition:	**v.** to require (something) or give (someone) authority to do something **n.** an official order or commission to do something; (in politics) strong approval for a course of action, presumed from wide margin of victory in an election
Sentence:	Hospital policy mandates that instruments be sterilized. The Democratic sweep of the presidency and both houses of Congress gave them a mandate to push through health care reform.

Indentation

Fr. Indentation
It. Indentazione
Port. Indentação
Sp. Hendidura

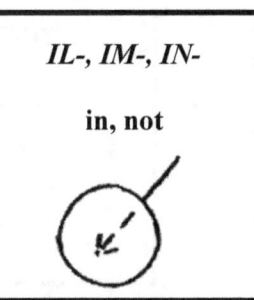

IL-, IM-, IN-

in, not

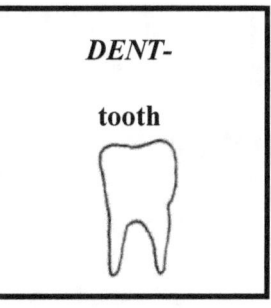

DENT-

tooth

Definition:	**n.** the action of indenting or the state of being indented; setting inward from the margin
Sentence:	A small indentation marked where a shotgun pellet had struck the car.

		TRI- three **3**	**DENT-** tooth 
Trident	Fr. Trident It. Tridente Port. Tridente Sp. Tridente		

Definition:	**n.** a three-pronged spear
Sentence:	Some gladiators used the trident and net as weapons.

		DICT- to say 
Dictator	Fr. Dictateur It. Dictatrice Port. Ditador Sp. Dictador	

Definition:	**n.** a ruler with total power over a country or institution
Sentence:	Hitler became a dictator after suspending most democratic rights.

		DICT- to say 
Diction	Fr. Diction It. Dizione Port. Dicção Sp. Dicción	

Definition:	**n.** the choice and use of words in speech or writing; enunciation
Sentence:	When writing a formal essay, it is important not to use colloquial diction.

Verdict

Fr. Verdict
It. Verdetto
Port. Veredicto
Sp. Veredicto

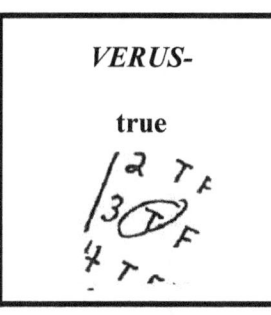

Definition: **n.** a final decision on the facts in a civil or criminal case, or at an inquest

Sentence: A jury is charged with rendering a verdict of guilt or innocence.

Docile

Fr. Docile
It. Docile
Port. Dócil
Sp. Dócil

Definition: **adj.** easily taught or managed; of an easy, compliant temperament

Sentence: The tutor was happy to teach the eager, docile pupils.

Domestic

Fr. Domestique
It. Domestico
Port. Doméstico
Sp. Doméstico

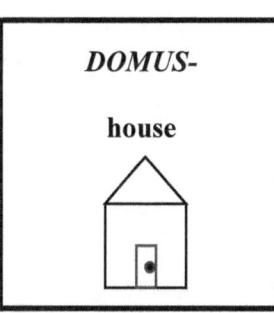

Definition: **adj.** relating to the home, family, or other matters near one's home; (in government) pertaining to national affairs (as opposed to international issues)
n. a household servant

Sentence: The president hired new advisors to counsel him on domestic problems.

The Industrial Revolution offered employment and independence to many workers who, in earlier times, would have sought work as domestics.

Dominant

Fr. Dominant
It. Dominante
Port. Dominante
Sp. Dominante

DOMIN-

to rule

Definition: **adj.** ruling or governing; occupying a commanding position or influence; major

Sentence: The New York Yankees are generally the dominant team in the American League East, although the Boston Red Sox have sometimes bested them.

Domain

Fr. Domaine
It. Dominio
Port. Domínio
Sp. Dominio

DOMIN-

to rule

Definition: **n.** (1) a territory where someone or something has influence or control
n. (2) a sphere of activity, concern, or focus

Sentence: No one can leave the king's domain.
The tenured professor's domain was ancient Chinese history.

Exercise A

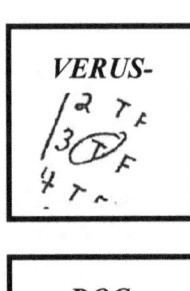 VERUS- _____

 DOC- _____

 DOMUS- _____

 DOMIN- _____

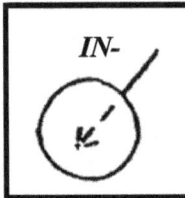 IN- _____

 CON- _____

Exercise B
Match the word with the letter of its definition:

1. ____ accrue
2. ____ concur
3. ____ crescendo
4. ____ cruciform
5. ____ culpable
6. ____ cupidity
7. ____ curriculum
8. ____ data
9. ____ dictator
10. ____ diction
11. ____ docile
12. ____ domain
13. ____ domestic
14. ____ dominant
15. ____ incumbent
16. ____ indentation
17. ____ mandate
18. ____ succumb
19. ____ trident
20. ____ verdict

a) controlling; most powerful
b) manner or clarity of speech
c) an area under control
d) a three-pronged weapon
e) to increase or add to over time
f) shaped like a cross
g) a household servant
h) the space set in from the margin of a document
i) a course of study
j) to agree
k) information for analysis
l) to demand action
m) a steady increase in volume
n) the current holder of a public office or post
o) submissive
p) extreme desire for riches
q) an absolute ruler
r) to yield; to give in to
s) deserving blame
t) a jury's decision

Exercise C

1. Ravel's stirring orchestral piece, *Bolero,* is one long, gradual _____.

2. No man could resist _____ to the sirens' call, despite its portent of doom.

3. The boy's parents weren't found guilty of the crimes he had committed, but many people considered them equally _____ because they had abused and neglected him.

4. Most Christian churches are built in a _____ shape.

5. The _____ mayor had two years remaining in his term.

6. The stockbroker's _____ eventually led him to steal from his clients.

7. Until he discovered an old IBM stock certificate in his attic, Enrique did not fully appreciate how an investment could _____ value over time.

8. It's a dire mistake to confuse a feral wolf with a _____ husky.

9. Coach Bill Parcells used fines to enforce his _____ that his players treat him and the staff with respect at all times.

10. MCAS tests, required for high school graduation, are part an attempt to standardize the _____ of Massachusetts public schools.

11. Sadly, many people confuse the splendor of Poseidon's _____ with the wickedness of the devil's pitchfork.

12. Although Stephen Hawking was fascinated by Homer Simpson's idea of a doughnut-shaped universe, Simpson had no _____ to support his theory.

13. It is rare for everyone to _____ with the president's policies, but most members of his party go along, in exchange for his support of their pet projects.

14. An _____ signifying a new paragraph should be used in written dialogue each time the speaker changes.

15. Even though she did well in school and her parents wanted her to go to college, she secretly dreamed of getting married, having children, and settling into a quiet, _____ life.

16. While the legal powers of the royal family have been supplanted by a parliamentary government, the British Isles are still considered the queen's _____.

17. His right hand is his _____ hand, but occasionally he bats lefty just to rattle the opposing pitcher.

18. Young writing students sometimes over-use imagery and metaphor while ignoring _____, the most powerful tool a writer has in setting a tone.

19. Kobe Bryant's reputation will be forever tainted by the sex scandal in Colorado, regardless of the _____ reached by the jury in his trial.

20. Fidel Castro, the former _____ of Cuba, openly aided the Soviet Union and its satellites during the cold war.

Exercise D

Latin words, roots, or fragments needed for some answers in the Puzzle:

Da, Do	Culpa
Domus	Verus
Cupi	Cumb
Curr	Doc
Dent	Cruc
Domin	

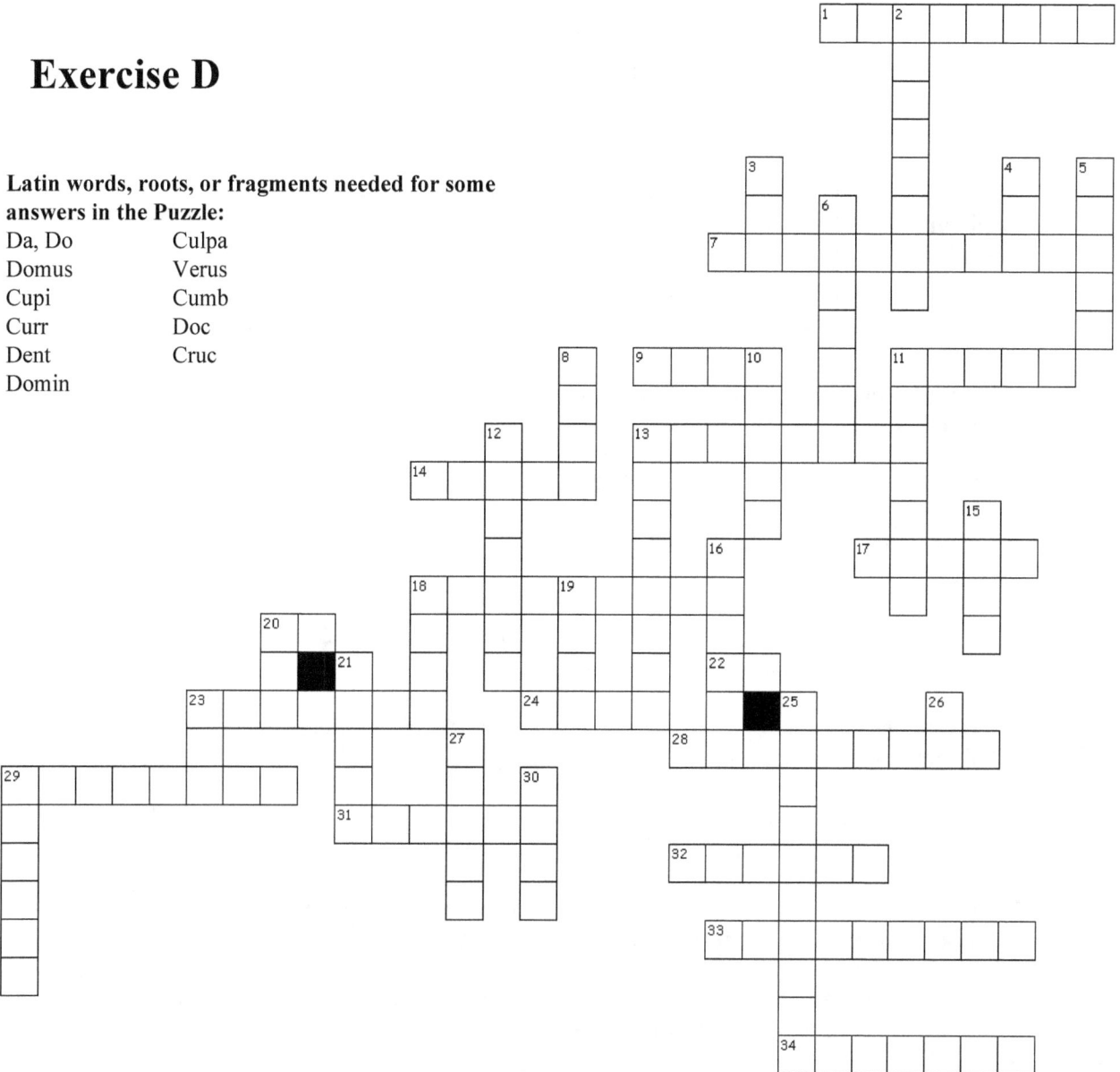

Across
1. an absolute ruler
7. the space set in from the margin of a document
9. cross (l)
11. to rule (l)
13. a household servant
14. shape (l)
17. house (l)
18. a steady increase in volume
20. to give (l)
22. to, toward (l)
23. to yield; to give in to
24. to say (l)
28. the current holder of a public office or post
29. deserving blame
31. to increase or add to over time
32. submissive
33. shaped like a cross
34. to demand action

Down
2. an extreme desire for riches
3. together (l)
4. three (l)
5. hand (l)
6. a jury's decision
8. information for analysis
10. to grow (l)
11. manner or clarity of speech
12. a three-pronged weapon
13. controlling; most powerful
15. to run (l)
16. an area under control
18. to lie down (l)
19. to desire (l)
20. to teach (l)
21. fault, guilt (l)
23. under (l)
25. a course of study
26. in, not (l)
27. true (l)
29. to agree
30. tooth (l)

Quiz 2

Quiz answers begin on page 318

> agility, civilization, alienated, amateur, verdict, corpse, incumbent, recluse, carnivorous, annuity, aptitude, amiable, acrid, artifacts, incorporate, agitate, inept, copious, crescendo, civilian, acute

1. In the Vietnam War, bombing tactics were inefficient and thus many _____ were killed.

2. The _____ in the infamous Casey Anthony trial was "not guilty."

3. Here in the tutoring office, we have a _____ supply of legal pads to write on.

4. When Howard Carter discovered the remains of King Tut in 1922, the world was amazed by the splendor of all the Ancient Egyptian _____.

5. The boy genius was _____ from the other college students by his age, but his professors considered him an _____ kid.

6. Because of a police dog's _____ sense of smell, it can detect human _____ even when their scent is obscured by _____ chemical fumes.

7. The _____ lived alone for many years, but then he befriended the priest in the nearby town, who encouraged him to _____ himself into the community.

8. The earliest signs of _____ can be found in Mesopotamia, the land between the Tigris and Euphrates Rivers.

9. Although the gymnast was an _____, she performed better than most professionals, amazing the crowd with her _____.

10. The power of financial compounding can be seen in an _____.

11. From an early age, the writer showed an _____ for creative expression.

12. Swimmers in Australian waters must take caution not to _____ predatory, _____ animals like great white sharks.

13. *"The din became a _____, like the roar of an oncoming train."* - The Red Badge of Courage

14. The _____ faces a tough reelection battle next November.

15. Despite standing 7 feet tall, the European basketball player proved _____ as the team's starting center because he wasn't fast enough to keep up with the smaller players.

Lesson XI

Dormant

Fr. Dormant
It. Dormiente
Port. Dormido
Sp. Dormido

DORMI-
to sleep

Definition: **adj.** in or seeming to be in a deep sleep; inactive

Sentence: A long dormant affection for the girl next door finally awakened when he reached adulthood.

Endorse

Fr. Endosser, Soutenir
It. Sostenere
Port. Endossar
Sp. Endosar

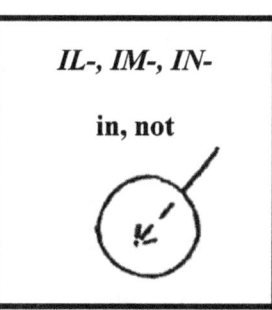

IL-, IM-, IN-
in, not

DORSUM-
back

Definition: **v.** to declare one's public approval of (someone or something); to sign a check on the back

Sentence: Sports stars are paid millions to endorse and promote athletic products.

Egocentric

Fr. Égocentrique
It. Egocentrico
Port. Egocêntrico
Sp. Egocéntrico

EGO-
I

Definition: **adj.** self-centered

Sentence: He who acts as if the world revolves around himself is egocentric.

Equal

Fr. Égal
It. Uguale
Port. Igual
Sp. Igual

EQU-
equal

Definition: **adj.** being the same in quantity, size, degree, value, or status
n. a person or thing that is equal to another

Sentence: One hundred pennies is equal in value to a dollar bill.
As a piano virtuoso, Mozart had no equal.

Erratic

Fr. Erratique
It. Erratico
Port. Errático
Sp. Errático

ERR-
to wander

Definition: **adj.** uneven or irregular in pattern or movement

Sentence: A performance that is not consistent and predictable is erratic.

Erroneous

Fr. Erroné
It. Erroneo
Port. Erróneo
Sp. Erróneo

ERR-
to wander

Definition: **adj.** wrong; incorrect

Sentence: His logic was faulty, so his conclusions were erroneous.

Facsimile

Fr. Fac-similé
It. Facsimile
Port. Fac-símile
Sp. Facsímil

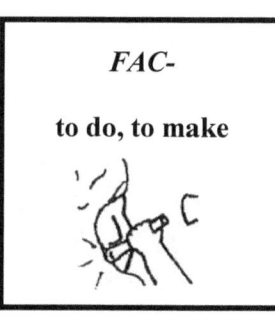

FAC-

to do, to make

SIMIL-

same

Definition: **n.** an exact copy of written or printed matter

Sentence: A fax machine scans documents and transmits their facsimiles to a distant machine.

Fiction

Fr. (Roman de) Fiction
It. Romanzo, Finzione
Port. Ficção
Sp. Ficción

FIGURA-, FING-

to shape

Definition: **n.** prose literature, especially novels; a thing that is invented, untrue

Sentence: Investigation proved the senator's claim of military service to be a fiction.

Deface

Fr. Dégrader
It. Deturpare
Port. Deformar
Sp. Deformar

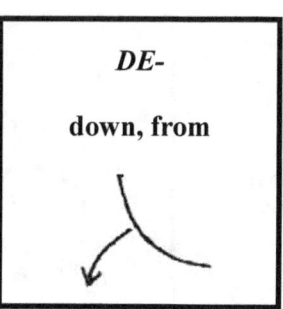

DE-

down, from

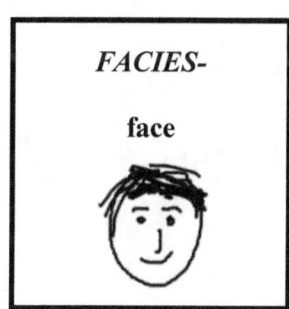

FACIES-

face

Definition: **v.** to spoil the surface or appearance of; to mar or disfigure

Sentence: The vandals defaced the gravestones with red spray paint.

Façade

Fr. Façade
It. Facciata, Apparenza
Port. Fachada
Sp. Fachada

FACIES-
face

Definition:	**n.** the decorative front of a building, facing the street; a deceptive appearance
Sentence:	The smile was a façade that masked his deep sorrow.

Falsify

Fr. Falsifier
It. Falsificare
Port. Falsidade
Sp. Falsedad

FALSUS-
false

F

FAC-
to do, to make

Definition:	**v.** to alter so as to mislead; to make false
Sentence:	A falsified signature on a tax form is grounds for imprisonment.

Infallible

Fr. Infaillible
It. Infallibile
Port. Infalível
Sp. Infalible

IL-, IM-, IN-
in, not

FALL-
to deceive, fail

Definition:	**adj.** incapable of making mistakes or being wrong; unfailing
Sentence:	Catholics believe the Pope is infallible because his pronouncements are inspired by God.

Confer

Fr. Conférer
It. Conferire
Port. Conferir
Sp. Conferir

CON- together	FER- to bring, to carry

Definition: **v.** to grant a title, degree, benefit, or right

Sentence: Only the king or queen may confer knighthood on a deserving subject.

Fertile

Fr. Fertile
It. Fertile
Port. Fértil
Sp. Fértil

FER-
to bring, to carry

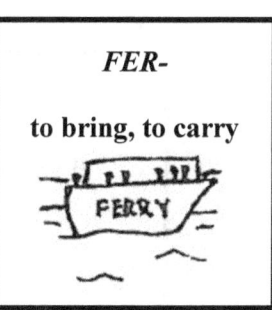

Definition: **adj.** producing or capable of producing abundant growth (vegetation)

Sentence: The housing projects proved to be fertile ground for gangs.

Fervor

Fr. Ferveur
It. Fervore
Port. Fervor
Sp. Fervor

FERV-
to boil

Definition: **n.** an intense and passionate feeling

Sentence: Jonathan Edwards' fervor erupted in hell-fire sermons.

Fidelity

Fr. Fidélité
It. Fedeltà
Port. Fidelidade
Sp. Fidelidad

Definition: **n.** loyalty to a person, cause, or belief; resemblance to reality

Sentence: Early stereo record players were known as 'hi-fis' for their high degree of fidelity in reproducing the original musical performance.

Affinity

Fr. Affinité
It. Affinità
Port. Afinidade
Sp. Afinidad

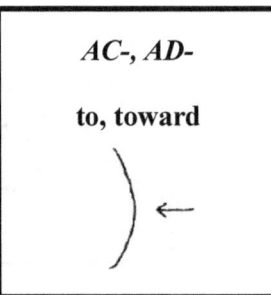 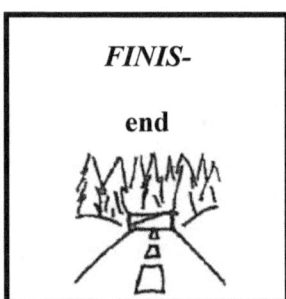

Definition: **n.** a spontaneous or natural liking or sympathy; a talent or leaning

Sentence: His affinity for animals made him an excellent veterinary technician.

Finite

Fr. Fini
It. Finito
Port. Finito
Sp. Finito

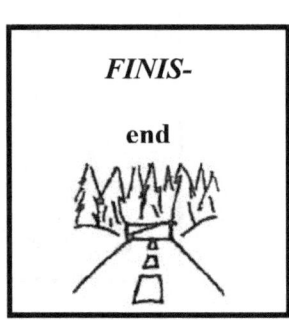

Definition: **adj.** limited in size or extent

Sentence: Though it is boundless, the universe contains a finite amount of matter.

Configuration

Fr. Configuration
It. Configurazione
Port. Configuração
Sp. Configuración

CON- together

FIGURA-, FING- to shape

Definition: **n.** an arrangement of parts or elements in a particular form or figure

Sentence: A baseball infield has a diamond-shaped configuration.

Figurative

Fr. Figuratif
It. Figurato
Port. Figurativo
Sp. Figurativo

FIGURATIVUS- symbolic

ω Δ א ■

Definition: **adj.** (1) representing symbolically or by a figure; resembling
adj. (2) characterized by figures of speech, especially metaphors; not literal

Sentence: The figurative sculpture of a broken window represented World War I.
He gave a figurative description of what happened to the officers.

Exercise A

Exercise B
Match the word with the letter of its definition:

1. ___ affinity
2. ___ confer
3. ___ configuration
4. ___ deface
5. ___ dormant
6. ___ egocentric
7. ___ endorse
8. ___ equal
9. ___ erratic
10. ___ erroneous
11. ___ façade
12. ___ facsimile
13. ___ falsify
14. ___ fervor
15. ___ fertile
16. ___ fiction
17. ___ fidelity
18. ___ figurative
19. ___ finite
20. ___ infallible

a) heightened passion
b) incorrect
c) to alter so as to mislead or make false
d) self-centered
e) to disfigure
f) an arrangement or pattern
g) a duplicate
h) to publicly support
i) prose literature that is not factual
j) having a limit
k) natural preference
l) using figures of speech
m) irregular
n) to consult with
o) foolproof
p) having the same value
q) asleep or inactive
r) loyalty
s) an illusion
t) capable of supporting abundant life

Exercise C

1. Celebrity athletes often let their status go to their heads, becoming hopelessly _____ and acting as if others exist only to flatter and serve them.

2. McDonald's and Burger King are an _____ distance from our home, but we usually go to the "Home of the Whopper" because there's less traffic that way.

3. The city of Pompeii was built at the base of Mount Vesuvius, a volcano that had been considered _____, but suddenly erupted after decades of inactivity.

4. The _____ comings and goings of the Mitfords caused much speculative talk in the village, as none of them appeared to hold a steady job.

5. The *New York Post* published an _____ report that John Kerry had chosen Dick Gephardt as his vice-presidential running mate.

6. John Kerry _____ Barack Obama over Hillary Clinton in the Democratic presidential primary.

7. Although Robin Hood wore a disguise to the archery contest, his expert marksmanship allowed the sheriff to see through the _____.

8. After the homecoming game victory, the _____ of the fans spilled over into a celebration on the field and an impromptu parade around campus.

9. When she traveled across Europe, Judith kept a _____ of her passport tucked into a separate bag, in case she lost the original.

10. It is likely that a Sufi monk tried to _____ the magnificent sphinx around 1100 A.D., as an insult to the Egyptian people.

11. Although Bill Gates once boasted that Windows XP would be _____, it proved to have as many bugs as its predecessors.

12. *To Kill A Mockingbird* is considered one of the greatest pieces of American _____, in part because the characters and plot are so realistic.

13. The teenager tried to _____ his age by tampering with his driver's license, but the bouncer spotted the fakery.

14. Nancy Kerrigan, like many competitive figure skaters, displayed an _____ for the sport at a young age.

15. A successful marriage must have a strong foundation of good communication and mutual _____.

16. He _____ a great honor on her when he chose her as chief operating officer.

17. The number of human beings that the earth can support is _____, although scientists do not agree on an exact figure.

18. The _____ valley of the Nile produces bountiful harvests.

19. Daniel's biting wit and clever use of _____ language caught the attention of Mr. Meade, his ninth-grade English teacher.

20. Astrologers believe that the _____ of the planets at a person's birth determines his or her unique personality.

Exercise D

Latin words, roots, or fragments needed for some answers in the Puzzle:

Simil   Fer
Equ   Fides
Dorsum   Fing
Ac   Com, Con
Dormi   Facies
Ferv   Fac, Fic
Figurativus

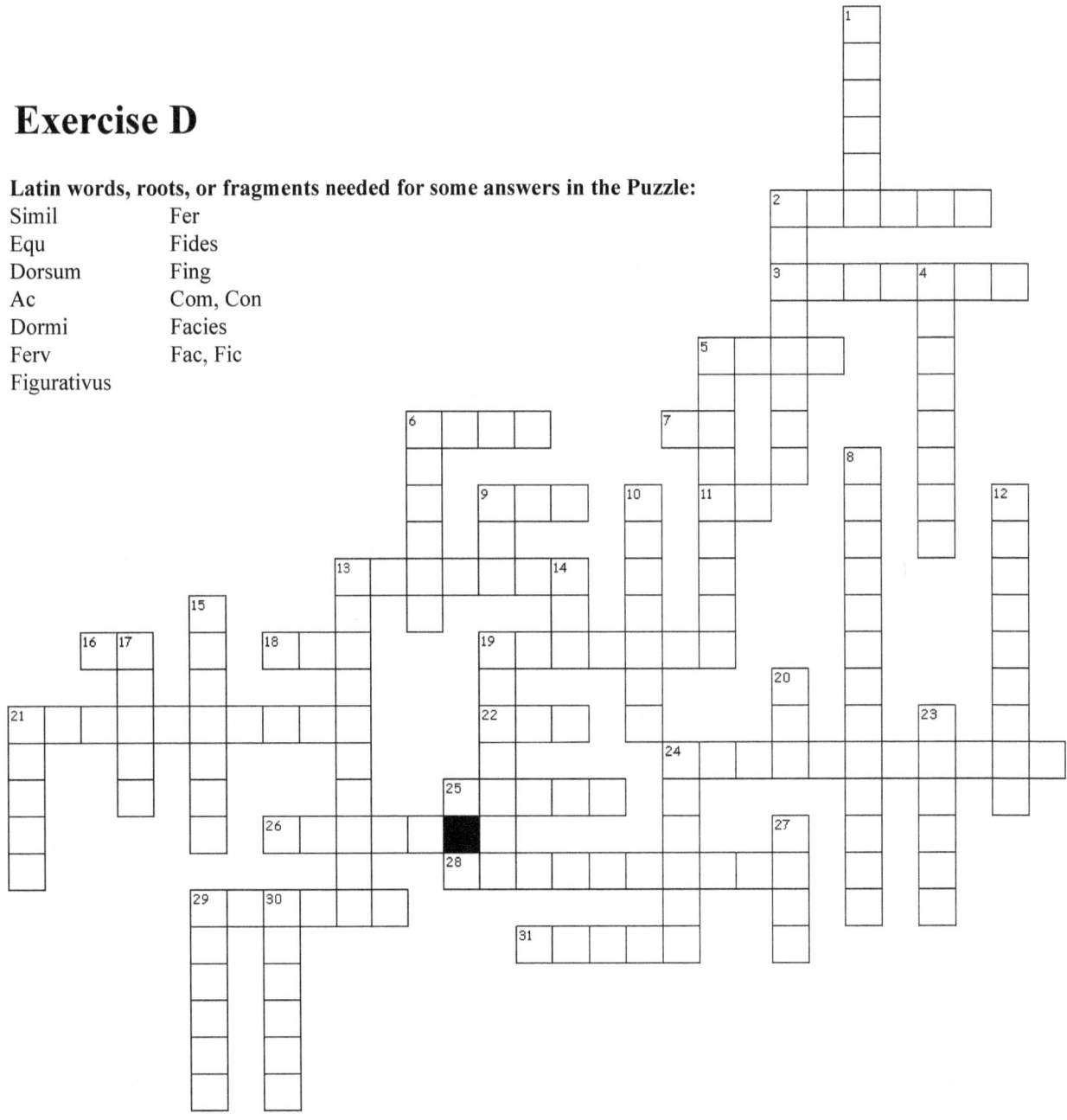

Across
2. heightened passion
3. asleep or inactive
5. to deceive, fail (l)
6. to shape (l)
7. to, toward (l)
9. to do, to make (l)
11. in, not (l)
13. to publicly support
16. down, from (l)
18. I (l)
19. capable of supporting abundant life
21. using figures of speech
22. together (l)
24. symbolic (l)
25. same (l)
26. to sleep (l)
28. foolproof
29. to disfigure
31. end

Down
1. to consult with
2. loyalty
4. natural preference
5. a duplicate
6. an illusion
8. an arrangement or pattern
9. to bring, to carry (l)
10. to alter so as to mislead or make false
12. incorrect
13. self-centered
14. to wander (l)
15. irregular
17. having the same value
19. prose literature that is not factual
20. equal (l)
21. faith (l)
23. having a limit
24. face (l)
27. to boil (l)
29. back (l)
30. false (l)

135

Lesson XII

Confirm

Fr. Confirmer
It. Confermare
Port. Confirmar
Sp. Confirmar

CON- together

FIRMUS- strong

Definition: **v.** to establish the truth or correctness of (something)

Sentence: The timely arrival of the comet confirmed Halley's prediction from years earlier.

Infirmary

Fr. Infirmerie
It. Infermeria
Port. Enfermaria
Sp. Enfermería

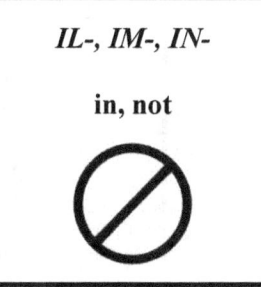

IL-, IM-, IN- in, not

FIRMUS- strong

Definition: **n.** a place within a larger institution for the care of those who are ill or injured; a hospital

Sentence: The outbreak of mononucleosis filled the beds of the college infirmary.

Deflect

Fr. Dévier
It. Deviare
Port. Deflectir
Sp. Desviar

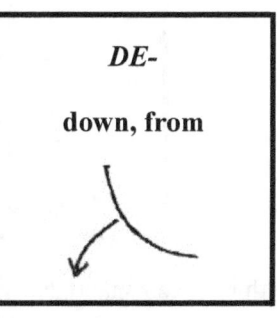

DE- down, from

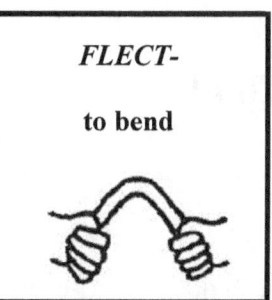

FLECT- to bend

Definition: **v.** to deviate or cause to deviate from a straight course

Sentence: The bullet was deflected by the wall and hit a bystander.

Inflection

Fr. Flexion, Modulation
It. Inflessione, Intonazione
Port. Inflexão
Sp. Infelxión

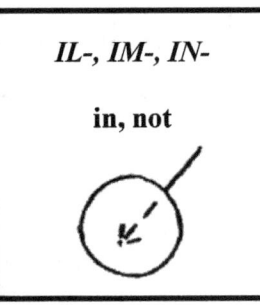

IL-, IM-, IN-
in, not

FLECT-
to bend

Definition: **n.** a change in the form of a word to express a grammatical function or attribute; specific pronunciation of a word or syllable

Sentence: One can tell the regional origins of a speaker based on his inflection.

Floral

Fr. Floral
It. Floreale
Port. Floral
Sp. Floral

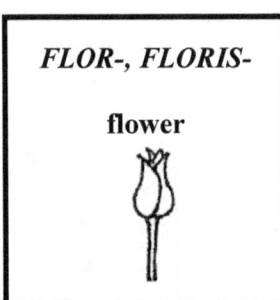

FLOR-, FLORIS-
flower

Definition: **adj.** involving or relating to flowers

Sentence: The tables were decorated with colorful floral arrangements.

Fluid

Fr. Fluide
It. Fluido
Port. Fluido
Sp. Fluido

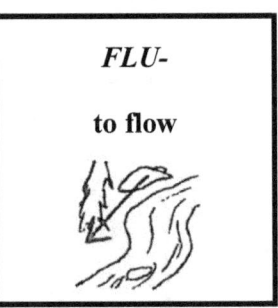

FLU-
to flow

Definition: **n.** a substance with no fixed shape that yields easily to pressure; a liquid or gas
adj. able to flow easily; not settled or stable

Sentence: The amber fluid spilled out of the bottle and onto the floor.
The game is still fluid; either side could win.

Fortunate

Fr. Fortuné
It. Fortunato
Port. Afortunado
Sp. Afortunado

Definition: **adj.** favored by or involving good luck

Sentence: Those still in perfect health in their 80s are fortunate indeed.

Forum

Fr. Forum
It. Forum
Port. Fórum
Sp. Foro

Definition: **n.** a meeting place or medium for an exchange of views

Sentence: PTA meetings constitute a forum for parents to air grievances and work with teachers to improve the school's performance.

Fragment

Fr. Fragment
It. Frammento
Port. Fragmento
Sp. Fragmento

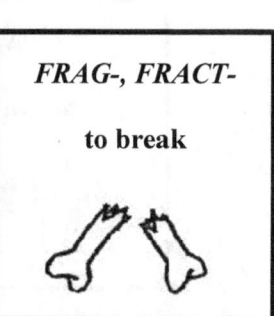

Definition: **n.** a small part broken off or detached

Sentence: The explosion sent scores of glass fragments flying through the air.

Fragile

Fr. Fragile
It. Fragile
Port. Frágil
Sp. Frágil

FRAG-, FRACT-
to break

Definition: **adj.** easily broken or damaged

Sentence: The starving refugees looked terribly fragile.

Fraternal

Fr. Fraternel
It. Fraterno
Port. Fraternal
Sp. Fraternal

FRATER-
brother

Definition: **adj.** of or like a brother(s)

Sentence: A club that admits males only is a fraternal organization.

Confront

Fr. Confronter, Affronter
It. Confrontare, Affrontare
Port. Confrontar
Sp. Confrontar

CON-
together

FRONS-, FRONT-
front

Definition: **v.** to stand or meet face to face

Sentence: A psychiatrist may help you to confront long-repressed emotions.

Fugitive

Fr. Fugitif
It. Fugitivo
Port. Fugitivo
Sp. Fugitivo

FUG-
to flee

Definition:
n. a person who has escaped from captivity or is in hiding
adj. quick to disappear; fleeting

Sentence:
Many fugitives head north through New Hampshire, hoping to reach the Canadian border before they are apprehended.
Fugitive shadows passed rapidly across the darkening sky.

Diffuse

Fr. adj. Diffus, v. Se diffuser
It. adj. Diffuso, v. Diffondere
Port. Difuso
Sp. Difuso

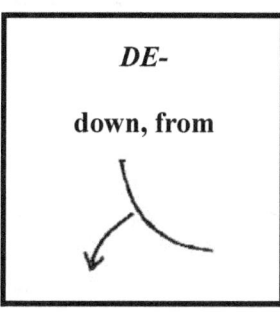

DE-
down, from

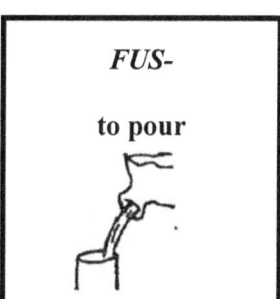

FUS-
to pour

Definition:
v. to spread over a wide area; to dilute
adj. spread out over a wide area; lacking clarity

Sentence:
He diffused the tension in the room by telling a joke.
He's a charming speaker, but unfortunately his attention is diffuse and he meanders along various tangents.

Fusion

Fr. Fusion
It. Fusione
Port. Fusão
Sp. Fusión

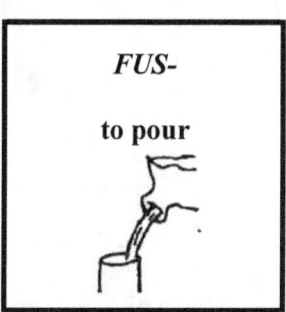

FUS-
to pour

Definition:
n. the process or result of joining together into a unit; a reaction in which light atomic nuclei meld to form a heavier nucleus

Sentence:
The fusion of nickel and chromium makes Nichrome coils.

Gorge

Fr. Gorge
It. Gola
Port. Garganta
Sp. Garganta

GURG-

throat

Definition: **n.** a steep, narrow valley or ravine; a ravine created by the flow of a river

Sentence: While hiking in the Grand Canyon, he fell into a small gorge and was never seen again.

Generate

Fr. Générer
It. Generare
Port. Gerar
Sp. Generar

GEN-

birth, family

Definition: **v.** to cause; to produce

Sentence: The shouting match over the controversial bill generated more heat than light.

Generous

Fr. Généreux
It. Generoso
Port. Generoso
Sp. Generoso

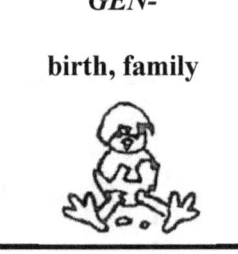

GEN-

birth, family

Definition: **adj.** freely giving more of something than is necessary or expected

Sentence: The teacher was generous with praise and encouragement."

Genuine	Fr. Sincère It. Genuino Port. Genuíno Sp. Genuino	*GEN-* **birth, family** 

Definition:	**adj.** truly what it is said to be; authentic; sincere and honest
Sentence:	The derringer was the genuine article, not a copy.

Genre	Fr. Genre It. Genere Port. Género Sp. Género	*GEN-* **birth, family** 

Definition:	**n.** a style or category of art or literature
Sentence:	Poetry, drama, and novels represent different literary genres.

Exercise A

Exercise B

Match the word with the letter of its definition:

1. ____ confirm
2. ____ confront
3. ____ diffuse
4. ____ deflect
5. ____ floral
6. ____ fluid
7. ____ fortunate
8. ____ forum
9. ____ fragment
10. ____ fragile
11. ____ fraternal
12. ____ fugitive
13. ____ fusion
14. ____ generate
15. ____ generous
16. ____ genre
17. ____ genuine
18. ____ gorge
19. ____ inflection
20. ____ infirmary

a) a piece of a whole
b) to face
c) a shapeless substance; a liquid or gas
d) a person who flees from the law
e) to cause to exist
f) a place for discussion
g) to spread over a wide area
h) favored by good luck
i) a steep valley; to eat greedily
j) freely giving
k) to acknowledge the truth of
l) to turn (something) aside
m) consisting of or relating to flowers
n) brotherly
o) easily breakable
p) the modulation of intonation in the voice
q) a hospital within a larger institution
r) authentic
s) a joining together
t) a category

Exercise C

1. The dancer's movements were _____ and graceful, even when she was doing something as ordinary as grocery shopping.

2. The wedding planner designed an intricate _____ arrangement for the head table.

3. His speech _____ my belief in the power of love to work miracles.

4. The linebacker tried to _____ Tom Brady's pass, but Troy Brown shifted direction and caught the ball anyway.

5. The army _____ was equipped to treat wounded soldiers and injured Iraqi civilians alike.

6. When the wind blew through the open window, the _____ vase fell from the shelf and shattered.

7. The philosopher used his college classroom as a _____ to test many of his controversial ideas, before subjecting them to the harsher criticism of his peers.

8. Her comical _____ belied the sad facts of her story.

9. The _____ hid in a dumpster for three days, surviving on leftovers in the garbage, until a police dog discovered him.

10. We were all _____ to graduate before the school lowered its standards and a degree became meaningless.

11. The boys had a _____ connection; they regarded each other as members of an extended family.

12. Archaeologists spend much of their time trying to piece together _____ of pottery to try and determine a vessel's shape and use.

13. The drunken teenager _____ the police officer and ended up getting charged with resisting arrest.

14. One classic example of chaos theory is that a drop of blue dye put into a beaker of water will never _____ through the liquid in the same pattern twice.

15. The Iron Chef's _____ of French cooking techniques with Asian ingredients and presentation created exciting and delicious new dishes.

16. The huge _____ known as the Grand Canyon was created by a combination of seismic activity and erosion by the Colorado River.

17. The _____ of science fiction has often predicted developments in science and technology.

18. Her parents are always very _____ with gifts for the holidays.

19. Although John McCain has voiced his support for President Bush, many experts believe his endorsement is not _____.

20. Nuclear plants can _____ enough electricity to power a sizeable city.

Exercise D

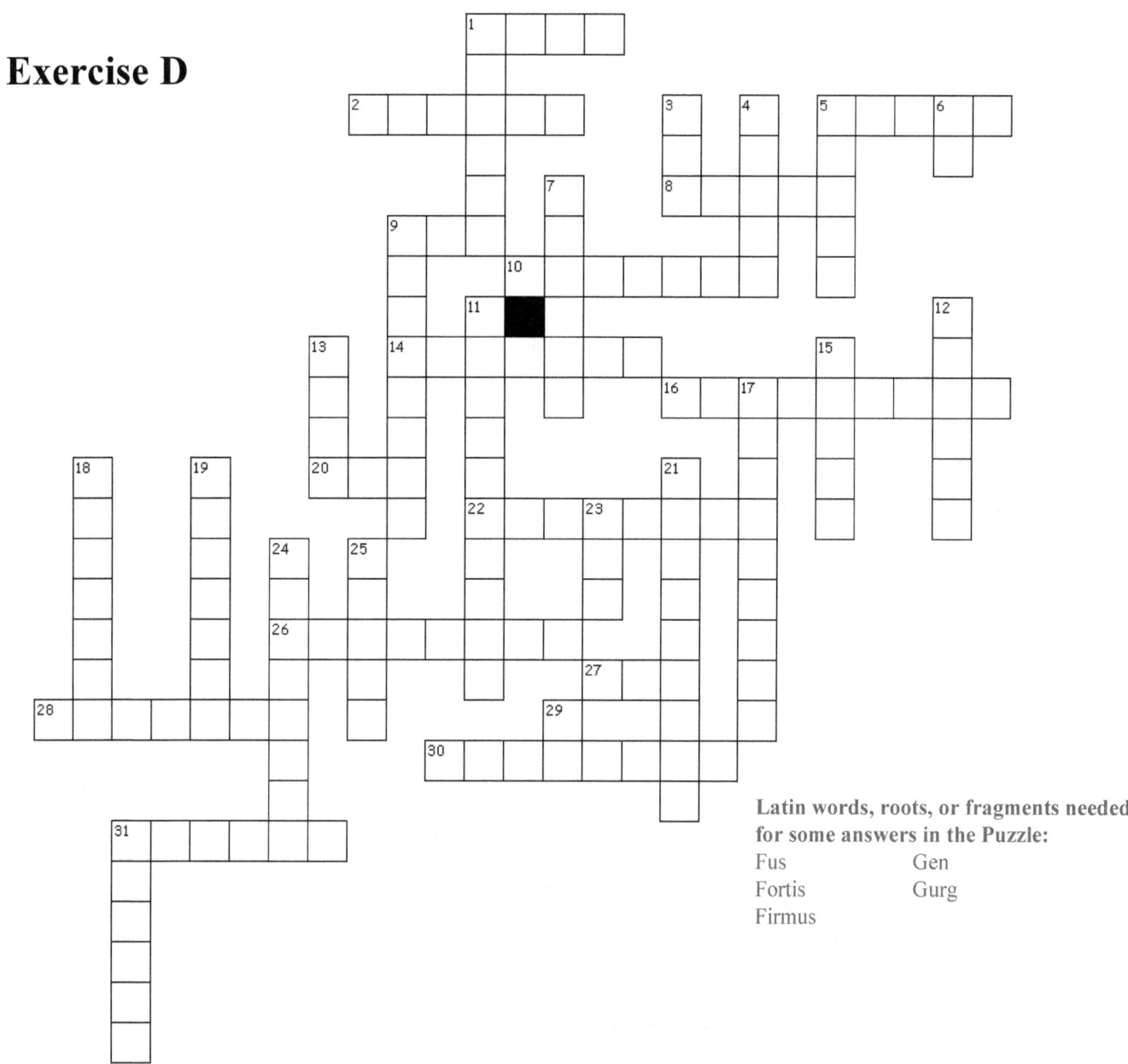

Latin words, roots, or fragments needed for some answers in the Puzzle:
Fus
Fortis
Firmus
Gen
Gurg

Across
1. to break (l)
2. consisting of or relating to flowers
5. a shapeless substance; a liquid or a gas
8. a steep valley; to eat greedily
9. to pour (l)
10. to acknowledge the truth of
14. authentic
16. a hospital within a larger institution
20. birth, family (l)
22. to face
26. freely giving
27. together (l)
28. to turn (something) aside
30. to cause to exist
31. brother (l)

Down
1. strong (l)
3. to flee (l)
4. a place for discussion
5. to bend (l)
6. in, not (l)
7. flower (l)
9. a piece of the whole
11. the modulation of intonation in the voice
12. luck (l)
13. throat (l)
15. front (l)
17. brotherly
18. easily breakable
19. to spread over a wide area
21. favored by good luck
23. to flow (l)
24. a person who flees from the law
25. a category
29. down, from (l)
31. joining together

Lesson XIII

GRAD-
step, advance

Gradual

Fr. Graduel
It. Graduale
Port. Gradual
Sp. Gradual

Definition:	**adj.** taking place in stages, or slowly, over an extended period
Sentence:	There has been a gradual decline in the number of patrons at our restaurant over the past three years.

GRAD-
step, advance

Graduate

Fr. Obtenir une licence
It. Laurearsi
Port. Graduado
Sp. Graduado

Definition:	**v.** to successfully complete a degree, course, or school; to mark with measurements **n.** a person who has been awarded an academic degree or high school diploma
Sentence:	An American yardstick is graduated by one sixteenth-inch lines. George W. Bush is a graduate of Phillips Academy, Andover.

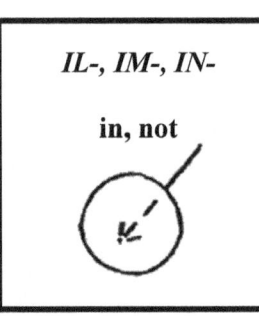 

IL-, IM-, IN- in, not   **GRAD-** step, advance

Ingredient

Fr. Ingrédient
It. Ingrediente
Port. Ingrediente
Sp. Ingrediente

Definition:	**n.** any of the foods or substances that are combined to make a particular dish; a component or element
Sentence:	Inspiration, hard work, and a little luck are the basic ingredients of success.

		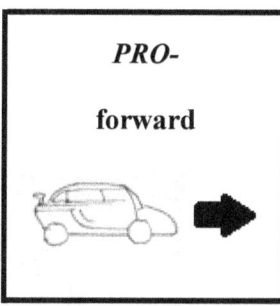	
Progress	Fr. v. Progresser, n. Progrès It. v. Progredire, n. Progresso Port. Progresso Sp. Progreso	PRO- forward	GRAD- step, advance

Definition: **n.** forward or onward movement toward a destination; development toward a better, more complete, or more modern condition
v. to move or develop toward a destination, goal, or better condition

Sentence: We've made progress; we are only a few miles from our destination.
Thomas Edison never progressed beyond grade school.

Congratulation(s) — Fr. Félicitation(s) / It. Congratulations / Port. Congratulação / Sp. Congratulacion

CON- together | GRAT- favor, please

Definition: **n.** praise or good wishes on a special occasion

Sentence: By way of congratulation, Mr. Smith bought his son a car.

Gratitude — Fr. Gratitude / It. Gratitudine / Port. Gratidão / Sp. Gratitud

GRAT- favor, please

Definition: **n.** appreciation of kindness; thankfulness

Sentence: The woman expressed gratitude to the firefighters who saved her kitten.

Congregation

Fr. Congrégation
It. Congregazione
Port. Congregação
Sp. Congregación

CON- — together

GREG- — flock, herd

Definition: **n.** a gathering of people or things; a group of people assembled for religious worship

Sentence: A congregation of crows blackened the crown of the tree.

Inherent

Fr. Intrinsèque
It. Intrinseco, Innato
Port. Inerente
Sp. Inherente

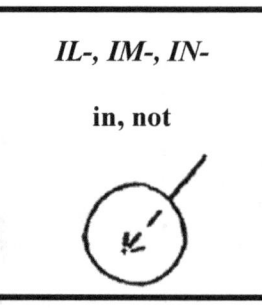

IL-, IM-, IN- — in, not

HER- — to stick

Definition: **adj.** existing in something as a permanent or essential attribute

Sentence: Flowers have inherent beauty, because they are designed to attract the insects or animals they depend on for reproduction.

Impel

Fr. Inciter
It. Incitare
Port. Impelir
Sp. Impulsar

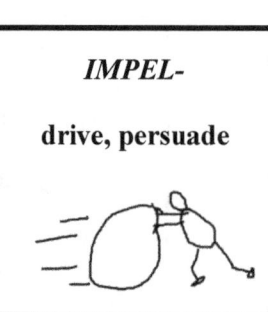

IMPEL- — drive, persuade

Definition: **v.** to drive or push toward; to persuade

Sentence: The terrorist attacks of Sept. 11, 2001 impelled him to join the Army.

Incense	Fr. v. Faire enrager, n. Encens It. v. Far inferocire, n. Incenso Port. Incenso Sp. Incienso	*INCEND-* **To set fire** 

Definition: **v.** to make very angry; to infuriate
n. a gum, spice, or other substance that is burned for the sweet smell it produces

Sentence: Her husband's flirtatious behavior incensed her.
The Wise Men brought gold and two precious incenses: frankincense and myrrh.

Irate	Fr. Furieux It. Irato Port. Irado Sp. Airado	*IRA-* **anger** 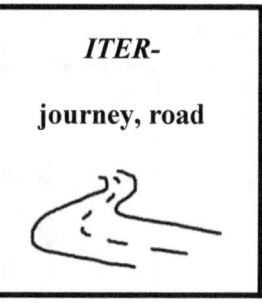

Definition: **adj.** extremely angry

Sentence: The irate customer dashed off a furious letter to the company.

Itinerary	Fr. Itinéraire It. Itinerario Port. Itinerário Sp. Itinerario	*ITER-* **journey, road**

Definition: **n.** a planned route of travel or journey

Sentence: My European itinerary includes Paris, Geneva, and Barcelona.

Transition	Fr. Transition It. Transizione Port. Transição Sp. Transición	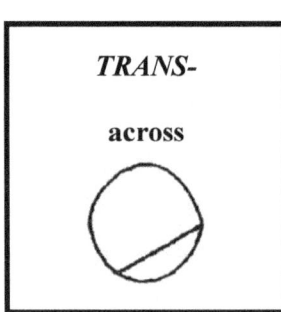	

Definition: **n.** the process or period of changing from one condition to another

Sentence: The Civil War marked the transition from a primarily agricultural economy to a more industrial one.

Transit	Fr. Transport, Transit It. Trasporto, Transit Port. Trânsito Sp. Transito	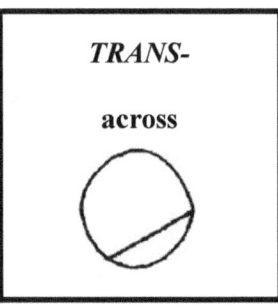	

Definition: **n.** the carrying of people or things from one place to another; an act of passing through or across a place

Sentence: Forms of mass transit include trains, buses, subways, and airplanes.

Inject	Fr. Injecter It. Iniettare Port. Injetar Sp. Inyectar	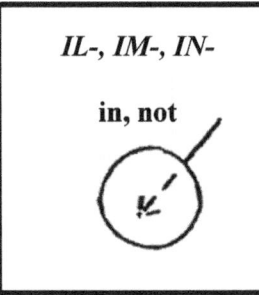	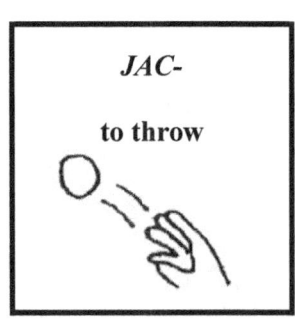

Definition: **v.** to force liquid into; to give a shot; to insert in the midst of something

Sentence: The porter in *Macbeth* injects a note of humor into an otherwise gloomy drama.

Projectile	Fr. Projectile It. Proiettile, Missile Port. Projétil Sp. Proyectil	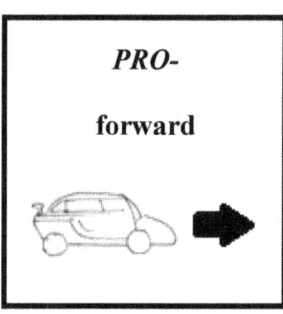 *PRO-* forward	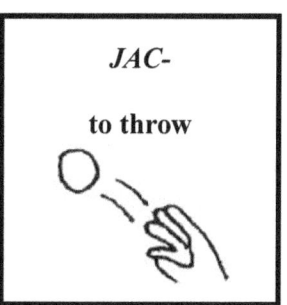 *JAC-* to throw

Definition: **n.** an object that can be thrown; a missile

Sentence: David's stone projectile struck Goliath in the temple and slew him.

Jocular	Fr. Jovial It. Giocoso Port. Jocoso Sp. Jocoso	 *JOCUS-* joke

Definition: **adj.** characterized by joking or wit

Sentence: Falstaff is Shakespeare's most famous jocular character.

Prejudice	Fr. Préjugé It. Pregiudizio Port. Prejuízo Sp. Prejuicio	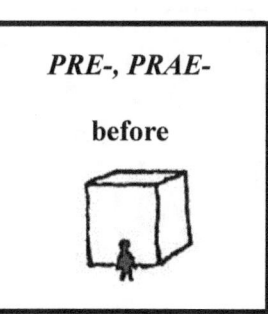 *PRE-, PRAE-* before	 *JUDIC-* to judge

Definition: **n.** a preconceived preference or idea formed without reason or experience; a biased opinion

Sentence: He bought only French wines, showing a snobbish prejudice against California wines of equal quality.

Junction

Fr. Intersection, Junction
It. Incrocio, Collegamento
Port. Junção
Sp. Unión

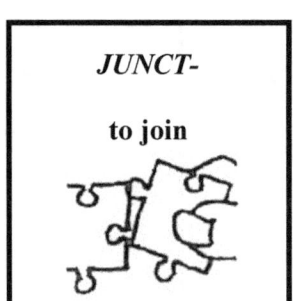

Definition: **n.** the act or process of joining; a place where two roads, railroad lines, or other things join

Sentence: Meet me at the junction of 7th Avenue and 107th Street.

Juncture

Fr. Giuntura, Moment critique
It. Giuntura, Occasione
Port. Juntura
Sp. Juntura

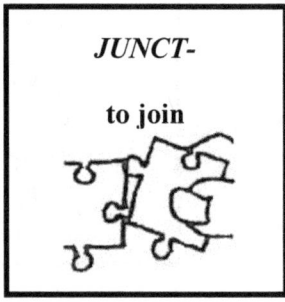

Definition: **n.** a point in time; a turning point or crisis; a joint or junction

Sentence: It's now five o'clock. At this juncture, we will recess until nine tomorrow morning.

Exercise A

_____

_____

_____

_____

Exercise B

Match the word with the letter of its definition:

1. ____ congratulation
2. ____ congregation
3. ____ impel
4. ____ gradual
5. ____ graduate
6. ____ gratitude
7. ____ ingredient
8. ____ inherent
9. ____ incense
10. ____ inject
11. ____ irate
12. ____ itinerary
13. ____ jocular
14. ____ junction
15. ____ juncture
16. ____ prejudice
17. ____ progress
18. ____ projectile
19. ____ transit
20. ____ transition

a) a critical point in time
b) to drive toward
c) extremely angry
d) to infuriate
e) the process of changing
f) a planned route
g) taking place in stages over a period of time
h) acknowledgement and approval
i) a preconceived idea or bias
j) the act of passing from one place to another
k) a component
l) to complete a diploma or degree
m) a gathering of people; a religious flock
n) thankfulness
o) to force liquid into something
p) permanent or essential (of a characteristic or attribute)
q) to move forward
r) humorous
s) a missile; something propelled with force
t) an intersection of two roads or rail lines

Exercise C

1. While some Episcopal _____ and ministers support the blessing of same-sex unions, others do not, which has caused a deep division within the church.

2. According to the map, the exit is at the _____ of Route 1 and Interstate 95.

3. Her _____ kindness and generosity helped her make new friends with ease.

4. The elderly lady's face glowed with _____ when the Boy Scout offered to carry her groceries.

5. _____ by white Americans toward racial and ethnic minorities has decreased significantly since the early 20th century.

6. The family's summer vacation _____ includes Cleveland, Chicago, and Michigan.

7. The day we _____ from high school was the happiest in our lives.

8. The most important _____ in steak au poivre is steak.

9. The doctor may _____ you with a contrast dye before your CT scan, because the resulting images are much clearer and easier to read.

10. At that _____, he saw there was no point in further argument; her mind was made up.

11. The prisoner became _____ when the one of the guards accused him of going to the infirmary under false pretenses.

12. The wise men gave frankincense and myrrh to the infant Jesus, which is why _____ is still used in formal church services.

13. We made excellent _____ on our trip from San Francisco to Chicago, traveling more than 500 miles each day.

14. The school did not allow _____ in the classroom; however, it did sponsor a paper airplane contest outside on the playground.

15. His brother's assassination _____ Robert Kennedy to run for president.

16. His students made the _____ from high school to college easily, because he prepared them so well.

17. The "T" subway in Boston is a popular form of mass _____.

18. Jesters were known as _____ entertainers who performed tricks for – and even poked fun at – kings and their courtiers.

19. The terraces the Incas carved into the mountainside formed a _____ staircase leading to the lofty peak.

20. The New England Patriots were thrilled to receive personal _____ from President Bush for winning the Super Bowl.

Exercise D

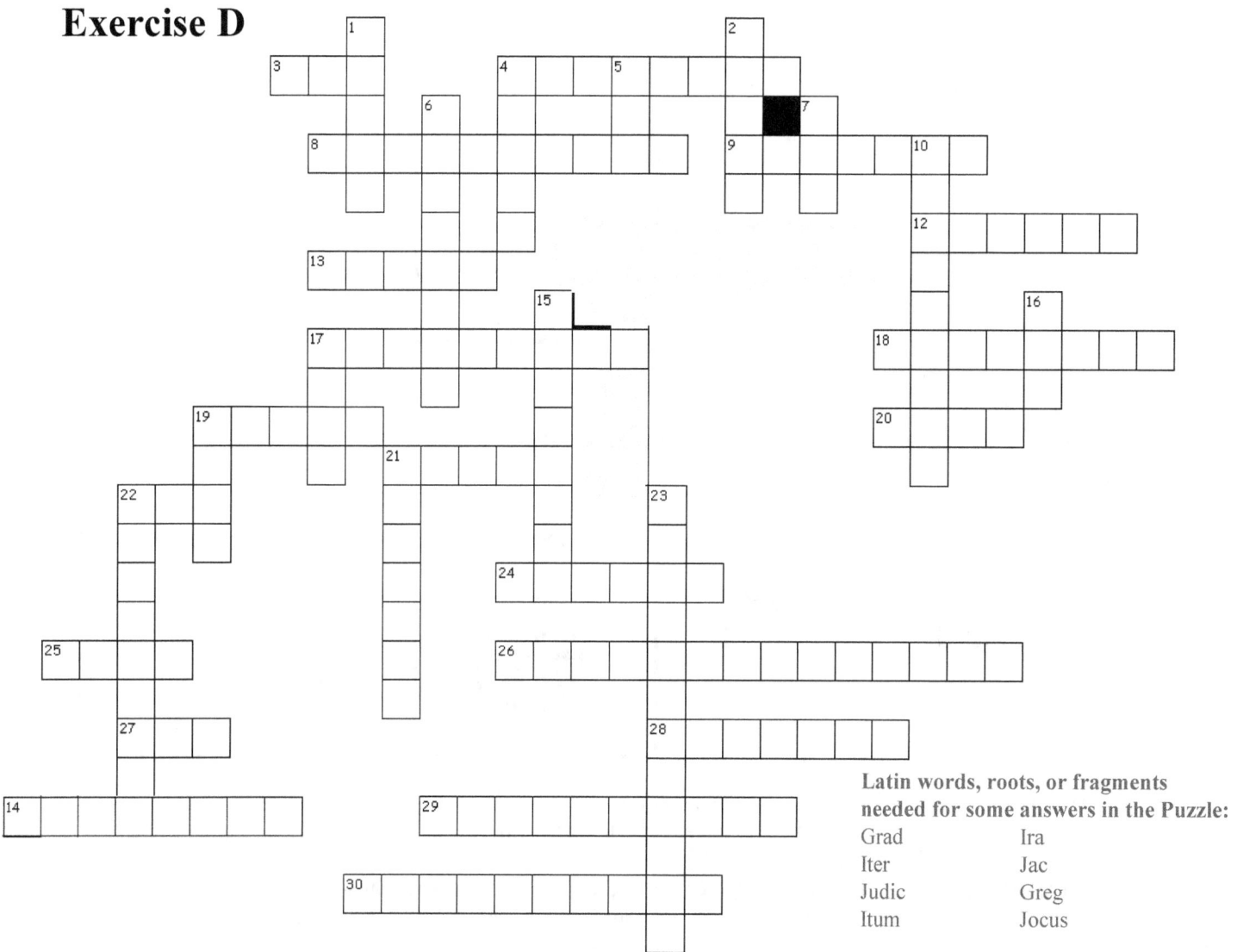

Latin words, roots, or fragments needed for some answers in the Puzzle:
Grad   Ira
Iter   Jac
Judic Greg
Itum   Jocus

Across
3. to stick (l)
4. a critical point in time
8. a component
9. the act of passing from one place to another
12. to force liquid into something
13. joke (l)
14. permanent or essential
17. thankfulness
18. to move forward
19. to drive toward
20. step (l)
21. to join (l)
22. before (l)
24. to set fire (l)
25. moved (l)
26. acknowledgement and approval
27. anger (l)
28. taking place in stages over a period of time
29. a missile; something propelled with force
30. the process of changing

Down
1. across (l)
2. extremely angry
4. to judge (l)
5. together (l)
6. to complete a diploma or degree
7. throw (l)
10. a planned route
15. an intersection of two roads or rail lines
16. forward (l)
17. flock, herd (l)
19. journey (l)
21. humorous
22. a preconceived idea or bias
23. a gathering of people; a religious flock

Lesson XIV

Laborious

Fr. Laborieux
It. Laborioso
Port. Laborioso
Sp. Laborioso

LABOR-
to work

Definition: **adj.** requiring considerable time and effort

Sentence: Digging the 100-foot ditch was laborious.

Collateral

Fr. Collatéral
It. Collaterale
Port. Collateral
Sp. Colateral

CON-
together

LATERAL-
side

Definition: **adj.** situated or running side by side; parallel
n. something pledged as security for repayment of a loan; additional but subordinate

Sentence: The bomb not only destroyed the military target, but caused a dozen civilian deaths, which the Army euphemistically called 'collateral damage.
The man gave his Rolex watch as collateral for the $500 loan.

Deluge

Fr. Déluge
It. Diluvio
Port. Dilúvio
Sp. Diluvio

DE-
down, from

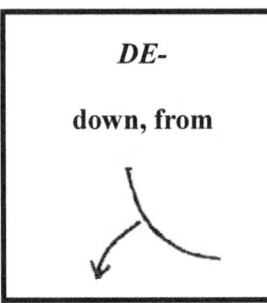

LAV-
to wash

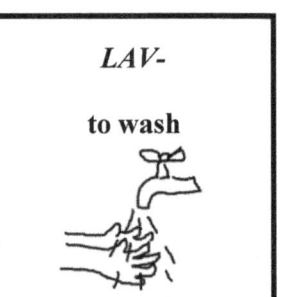

Definition: **v.** to overrun with water; to inundate
n. a flood; a drenching downpour of rain

Sentence: The president was deluged with angry e-mails after the preemptive attack.
The deluge after the earthquake multiplied the damage.

Legitimate	Fr. Légitimate It. Legittimo Port. Legítimo Sp. Legítimo	 *LEGIS-* **law**

Definition: **adj.** conforming to the law or to the rules; defensible with logic or justification; (of a child) born to a married couple

Sentence: The eldest son born to the king and queen is the legitimate heir to the throne.

Legacy	Fr. Héritage It. Eredità Port. Legado Sp. Legado	 *LEGIS-* **law**

Definition: **n.** an amount of money or property left to someone in a will; something intangible that has been bequeathed or inherited

Sentence: His father's reputation as a ne'er-do-well was an unwanted legacy that hindered his own career.

Delegate	Fr. v. Déléguer, n. Délégué It. v. Delegare, n. Delegato Port. Delegado Sp. Delegado	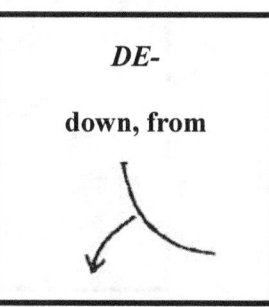 *DE-* **down, from**	 *LEGIS-* **law**

Definition: **n.** a person sent or authorized to represent others; a member of a committee
v. to entrust to another person, typically one who is less senior than oneself

Sentence: The U.S. sent the vice president as a delegate to the international climate summit.
If the boss did not delegate tasks, nothing would be completed on time.

Levity

Fr. Légèreté
It. Leggerezza
Port. Leveza
Sp. Levedad

LEVIS-

to rise

Definition: **n.** the treatment of a serious matter with humor or lack of respect

Sentence: Making jokes at his friend's expense was unpardonable levity.

Liberal

Fr. Libéral
It. Liberale
Port. Liberal
Sp. Liberal

LIBER-

free

Definition: **adj.** having or giving freely; respectful and accepting of behavior or opinions different from one's own; ample

Sentence: The homeowner spread liberal amounts of fertilizer to assure a thick lawn.

Liberty

Fr. Liberté
It. Libertà
Port. Liberdade
Sp. Libertad

LIBER-

free

Definition: **n.** freedom; the state of being free from oppression or imprisonment; (pl.) overly free or unrestricted actions

Sentence: The father warned the young man not to take any liberties with his underage daughter.

License	Fr. Licence It. Licenza Port. Licença Sp. Liciencia	 *LICENCIA-* **freedom**
Definition:	**n.** 1) a permit from an authority to own or use something, do a particular thing, or carry on a trade; formal or official permission **n.** 2) deviation from normal rules	
Sentence:	Many teenagers are excited to get a driver's license. A poet will often take license with standard English usage to better express himself.	

League	Fr. Ligue It. Lega Port. Liga Sp. Liga	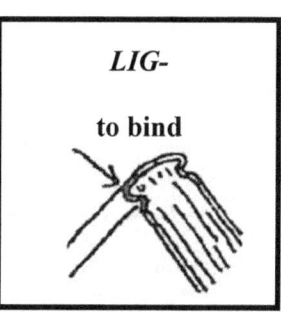 *LIG-* **to bind**
Definition:	**n.** a union of persons with common aims; a collection of people, countries, or groups that combine for mutual protection or cooperation	
Sentence:	The buccaneers were in league with Andrew Jackson at the Battle of New Orleans.	

Lingual	Fr. Linguistique, Lingual It. Linguistico Port. Lingual Sp. Lingual	 *LINGUA-* **language**
Definition:	**adj.** relating to or near the tongue; relating to speech or language	
Sentence:	He grew up in a multi-lingual household; his parents spoke Spanish, English, and Russian.	

Literal	Fr. Littéral It. Letterale Port. Literal Sp. Literal	 *LITTERA-* letter
Definition:	**adj.** straightforward, not figurative; taking words in their concrete or usual sense; representing the exact words of the original text	
Sentence:	The literal meaning of 'star' is a heavenly body; the figurative meaning refers to a famous person.	

Locality	Fr. Localité It. Località Port. Localidade Sp. Localidad	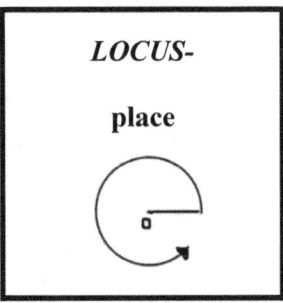 *LOCUS-* place
Definition:	**n.** a particular neighborhood, place, or district; a specific place	
Sentence:	It was in this locality that the series of brutal muggings took place.	

Eloquent	Fr. Éloquent It. Eloquente Port. Eloquente Sp. Elocuente	 *LOQU-* to talk
Definition:	**adj.** forceful and expressive; fluent and expressive (speech)	
Sentence:	The rows of graves in Arlington are eloquent testimony to American war sacrifices.	

Colloquial	Fr. Familier, Parlé It. Colloquiale Port. Coloquial Sp. Coloquial	*LOQU-* **to talk** 

Definition: **adj.** conversational or informal speech or writing (not formal or literary)

Sentence: 'Colloquial' describes everyday spoken English as opposed to formal, written English.

Illuminate	Fr. Illuminer It. Illuminare Port. Iluminar Sp. Iluminar	*LUMIN-* **to light up** 

Definition: **v.** to light up; to make bright; to shed light on a subject

Sentence: Hundreds of Japanese lanterns illuminate the tiny cottages at the Oak Bluffs campground once a year on 'Illumination Night.'

Lucid	Fr. Lucide It. Lucido Port. Lúcido Sp. Lúcido	*LUCIS-* **light** 

Definition: **adj.** easy to follow; clear

Sentence: As the general anesthesia wears off, it may take a while for the patient to become lucid again.

Delusion

Fr. Illusion
It. Illusione
Port. Delusão
Sp. Delusión

DE-
down, from

LUD-, LUS-
to play, game

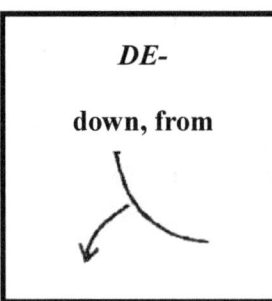

Definition: **n.** an idiosyncratic belief or impression that is not in accordance with generally accepted reality; an incorrect idea or belief

Sentence: Hitler's belief that Germany could quickly conquer England proved to be a delusion.

Elusive

Fr. Élusif
It. Elusivo
Port. Elusivo
Sp. Elusivo

EX-
out

LUD-, LUS-
to play, game

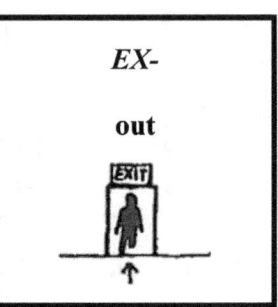

Definition: **adj.** difficult to find, catch, or achieve

Sentence: Despite his determination, straight As proved an elusive goal.

Exercise A

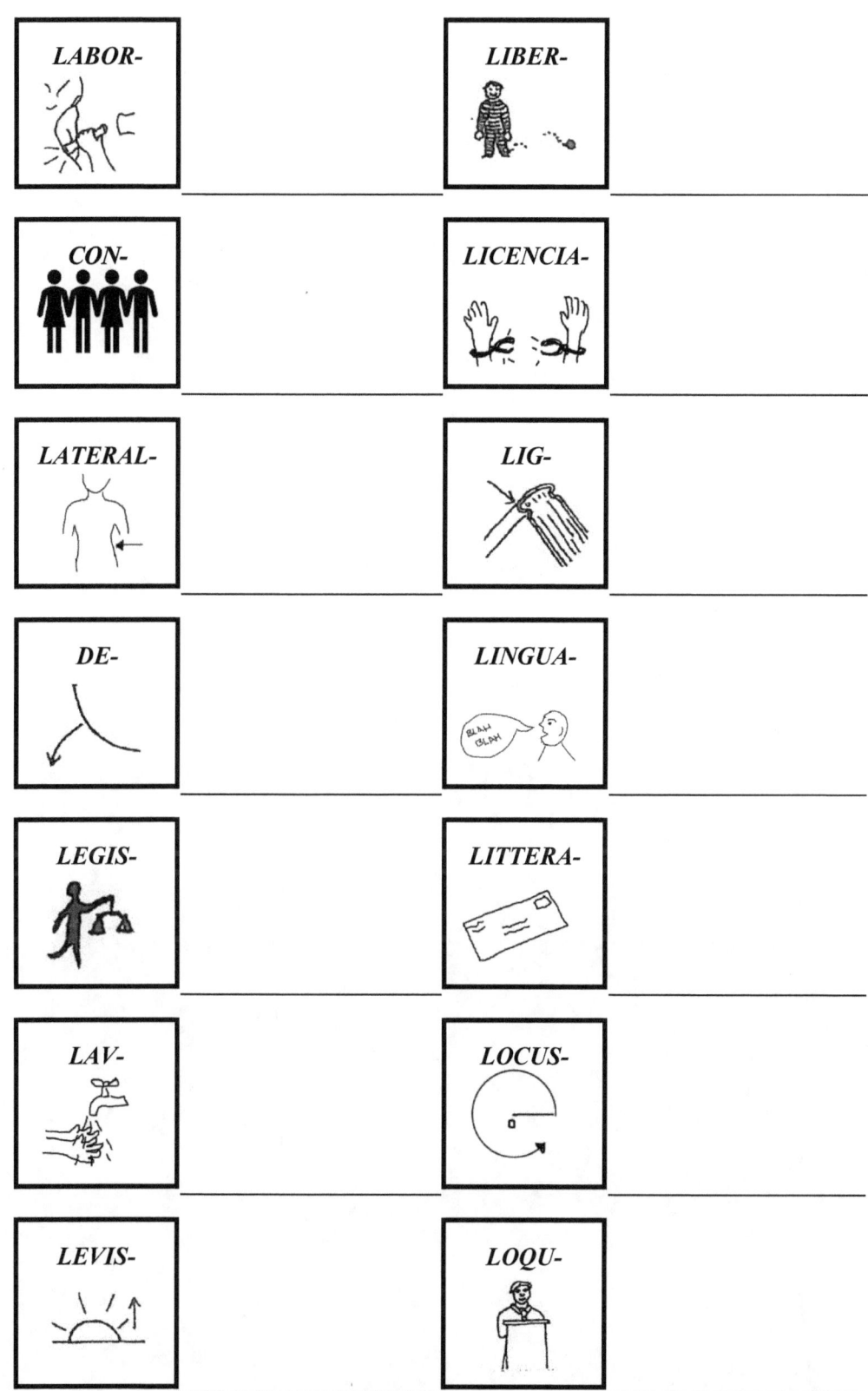

 _____

 _____

 _____

 _____

Exercise B
Match the word with the letter of its definition:

1. ____ **collateral**
2. ____ **colloquial**
3. ____ **delegate**
4. ____ **delusion**
5. ____ **deluge**
6. ____ **eloquent**
7. ____ **elusive**
8. ____ **illuminate**
9. ____ **laborious**
10. ____ **legitimate**
11. ____ **levity**
12. ____ **league**
13. ____ **legacy**
14. ____ **liberal**
15. ____ **liberty**
16. ____ **license**
17. ____ **lingual**
18. ____ **literal**
19. ____ **locality**
20. ____ **lucid**

a) articulate and expressive
b) freedom
c) something bequeathed at death
d) familiar and conversational
e) to shed light on
f) lighthearted or humorous speech
g) relating to the tongue
h) an area or specific site
i) requiring considerable time and effort
j) to entrust to someone
k) something pledged as security for a loan
l) having or giving freely
m) straightforward; using the exact words
n) conforming to the law
o) clear
p) an unrealistic idea or belief
q) to flood or inundate
r) difficult to find or achieve
s) a union of persons or countries
t) a permit or official permission

Exercise C

1. The graduation speaker was so _____ that the students and faculty gave her a standing ovation.

2. Major _____ Baseball employs only the best baseball players in the country.

3. After Michelle Obama did an in-depth radio interview, there was a _____ of phone calls from listeners.

4. Julia Child often added a _____ quantity of wine to her sauces and entrées.

5. According to the local court, the homeowner had a _____ claim to the piece of land in dispute.

6. Even though most of the movie was filmed on the set in Hollywood, the director cut in street scenes from Charlestown to establish the film's fictional _____.

7. She went to the Democratic National Convention as a _____ for John Edwards, but ended up voting for Barack Obama.

8. His only _____ to his children was a small investment portfolio.

9. The bank accepted the property as _____ to secure the new business loan.

10. "Get the lead out" is a _____ expression for "Please, move faster!"

11. The moderator was expert at using _____ to keep the audience's attention focused.

12. "Give me _____ or give me death" is a famous quotation attributed to Patrick Henry at the time of the Revolutionary War.

13. Every set of new parents operates under the _____ that their baby is the cutest in the entire world.

14. The _____ area was very sore, so the patient had to "eat" a liquid diet through a straw.

15. Those who suffer from autism spectrum disorders often have difficulty understanding humor based on wordplay, as their minds are very _____.

16. Strategically placed solar lights will _____ the borders of the driveway at night.

17. Because restaurant work is so _____ and low-paid, the burnout rate is high for people who work in the kitchens.

18. We could hear the spring peepers all around us, but when we tried to spot them, they proved _____.

19. The robbers were under the false impression that an "open door policy" gave them a _____ to steal.

20. Her thinking and speech were _____ until she suffered a second stroke.

Exercise D

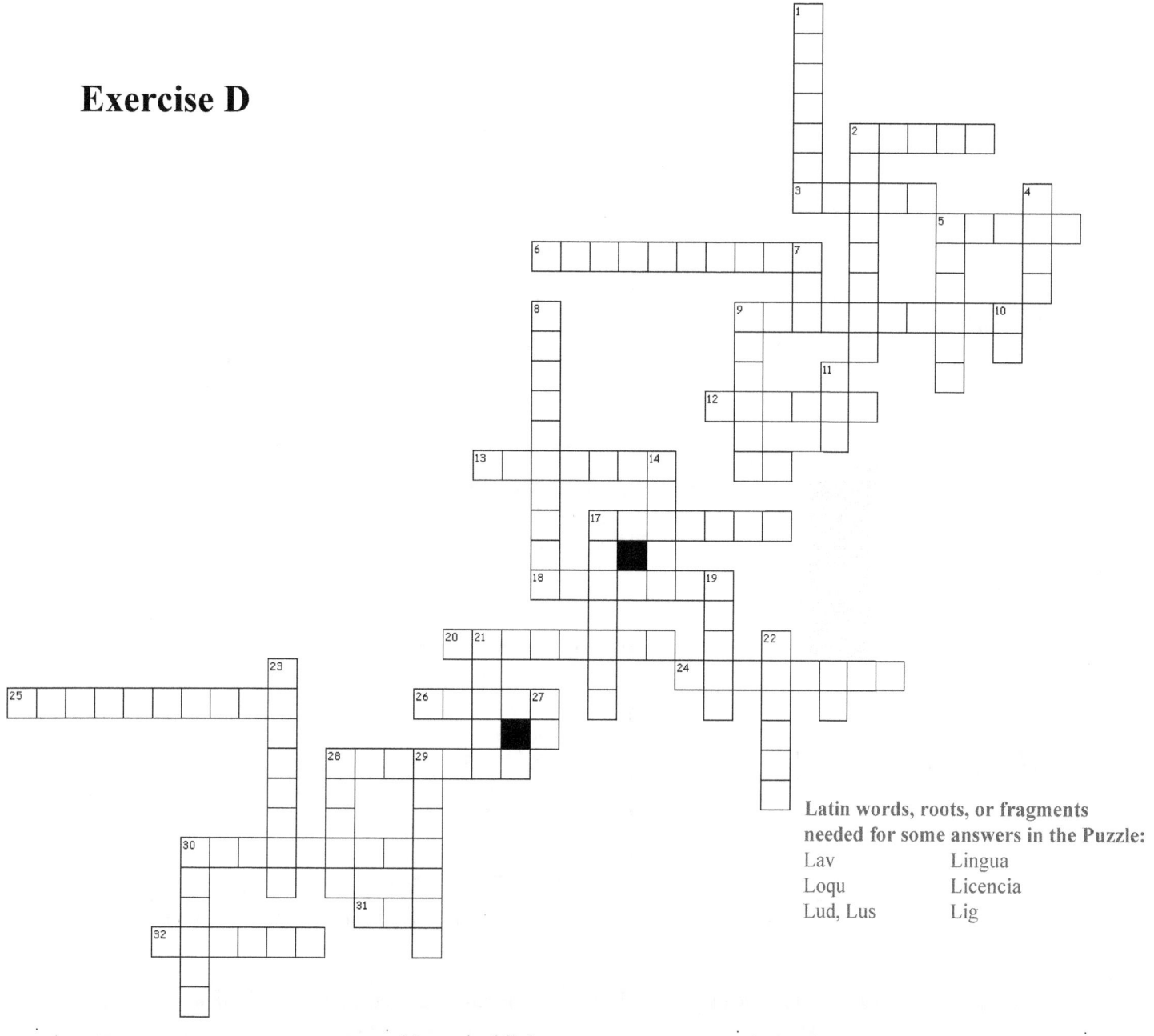

Latin words, roots, or fragments needed for some answers in the Puzzle:
Lav
Loqu
Lud, Lus
Lingua
Licencia
Lig

Across
2. to light up (l)
3. place (l)
5. to work (l)
6. familiar and conversational speech
9. conforming to the law
12. a union of persons or countries
13. straightforward; using the exact words
15. together (l)
17. having or giving freely
18. side (l)
20. articulate and expressive
24. freedom (l)
25. to shed light on
26. clear
28. a permit or official permission
30. requiring considerable time and effort
31. wash away (l)
32. language (l)

Down
1. relating to the tongue
2. an area or specific site
4. to talk (l)
5. something bequeathed at death
7. to bind (l)
8. something pledged as security for a loan
9. freedom
10. out (l)
11. to play, game (l)
14. free (l)
16. letter (l)
19. to rise (l)
21. light (l)
22. to flood or inundate
23. an unrealistic idea or belief
27. down, from (l)
28. law (l)
29. difficult to find or achieve
30. lighthearted or humorous speech

Lesson XV

Mandatory

Fr. Mandaté
It. Mandatorio
Port. Mandatário
Sp. Mandatario

MANUS-
hand

DO-, DA-, DAT-
to give

Definition: **adj.** required by law, rule, or other obligation

Sentence: Military service was mandatory for all Spartan males from the age of 8.

Manipulate

Fr. Manipuler
It. Manipolare
Port. Manipular
Sp. Manipular

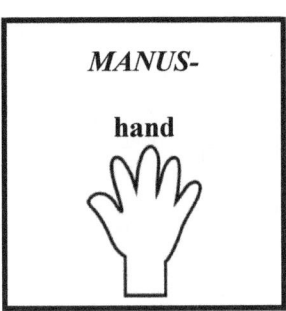

MANUS-
hand

Definition: **v.** to handle or control with dexterity; to control or influence; to change to serve one's own ends

Sentence: Dictators typically manipulate vote-counting to guarantee their reelection.

Manufacture

Fr. Manufacturer
It. Fabbricare
Port. Manufacturar
Sp. Manufacturar

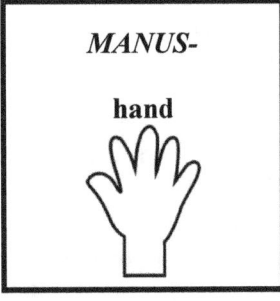

MANUS-
hand

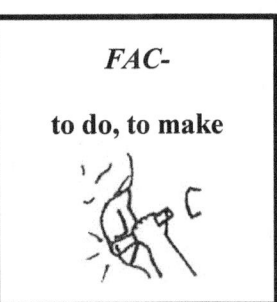

FAC-
to do, to make

Definition: **v.** to make or process into a finished product; to fabricate

Sentence: The tardy student's excuse of a flat tire was manufactured.

Maritime	Fr. Maritime It. Marittimo Port. Marítimo Sp. Marítimo	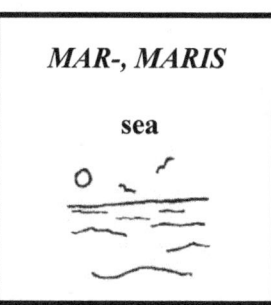 *MAR-, MARIS* sea

Definition: **adj.** of, relating to, or along the sea

Sentence: The Canadian Maritimes is the name given to those provinces bordering the Atlantic Ocean.

Maternal	Fr. Maternel It. Materno Port. Maternal Sp. Maternal	 *MATER-* mother

Definition: **adj.** related through one's mother; concerning motherhood

Sentence: My mother's sisters and brothers are my maternal aunts and uncles.

Matrimony	Fr. Mariage It. Matrimonio Port. Matrimônio Sp. Matrimonio	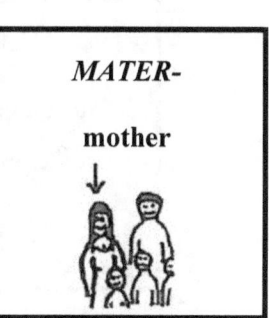 *MATER-* mother

Definition: **n.** the rites of marriage; the state of being married

Sentence: Holy matrimony is a sacred rite in the Roman Catholic Church.

Medieval

Fr. Médiéval
It. Medievale
Port. Medieval
Sp. Medieval

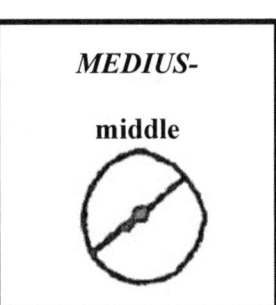

Definition: **adj.** belonging to or having to do with the Middle Ages; antiquated or outdated

Sentence: Some countries continue to use medieval punishments, such as amputation of a hand for theft.

Mediocre

Fr. Médiocre
It. Mediocre
Port. Medíocre
Sp. Mediocre

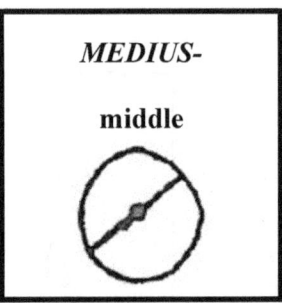

Definition: **adj.** of average to inferior quality

Sentence: The middle school students' mediocre performance on the standardized tests lowered the entire school district's ranking.

Memorabilia

Fr. Souvenirs
It. Memorabilia, Cimeli
Port. Memorabilia
Sp. Memorabilia

Definition: **n.** objects kept or collected because of their associations with memorable people or events

Sentence: Souvenirs are often memorabilia of places we have visited.

Memory	Fr. Mémoire It. Memoria Port. Memória Sp. Memoria	 *MEM-* to remember

Definition: **n.** the mental faculty of retaining and recalling past experience

Sentence: "Memory" is the capacity of men or machines to embed and later retrieve information.

Mend	Fr. Réparer It. Rammendare Port. Emendar Sp. Enmendar	 *MENDUM-* defect, fault

Definition: **v.** to fix something broken or torn; to restore to good condition

Sentence: Mending fences' means to make up for past disputes and become friendly again.

Immersion	Fr. Immersion It. Immersione Port. Imersão Sp. Inmersión	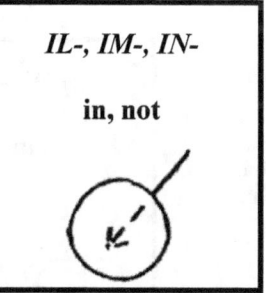 *IL-, IM-, IN-* in, not	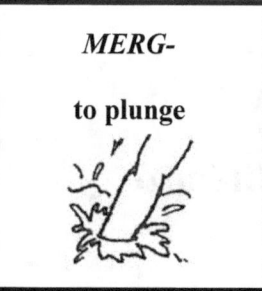 *MERG-* to plunge

Definition: **n.** the act of covering completely in liquid; complete absorption in a situation or subject

Sentence: The Army uses the immersion method to teach languages.

Merge

Fr. Mêler, Se fondre
It. Mescolarsi
Port. Mesclar
Sp. Mezclar

MERG-
to plunge

Definition:	**v.** to combine or be combined into a single entity
Sentence:	One of the most difficult tasks for new drivers is learning to merge onto an interstate.

Minimal

Fr. Minimal
It. Minimo
Port. Mínimo
Sp. Mínimo

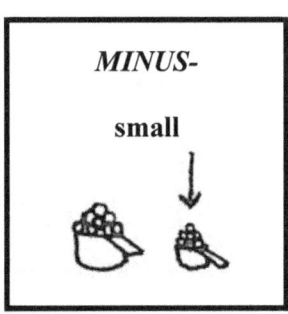

MINUS-
small

Definition:	**adj.** the least amount; of the smallest amount, quantity, or degree
Sentence:	Even a minimal amount of gluten in her food can make her deathly ill.

Minimize

Fr. Minimiser
It. Minimizzare
Port. Minimizar
Sp. Minimizar

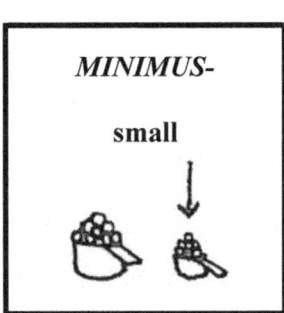

MINIMUS-
small

Definition:	**v.** to reduce to the least or smallest size
Sentence:	A flu shot should minimize your chances of coming down with the disease.

Missile

Fr. Missile
It. Missile
Port. Míssil
Sp. Misil

MISSUS- — thrown

Definition:	**n.** an object that is fired, thrown, dropped, or otherwise projected at a target; a projectile
Sentence:	There is an international ban on intercontinental ballistic missiles, or ICBMs.

Promise

Fr. Promesse
It. Promessa
Port. Prometer
Sp. Prometer

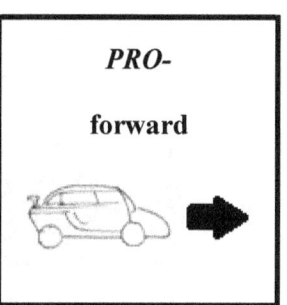 

PRO- — forward   *MITT-, MISS-* — to send forth

Definition:	**n.** a written or spoken statement binding a person to an action
Sentence:	I promise to tell the truth, the whole truth, and nothing but the truth.

Moment

Fr. Moment, Instant
It. Momento
Port. Momento
Sp. Momento

MOT-, MOV- — to move

Definition:	**n.** a very brief period of time; importance or consequence; a particular time (in history)
Sentence:	For a moment, I thought the woman was my dead aunt, but I realized immediately that she couldn't be.

Momentum

Fr. Élan
It. Impeto
Port. Momentum
Sp. Impulso

Definition: **n.** the impetus gained by a moving object

Sentence: Trains build great momentum and cannot stop quickly.

Motion

Fr. Mouvement
It. Movimento
Port. Movimiento
Sp. Movimiento

Definition: **n.** the action or process of moving

Sentence: The ball was in motion while it was rolling down the hill.

Exercise A

Exercise B
Match the word with the letter of its definition:

1. ____ immersion
2. ____ manipulate
3. ____ mandatory
4. ____ manufacture
5. ____ maritime
6. ____ maternal
7. ____ matrimony
8. ____ medieval
9. ____ mediocre
10. ____ memorabilia
11. ____ memory
12. ____ mend
13. ____ merge
14. ____ minimal
15. ____ minimize
16. ____ missile
17. ____ moment
18. ____ momentum
19. ____ motion
20. ____ promise

a) a projectile
b) related through one's mother
c) the action or process of moving
d) the mental faculty of retaining information
e) belonging to the Middle Ages
f) to cleverly control or influence, especially for one's own benefit
g) the least possible
h) to combine into a single entity
i) of average quality
j) covering completely with liquid
k) a very brief period of time
l) relating to the sea
m) to fabricate
n) the rite of marriage
o) to reduce to the least possible amount
p) a binding statement of intent
q) to restore to a sound condition
r) required
s) the impetus gained by a moving object
t) objects kept in association with memorable events

Exercise C

Use the word box at the beginning of the lesson to fill in the blanks below:

1. The toy company tried, but failed, to _____ enough action figures to meet holiday demand.

2. Jesus was baptized by _____ in the Jordan River.

3. In comparison to Krispy Kreme doughnuts, Dunkin' Donuts treats are only _____.

4. A person used to public speaking can prepare a speech with _____ notice, but I need at least a week.

5. In _____ times, there was a strict social caste system with little opportunity for upward mobility.

6. The _____ of the roller-coaster left him nauseated and dizzy.

7. He made a solemn _____ at his swearing-in to uphold the U.S. Constitution.

8. The business executives _____ the accounts to show greater sales revenues than they actually had, artificially driving up the stock's share price.

9. Sports fanatics often collect _____ of their favorite teams.

10. _____ can be a big adjustment for older newlyweds who have been used to living on their own.

11. "To take a trip down _____ lane" is to indulge in pleasant or sentimental memories.

12. After much deliberation, the two local banks decided to _____ so as to withstand competition from larger, regional banks.

13. The little girl was devoted to her _____ grandmother, who often took care of her when her mother had to work late.

14. Once the _____ is airborne, it is monitored by NASA with instruments on the ground.

15. The _____ came when he needed to act decisively or risk losing her.

16. At most liberal arts colleges, writing courses are _____, but at others they are optional.

17. Many New England states sponsor a _____ academy to train those who wish to join the Coast Guard or make their living on the sea.

18. I told him to _____ his ways, or I would fire him.

19. The _____ of the sled carried him into the tree before he had time to correct course.

20. Botox injections can _____ wrinkles by paralyzing the tiny muscles that cause them.

Exercise D

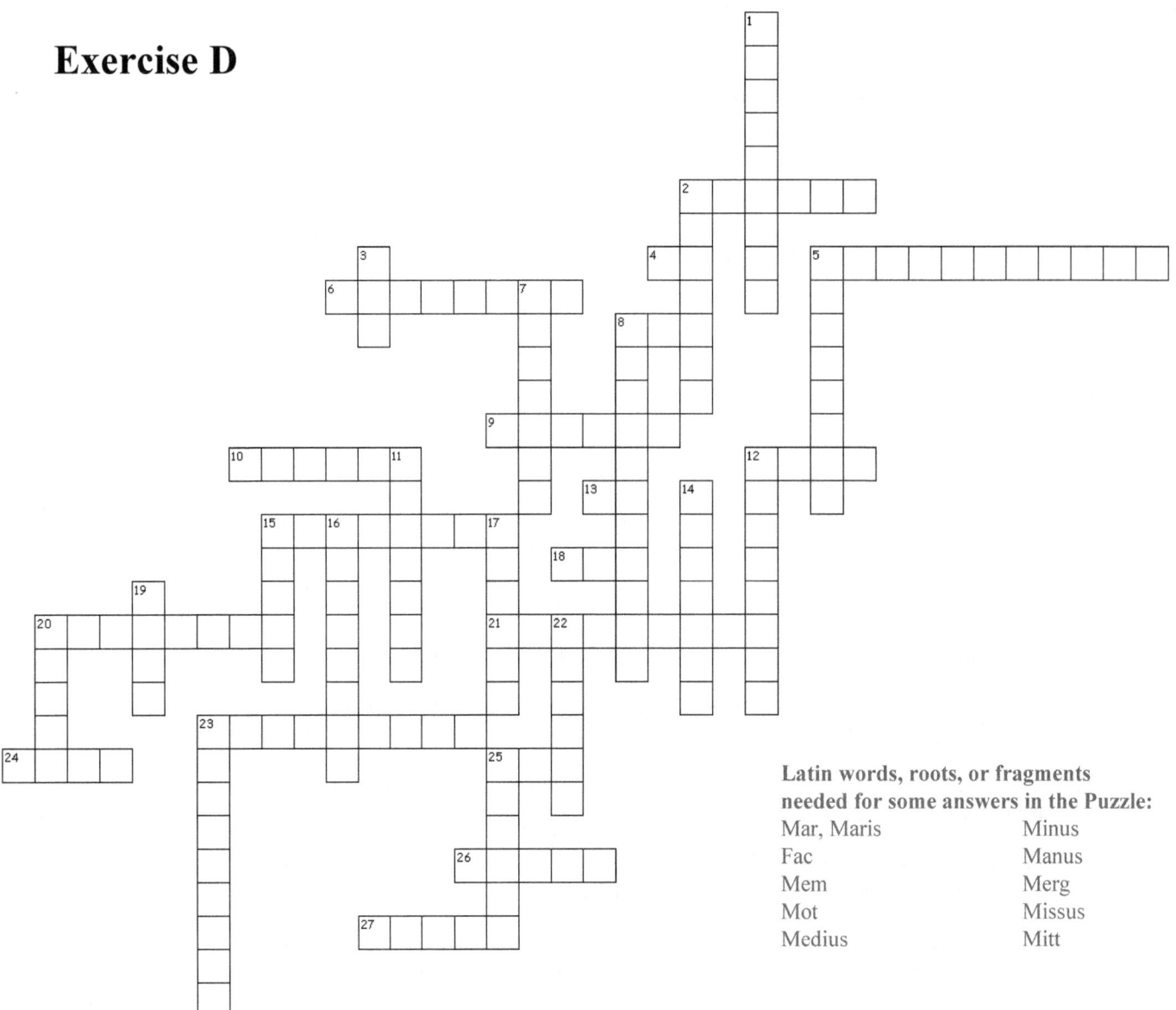

Latin words, roots, or fragments needed for some answers in the Puzzle:
Mar, Maris
Fac
Mem
Mot
Medius
Minus
Manus
Merg
Missus
Mitt

Across
2. a very brief period of time
4. in, not (l)
5. objects kept in association with memorable events
6. relating to the sea
8. to remember (l)
9. thrown (l)
10. defect, fault (l)
12. to plunge (l)
13. to give (l)
15. the impetus gained by a moving object
18. to move (l)
20. to reduce to the least possible amount
21. covering completely with liquid
23. required
24. to restore to a sound condition
25. sea (l)
26. small (l)
27. hand (l)

Down
1. the rite of marriage
2. small
3. to do, to make (l)
5. of average quality
7. a projectile
8. to fabricate
11. the least possible
12. related through one's mother
14. a binding statement of intent
15. mother (l)
16. belonging to the Middle Ages
17. the action or process of moving
19. to send forth (l)
20. to combine into a single entity
22. the mental faculty of retaining information
23. to cleverly control or influence, especially for one's own benefit
25. middle (l)

Quiz 3

Quiz answers begin on page 318

> transition, dormant, genuine, levity, fragment, immersion, fragile, legacy, congregation, progress, lucid, irate, fortunate, elusive, mediocre, liberal, deface, fertile, mandatory, incense

1. The _____ from high school to college often causes much anxiety for students and parents alike.

2. My mother became _____ after the store manager refused to let her return the defective towels.

3. The teacher left a rich intellectual _____, but her children didn't inherit much money.

4. The vase was quite _____, and she was _____ that it did not break when she dropped it.

5. Although the Nile River Valley remains _____, many of its ancient tombs have been _____ by grave robbers seeking archaeological treasures.

6. When the window shattered, a _____ of glass struck his eye.

7. Harold Bloom's lectures were filled with obscure references, but his teaching assistant gave _____ explanations afterward to the confused undergraduates.

8. While I was in the hospital, my friend tried to cheer me up with _____, but I knew that underneath his humorous facade, he felt _____ concern.

9. At some colleges, mastery of a foreign language is _____; as a result, many students travel abroad for language _____ programs.

10. The labor union and management negotiators made some _____ on minor issues, but an agreement on wages and benefits remained _____.

11. Despite the student's powerful intellect, his essay was disappointingly _____.

12. Antigua, Guatemala is surrounded by three _____ volcanoes.

13. The _____ bowed their heads in prayer as the priest processed down the aisle, swinging a censer filled with burning _____.

14. A supporter of gay marriage and abortion rights, he was much more _____ than his sister, a Catholic and staunch Republican.

Lesson XVI

Monitor

Fr. n. Moniteur, v. Surveiller
It. n. Monitor, v. Monitorare
Port. Monitor
Sp. Monitor

MON-
to warn, to advise

Definition: **v.** to observe and check over a period of time
n. a person or device that watches over something

Sentence: Teachers are required to monitor their students' academic progress.
Andy used a baby monitor so he'd hear when his son woke from his nap.

Muster

Fr. Rassembler
It. Raccogliere
Port. Juntar
Sp. Juntar

MON-
to warn, advise

Definition: **v.** to gather together; to collect; to summon for military service

Sentence: A sip of wine may aid in mustering the courage to go on stage and speak.

Mountain

Fr. Montagne
It. Montagna
Port. Montanha
Sp. Montaña

MONS-
mountain

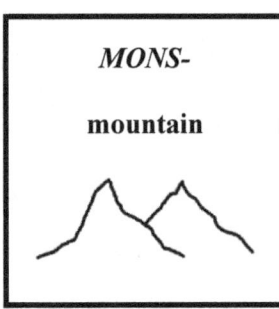

Definition: **n.** a conical elevation of the earth's surface, rising to a summit

Sentence: One of my favorite pastimes is mountain climbing.

Morality	Fr. Moralité It. Moralità Port. Moralidade Sp. Moralidad	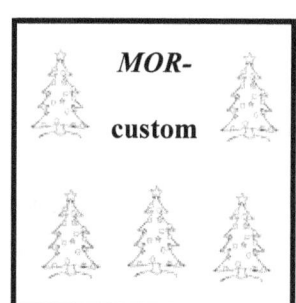  

Definition: **n.** a set of principles of conduct; a system of ideas of right and wrong

Sentence: In response to the Civil Rights Movement, some Southerners argued that morality could not be legislated.

Immortal	Fr. Immortel It. Immortale Port. Imortal Sp. Inmortal	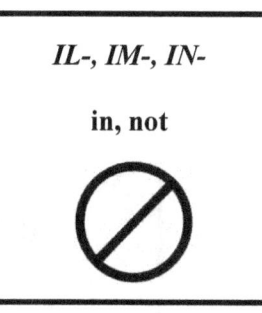 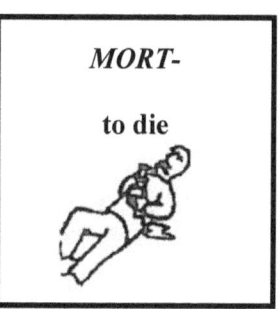

Definition: **adj.** living forever; unable to die; deathless

Sentence: 'Ozymandias' is a Keats' poem reminding that even a pharaoh is not immortal.

Mortify	Fr. Mortifier It. Mortificare Port. Mortificar Sp. Mortificar	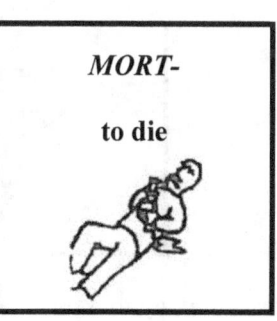 

Definition: **v.** to humiliate or embarrass

Sentence: Nude beaches still mortify most Americans; Europeans are much more accepting of public nudity.

			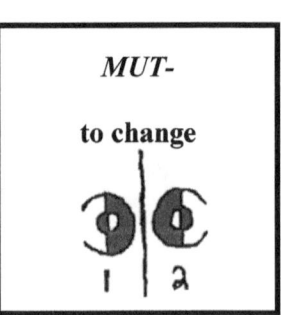
Commute	Fr. Faire la navette, Commuer It. Fare il pendolare Port. Comutar Sp. Conmutar	COM- together	MUT- to change

Definition: **v.** to go from one place to another; to travel the distance between one's home and place of work on a regular basis; to substitute or to exchange

Sentence: The murderer's death sentence was commuted by the governor to life without parole.

		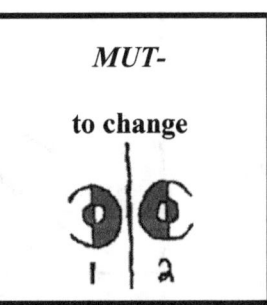
Mutate	Fr. Muter It. Mutare Port. Mudar Sp. Mutar	MUT- to change

Definition: **v.** to undergo or cause to undergo mutation (change or alteration)

Sentence: Alchemists sought a Philosopher's Stone to mutate common metals into gold.

Native	Fr. Natif (de) It. Nativo (di) Port. Nativo Sp. Nativo	NAT- born

Definition: **adj.** existing in or belonging to by nature
n. one born in or connected with a place of birth; an original inhabitant of a place; aborigine

Sentence: Tomatoes, potatoes, cocoa, and tobacco are native to the Americas.
Michael Jordan is a native of Brooklyn, where he learned to play basketball at an early age.

Naval

Fr. Naval
It. Navale
Port. Naval
Sp. Naval

NAVIS- ship

Definition: **adj.** relating to ships or shipping; relating to a navy

Sentence: Land-locked Switzerland is not a naval power.

Navigate

Fr. Naviguer
It. Navigare
Port. Navegar
Sp. Navegar

NAVIS- ship

AG- to drive, to urge

Definition: **v.** to plan or direct the route or course of a ship, airplane, etc; to sail or travel; to find one's way

Sentence: Strangers have difficulty navigating Boston's winding and often unmarked streets.

Negate

Fr. Nier
It. Negare
Port. Negar
Sp. Negar

NEG- to deny

Definition: **v.** to make ineffective or invalid; to nullify; to deny the existence of

Sentence: The apparent goal was negated by the referee's offsides call.

Negative	Fr. Négatif It. Negativo Port. Negativo Sp. Negativo	 *NEG-* to deny

Definition: **n.** a statement or act indicating or expressing a contradiction, denial, or refusal; describing a number less than zero; exposed film, in which the colors (or black and white) are inverted
adj. the absence of something

Sentence: In radio transmissions, military personnel and airline pilots say 'Negative' instead of 'No.'
There is much negative space in an atom.

Annihilate	Fr. Annihiler It. Annientare Port. Aniquilar Sp. Aniquilar	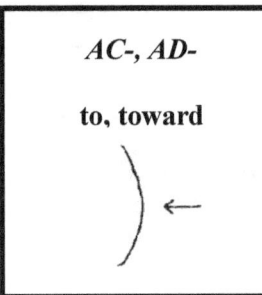 *AC-, AD-* to, toward	 *NIHIL-* nothing

Definition: **v.** to destroy completely

Sentence: The Romans annihilated Carthage, razing the city and plowing salt into its fields.

Nominal	Fr. Nominal It. Nominale Port. Nominal Sp. Nominal	 *NOMEN-* name

Definition: **adj.** existing in name only; very small; far below real value or cost

Sentence: 'To get it for a song' means to pay a nominal price for a thing.

Innovation	Fr. Innovation It. Innovazione Port. Inovação Sp. Innovación	*IL-, IM-, IN-* **in, not**	*NOV-* **to make new**

Definition: **n.** the act of beginning or introducing something for the first time

Sentence: The transistor was the crucial innovation that led to microchip technology.

Novelty	Fr. Nouveauté It. Novità Port. Novidade Sp. Novedad	*NOV-* **to make new**

Definition: **n.** something new and unusual; the quality of being novel

Sentence: The automobile was a novelty until mass production and extensive paved roads brought down the price and made it practical to use.

Novice	Fr. Novice It. Novellino Port. Noviço Sp. Novato	*NOV-* **to make new**

Definition: **n.** someone who is beginning; a person who is new to and inexperienced in a job or situation; a rookie

Sentence: When he was a novice at golf, he had a high handicap, but it quickly dropped after he took lessons.

Nocturnal

Fr. Nocturne
It. Notturno
Port. Noturno
Sp. Nocturno

Definition: **adj.** occurring or active at night

Sentence: Owls and bats are nocturnal creatures: They hunt at night and sleep during the day.

Announce

Fr. Annoncer
It. Annunciare
Port. Anunciar
Sp. Anunciar

Definition: **v.** to make known publicly

Sentence: 'The Wedding March' traditionally announces that the bride is starting down the aisle.

Exercise A

 _____

 _____

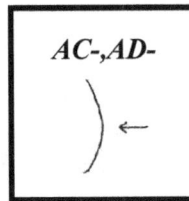 _____

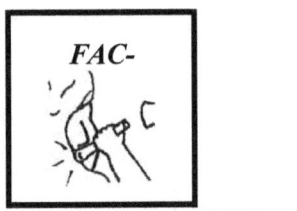 _____

Exercise B

Match the word with the letter of its definition:

1. ____ annihilate
2. ____ announce
3. ____ commute
4. ____ immortal
5. ____ innovation
6. ____ monitor
7. ____ morality
8. ____ mortify
9. ____ mountain
10. ____ muster
11. ____ mutate
12. ____ naval
13. ____ native
14. ____ navigate
15. ____ negate
16. ____ negative
17. ____ nocturnal
18. ____ nominal
19. ____ novelty
20. ____ novice

a) active at night
b) to travel a certain distance regularly
c) something new and/or unusual
d) to make known publically
e) a set of principles of conduct
f) to undergo a change or alteration
g) relating to ships
h) a conical, natural elevation of the earth's surface
i) to invalidate
j) original to a particular person or place
k) to destroy completely
l) an inexperienced person
m) to humiliate
n) a contradiction, denial, or refusal
o) to gather together
p) a new method, idea, or product
q) symbolic or minimal; existing in name only
r) to travel on a desired course
s) living forever
t) to observe over time

Exercise C

1. _____ people inhabited North America at least 10,000 to 12,000 years ago.

2. In Greek mythology, the _____ gods live on Mount Olympus.

3. To make "a _____ out of a molehill" is an expression meaning to exaggerate something or to make a huge fuss over a minor problem.

4. The _____ of the printing press made books available and affordable beyond the aristocracy and religious orders.

5. He decided to _____ his former girlfriend by posting embarrassing photos of her on Facebook.

6. She used to spend two or more hours each day on her _____ into the city.

7. In 1492, Christopher Columbus _____ across the Atlantic ocean to the New World, thinking he was going to India.

8. Animals that are more active at night than during the day are _____.

9. At first, Powerpoint presentations were a _____, but now few people dare to lecture without one.

10. The anchors will _____ the Powerball lottery winner on the evening news.

11. In Robert Louis Stevenson's famous novel about a man with a split personality, the amiable and moral Dr. Jekyll _____ into his brutish and misanthropic alter-ego, Mr. Hyde.

12. The Minutemen _____ on the town green in Lexington to confront the Redcoats.

13. Although he invested steadily in his retirement plan, a sudden decline in the stock market threatened to _____ most of his gains.

14. During the Crusades, it was not unusual for one force to _____ another on the battlefield.

15. A special device linked to the thermostat will _____ the temperature and humidity inside the library, and sound an alarm if they sink too low.

16. _____ as well as land battles were fought in the Revolutionary War, as England was a major maritime power.

17. A _____ sales tax increase of ¼ percent allowed Arkansas to better fund its fish and wildlife agency.

18. The mother's _____ comments hurt her sensitive son's feelings.

19. The _____ of the times allowed the English to capture Native Americans to act as guides in New England.

20. At the ski resort, my friends and I will stick to the _____ trails until we get more practice.

Exercise D

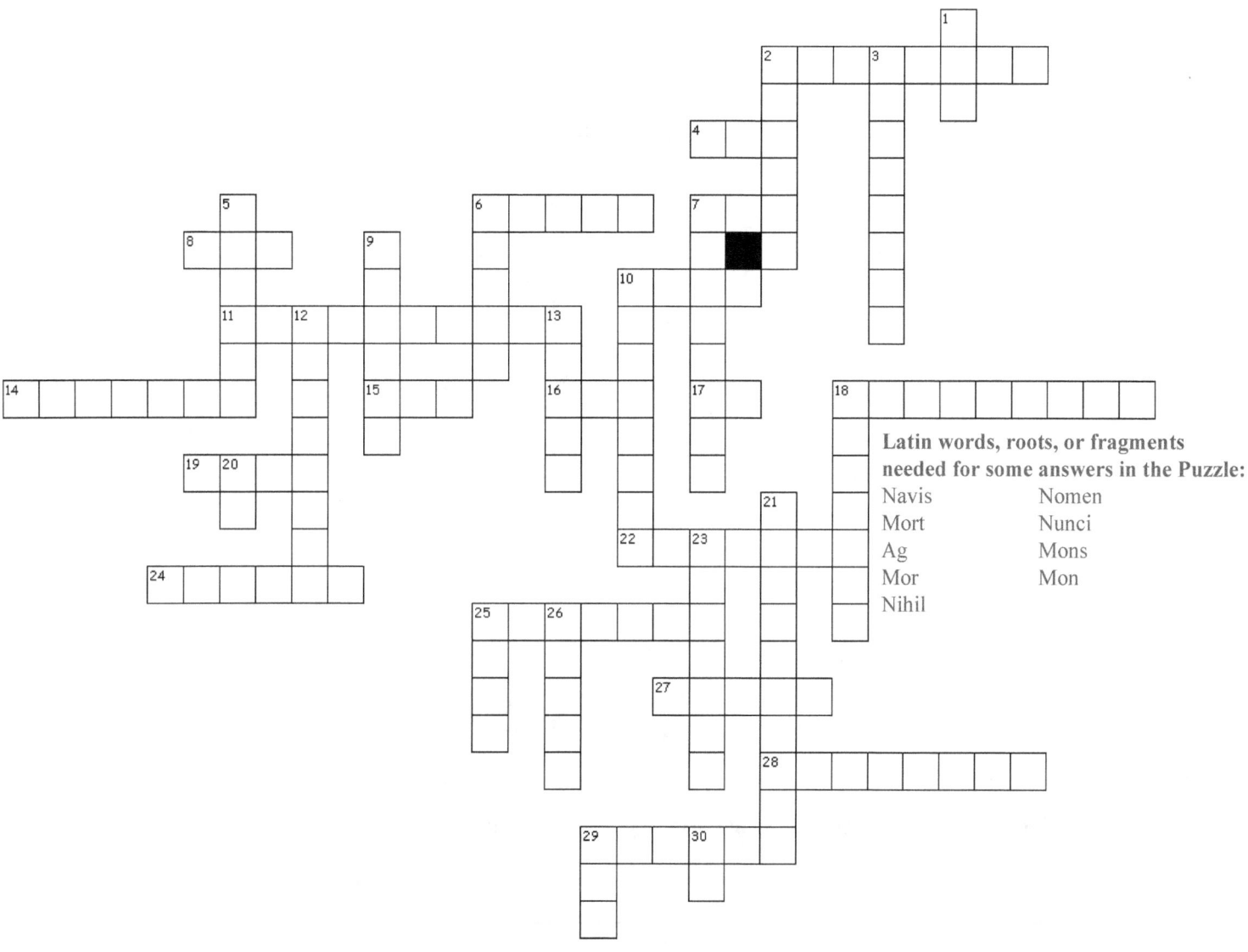

Latin words, roots, or fragments needed for some answers in the Puzzle:
Navis
Mort
Ag
Mor
Nihil
Nomen
Nunci
Mons
Mon

Across
2. to travel on a desired course
4. to deny (l)
6. to announce (l)
7. to change (l)
8. to do, to work (l)
10. to die (l)
11. a new method, idea, or product
14. to travel a certain distance regularly
15. together (l)
16. to warn, to advise (l)
17. in, not (l)
18. active at night
19. night (l)
22. symbolic or minimal; existing in name only
24. to gather together
25. to observe over time
27. nothing (l)
28. to make known publicly
29. to undergo a change or alteration

Down
1. born (l)
2. to invalidate
3. living forever
5. original to a particular person or place
6. ship (l)
7. a set of principles of conduct
9. an inexperienced person
10. a conical, natural elevation of the earth's surface
12. a contradiction, denial, or refusal
13. name (l)
18. something new and/or unusual
20. to make new (l)
21. to destroy completely
23. to humiliate
25. mountain (l)
26. relating to ships
29. custom (l)
30. to drive, to urge (l)

Lesson XVII

Oculist

Fr. Oculiste
It. Oculista
Port. Oculista
Sp. Oculista

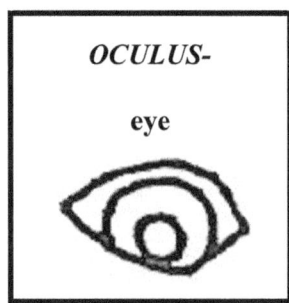
OCULUS- eye

Definition: **n.** a person who treats diseases or defects of the eye

Sentence: Ben Franklin proved himself an amateur oculist with his invention of bifocals.

Odious

Fr. Odieux
It. Odioso
Port. Odioso
Sp. Odioso

ODI- to hate

Definition: **adj.** extremely unpleasant; repulsive; hateful

Sentence: Cleaning a septic tank is an odious task, even to professionals.

Olfactory

Fr. Olfactif
It. Olfattivo
Port. Olfativo
Sp. Olfativo

OLE- smell

Definition: **adj.** relating to the sense of smell

Sentence: Most of the sense of taste in fact derives from the olfactory organ: the nose.

Operate

Fr. Opérer, Diriger
It. Operare. Dirigere
Port. Operar
Sp. Operar

OPER-
work

Definition: **v.** to function or control the function of; to manage or run

Sentence: Mob bosses stereotypically operate out of pizza parlors and bars.

Orator

Fr. Orateur
It. Oratore
Port. Orador
Sp. Orador

ORA-
to speak, to pray

Definition: **n.** a public speaker, especially one who is proficient

Sentence: With his masterful speech, orator Daniel Webster overwhelmed the Devil.

Orbit

Fr. n. Orbite, v. Orbiter
It. n. Orbita, v. Orbitare
Port. Órbita
Sp. Órbita

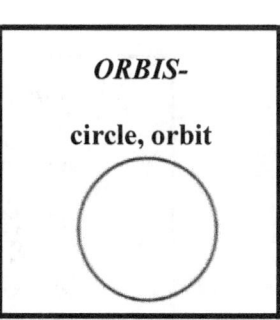
ORBIS-
circle, orbit

Definition: **n.** the regular elliptical course of a smaller celestial object around a larger one; the network of people who come into contact with a person or family; proximity
v. to revolve around (literally or figuratively)

Sentence: Wealthy families rarely admit the financially inferior into their social orbit.
Earth orbits the Sun once every year.

Ordain

Fr. Ordonner
It. Ordinare
Port. Ordenar
Sp. Ordenar

ORDO-
rank
1 2 3
4 5 6

Definition: **v.** to confer holy orders upon; to order or appoint officially

Sentence: After years of study in a seminary, a theologian may be ordained as a minister.

Ornament

Fr. Ornement
It. Ornamento
Port. Ornamento
Sp. Ornamento

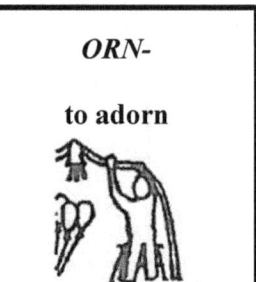

Definition: **n.** an object used or serving to decorate something

Sentence: A car's hood ornament serves no purpose beyond decoration and branding.

Ornate

Fr. Orné
It. Ornato
Port. Ornamentado
Sp. Ornamentado

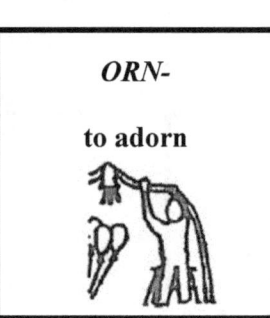

Definition: **adj.** extremely decorated; elaborately covered; extensively designed

Sentence: Notre Dame has many ornate statues and carvings on its exterior.

Ostentatious

Fr. Ostentatoire, Prétentieux
It. Ostentatore, Appariscente
Port. Ostentoso
Sp. Ostentoso

OSTEND- to exhibit

Definition:	**adj.** characterized by pretentious or showy display; designed to impress
Sentence:	Those from monied families often complain that the nouveaux riches are too ostentatious, announcing their wealth with gaudy jewelry and flashy cars.

Repast

Fr. Repas
It. Pasto
Port. Repasto
Sp. Comida

RE- back, again

PASC- to feed

Definition:	**n.** a meal
Sentence:	A roasted, stuffed turkey is the standard centerpiece of the Thanksgiving repast.

Passionate

Fr. Passionné
It. Appassionato
Port. Apaixonado
Sp. Apasionado

PASS- to suffer

Definition:	**adj.** having or showing strong feelings; unstinting devotion
Sentence:	Anthony and Cleopatra pursued a passionate love affair before their mutual suicide.

Patriotism	**Fr.** Patriotisme **It.** Patriottismo **Port.** Patriotismo **Sp.** Patriotismo	

Definition:	**n.** love of one's country and a willingness to defend it
Sentence:	Americans display their patriotism with parades, and fireworks on July Fourth.

Patron	**Fr.** Patron, Mécène **It.** Patrono, Mecenate **Port.** Patrono **Sp.** Patrono	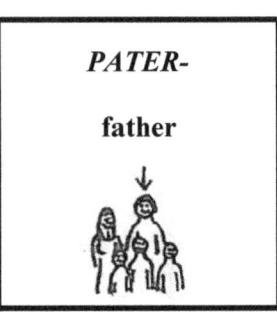

Definition:	**n.** a person who gives financial and other support
Sentence:	Theater patrons are asked to switch off their cell phones during performances.

Pacify	**Fr.** Pacifier **It.** Pacificare **Port.** Pacificar **Sp.** Pacificar	

Definition:	**v.** to quiet; to bring peace to
Sentence:	Unable to pacify the savage Picts, Hadrian built a wall along the Scottish border.

Impeccable	Fr. Impeccable It. Impeccabile Port. Impecável Sp. Impecable	 *IL-, IM-, IN-* in, not	 *PEC-* to sin

Definition: **adj.** flawless; perfect; in accordance with the highest standards

Sentence: The credentials of the Supreme Court candidate were impeccable.

Pecuniary	Fr. Pécuniaire It. Pecuniario Port. Pecuniário Sp. Pecuniario	 *PECUNIA-* money

Definition: **adj.** pertaining to money

Sentence: A pecuniary reward was offered for information leading to the suspect's arrest.

Propeller	Fr. Hélice It. Elica Port. Hélice Sp. Hélice	 *PRO-* forward	 *PELL-* to drive

Definition: **n.** a rotating, fan-like device for driving an aircraft or boat

Sentence: A jet's turbine engines outperform an airplane's propellers.

Pendant

Fr. Pendentif
It. Pendente
Port. Pingente
Sp. Colgante

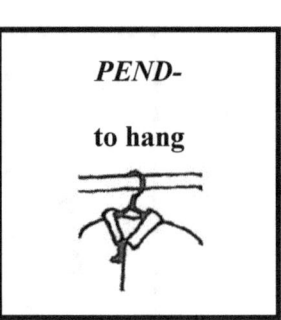

Definition: **n.** an ornament suspended from something else, usually a necklace

Sentence: After she developed arthritis in her hands, she wore her wedding ring as a pendant on a gold chain.

Pedestrian

Fr. Piéton
It. Pedone
Port. Pedestre
Sp. Peatón

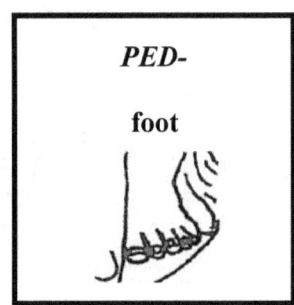

Definition: **n.** a person traveling by foot; common, ordinary

Sentence: Even though pedestrians have the right of way at intersections, many drivers believe that might makes right.

Pedal

Fr. Pédale
It. Pedale
Port. Pedal
Sp. Pedal

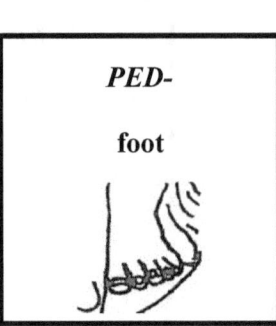

Definition: **n.** a foot-operated lever

Sentence: A foot pedal operated the spinning wheel and spinning Jenny.

Exercise A

 *PEC-* _____

 *PECUNIA-* _____

 *PELL-* _____

 *PEND-* _____

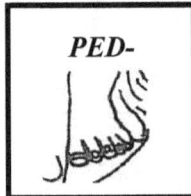 *PED-* _____

 *IM-* _____

Exercise B

Match the word with the letter of its definition:

1. ____ impeccable
2. ____ oculist
3. ____ odious
4. ____ olfactory
5. ____ operate
6. ____ orator
7. ____ orbit
8. ____ ordain
9. ____ ornate
10. ____ ostentatious
11. ____ pacify
12. ____ passionate
13. ____ patriotism
14. ____ patron
15. ____ pecuniary
16. ____ pedal
17. ____ pedestrian
18. ____ pendant
19. ____ propeller
20. ____ repast

a) characterized by pretentious display
b) to manage or function
c) the rotation of a smaller heavenly body around a larger one
d) strong support for one's country
e) hateful; extremely unpleasant
f) to make quiet; to bring peace
g) relating to money
h) a foot-operated lever or control
i) a person who gives financial support
j) faultless
k) to appoint officially
l) highly decorated
m) a person travelling by foot
n) one who treats eye diseases
o) having or showing powerful emotions
p) a suspended ornament
q) a meal
r) a proficient public speaker
s) relating to the sense of smell
t) a fan-like device that drives an aircraft or boat

Exercise C

1. Lorenzo de Medici, a _____ of the arts during the Renaissance, supported Michelangelo and Leonardo da Vinci.

2. Although forklifts look easy to _____, they are frequently involved in workplace accidents because they tip over easily.

3. She gave a bottle to the crying baby to _____ him, and he quickly went to sleep.

4. Gaudy costume jewelry is too _____ for my taste; I prefer simple, delicate earrings and necklaces.

5. The midday _____ was enormous, so afterwards he took a nap.

6. If you are fortunate enough to find a vocation you are _____ about, you will never regret your everyday employment.

7. The bishop prepared to _____ her as a minister, despite the controversy within the church over women clergy.

8. The candidate for student council president had an _____ reputation and was easily elected.

9. Once he enters a crosswalk, a _____ has the right of way.

10. The _____ sense is closely related to the sense of taste; if something smells good, it probably tastes good as well.

11. When bicycling uphill, you need to _____ faster in a lower gear.

12. A patient with pink eye should be checked out by an _____.

13. Students might calculate the _____ of a planet in an astronomy class.

14. The bully's _____ behavior offended the entire school.

15. After the terrorist attacks of Sept. 11, 2001 stalled the economy, President George W. Bush declared that shopping was an act of _____.

16. The valedictorian is typically the student _____ at high school graduation.

17. She was looking for a suitable _____ to put on her antique gold chain.

18. Rococo architecture is characterized by its use of elaborate decorative elements, such as _____ statues and florid, gold-painted moldings.

19. Every year, hundreds of manatees, whales, dolphins, and other marine mammals are fatally injured by boat _____.

20. The hospital had to pay _____ damages and change its policies after the successful malpractice lawsuit.

Exercise D

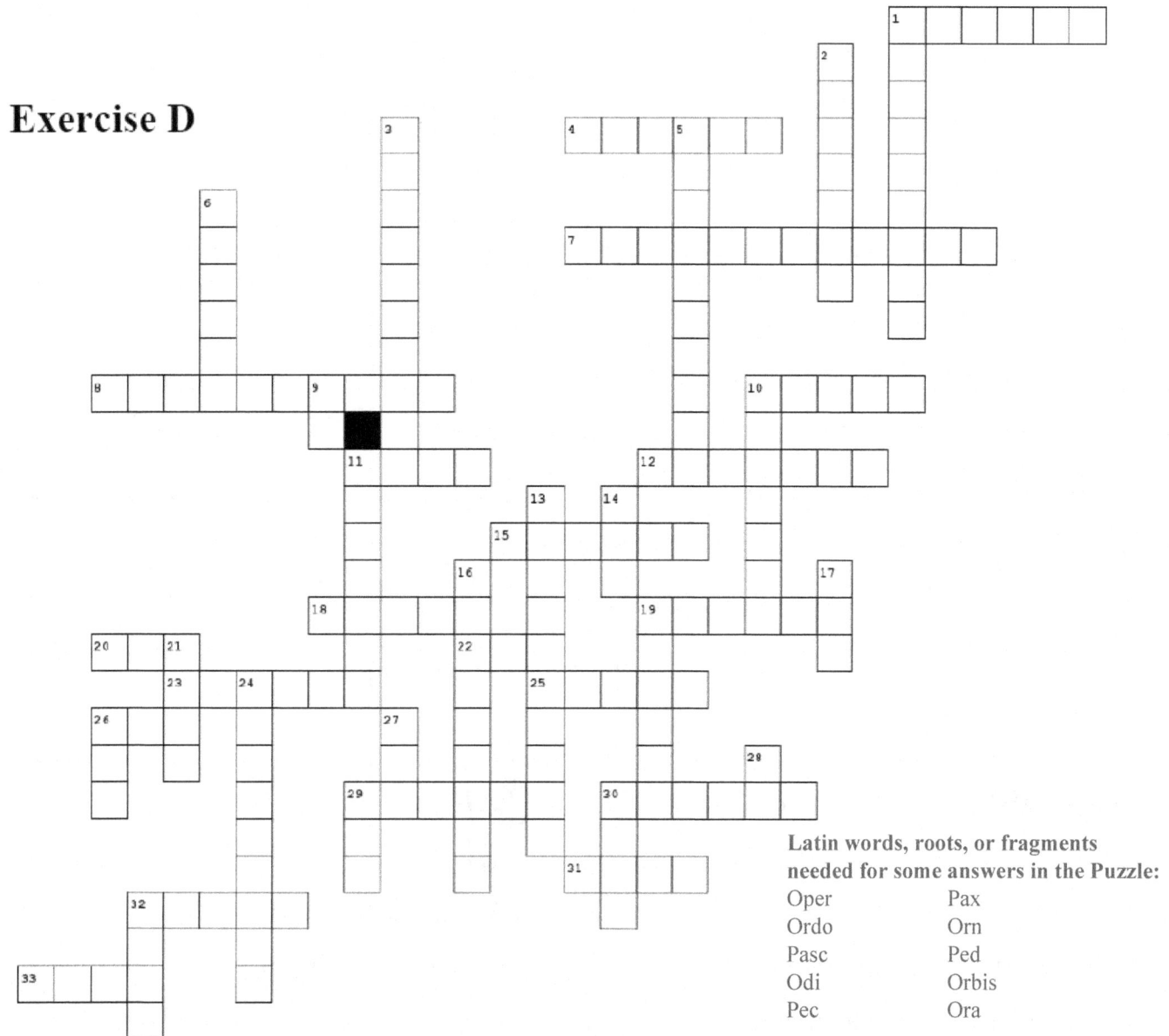

Latin words, roots, or fragments needed for some answers in the Puzzle:
Oper   Pax
Ordo   Orn
Pasc   Ped
Odi   Orbis
Pec   Ora

Across
1. to appoint officially
4. to make quiet; to bring peace
7. characterized by pretentious display
8. a person traveling by foot
10. the rotation of a smaller heavenly body around a larger one
11. to hang (l)
12. money (l)
15. a person who gives financial support
18. father (l)
19. a proficient public speaker
20. forward (l)
22. to hate (l)
23. a meal
25. circle (l)
26. foot (l)
29. eye (l)
30. to exhibit (l)
31. to drive (l)
32. a foot-operated lever or control
33. to suffer (l)

Down
1. relating to the sense of smell
2. to manage or function
3. having or showing powerful emotions
5. faultless
6. highly decorated
9. back, again (l)
10. one who treats eye diseases
11. a suspended ornament
13. strong support for one's country
14. to speak, to pray (l)
16. a fan-like device that drives an aircraft or boat
17. to adorn (l)
19. hateful; extremely unpleasant
21. rank (l)
24. relating to money
26. peace (l)
27. to sin (l)
28. in, not (l)
29. smell (l)
30. to work (l)
32. to feed (l)

205

Lesson XVIII

Appetite

Fr. Appétit
It. Appetito
Port. Apetite
Sp. Apetito

AC-, AD-
to, toward

PET-
to seek

Definition: **n.** an instinctive physical desire, especially for food or drink

Sentence: The bone-weary soldiers had no appetite for battle that day.

Petition

Fr. Pétition
It. Petizione
Port. Petição
Sp. Petición

PET-
To seek

Definition: **n.** a formal request to a superior authority for a right or benefit

Sentence: The Magna Carta ensued from the nobles' petition for rights from King John.

Depict

Fr. Dépeindre
It. Dipingere
Port. Representar
Sp. Representar

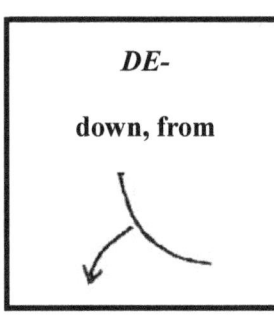

DE-
down, from

PICTUS-
painted

Definition: **v.** to represent in a picture or sculpture

Sentence: The face of George Washington is depicted on both the quarter and dollar bill.

Piety

Fr. Piété
It. Pietà
Port. Piedade
Sp. Piedad

PIUS- religiously devoted

Definition: **n.** reverence or devotion to God

Sentence: A pilgrimage to Mecca is a prescribed act of piety for all Muslims.

Pittance

Fr. Misère
It. Miseria
Port. Miséria
Sp. Miseria

PIUS- religiously devoted

Definition: **n.** a small amount of money; the ration in a religious order

Sentence: The cost of a meal at McDonald's is a pittance compared to the tab at the Four Seasons.

Placid

Fr. Placide
It. Placido
Port. Plácido
Sp. Plácido

PLAC- to appease

Definition: **adj.** (of water) having an undisturbed appearance; not easily upset or excited; calm

Sentence: The Buddha's placid expression is the outward face of inner peace.

		IL-, IM-, IN-	PON-
Imposter	Fr. Imposteur It. Impostore Port. Impostor Sp. Impostor	in, not	to put

Definition: **n.** a person who deceives by taking a false identity

Sentence: A wolf in sheep's clothing is a familiar metaphor for an imposter.

		POST-	PON-
Postpone	Fr. Reporter, Postposer (Belgian) It. Posticipare Port. Posponde Sp. Posponer	after	to put

Definition: **v.** to put off until later

Sentence: He decided to postpone the wedding until he finished his tour in Iraq.

		PRO-	PON-
Proponent	Fr. Advocat It. Proponente, Sostenitore Port. Proponente Sp. Proponente	forward	to put

Definition: **n.** an advocate; an open supporter

Sentence: An atomic power proponent, Admiral Rickover lobbied for the nuclear submarine.

Ponderous

Fr. Pesant
It. Ponderoso, Pesante
Port. Ponderoso
Sp. Ponderoso

PONDUS-
weight

Definition:	**adj.** having great weight; labored and dull
Sentence:	The windy and dull keynote speaker gave a ponderous speech.

Pontiff

Fr. Pontife
It. Pontefice
Port. Pontífice
Sp. Pontífice

PONS-
bridge

FAC-
to do, to make

Definition:	**n.** the Pope or a bishop
Sentence:	Pope John Paul II was the first Polish pontiff.

Portable

Fr. Portable
It. Portatile
Port. Portátil
Sp. Portátil

PORT-
to carry

Definition:	**adj.** easily carried or moved
Sentence:	A picnic involves a portable feast.

Opportune

Fr. Opportun
It. Opportuno
Port. Oportuno
Sp. Oportuno

OB-
over, towards, against

PORTUS-
harbor

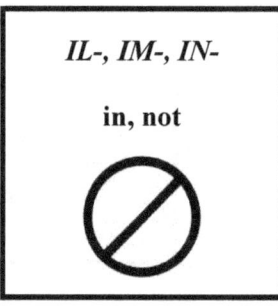

Definition: **adj.** suited or right for a particular purpose; especially convenient or appropriate

Sentence: Mistletoe provides an opportune excuse to kiss someone.

Impotent

Fr. Impuissant
It. Impotente
Port. Impotente
Sp. Impotente

IL-, IM-, IN-
in, not

POTEN-
powerful

Definition: **adj.** weak; helpless; powerless

Sentence: Samson was rendered impotent when Delilah cut off his hair.

Potential

Fr. Potentiel
It. Potenziale
Port. Potencial
Sp. Potencial

POTEN-
powerful

Definition: **adj.** having the capacity to develop into something in the future

Sentence: The threat of a scandal had the potential to derail his candidacy.

Potable	Fr. Potable It. Potabile Port. Portável Sp. Portable	*POT-* to drink 

Definition: **adj.** drinkable

Sentence: Desalinization makes seawater potable.

Potion	Fr. Potion It. Pozione Port. Poção Sp. Poción	*POT-* to drink 

Definition: **n.** a liquid with healing, magical, or poisonous powers

Sentence: Absinthe liqueur contains wood alcohol, making the drink a poisonous potion.

Predatory	Fr. Prédateur It. Predatore Port. Predador Sp. Predador	*PRAEDA-* spoils of war 

Definition: **adj.** characterized by plundering; preying naturally on others

Sentence: Loan sharks charge such predatory interest rates that their dealings are illegal.

Apprehend

Fr. Appréhender
It. Apprendere
Port. Apreender
Sp. Aprender

AC-, AD-
to, towards

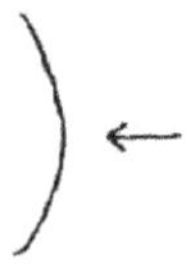

PREHEND-
to catch

Definition: **v.** to take into custody; to arrest for a crime; to perceive or understand

Sentence: Robert E. Lee apprehended John Brown in the Harper's Ferry armory.

Reprisal

Fr. Représailles
It. Rappresaglia
Port. Replesália
Sp. Represalia

RE-
back, again

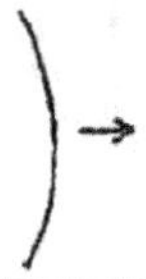

PREHEND-
to catch

Definition: **n.** an act of retaliation

Sentence: A trade embargo was the U.S. reprisal for Castro's ties to the Soviet Union.

Exercise A

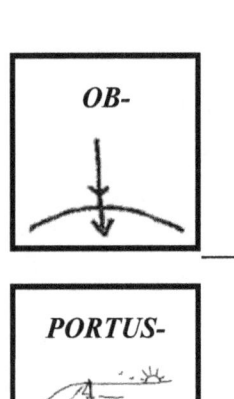 OB- _____

 PORTUS- _____

 POTEN- _____

 POT- _____

 PRAEDA- _____

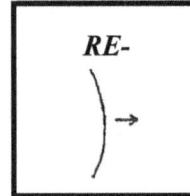 PREHEND- _____

RE- _____

Exercise B
Match the word with the letter of its definition:

1. ____ appetite
2. ____ apprehend
3. ____ depict
4. ____ imposter
5. ____ impotent
6. ____ opportune
7. ____ petition
8. ____ piety
9. ____ pittance
10. ____ placid
11. ____ ponderous
12. ____ pontiff
13. ____ portable
14. ____ postpone
15. ____ potable
16. ____ potential
17. ____ potion
18. ____ predatory
19. ____ proponent
20. ____ reprisal

a) weighty; heavy
b) a formal request
c) the Pope
d) to show through an art form
e) a very small amount of money
f) an advocate
g) a liquid mixture with magical, healing, or poisonous properties
h) someone using a false identity
i) to arrest for a crime; to perceive
j) reverence; devotion to God
k) an instinctive physical desire, especially hunger
l) an act of retaliation
m) preying on others
n) helpless; powerless
o) easily carried or moved
p) capacity to develop for the future
q) especially convenient or appropriate
r) calm; peaceful
s) drinkable
t) to put off until later

Exercise C

1. To indicate that the water is restricted to hand-washing only and should not be drunk, a sign over a restroom sink will state "not _____."

2. The _____ pirate lives off the theft of other peoples' goods.

3. "An eye for an eye, a tooth for a tooth" is a Biblical proverb used to justify _____ for wrongs or injuries inflicted on a person or society.

4. The "Pen Hens" decided they would _____ their meeting, as three members could not attend on the scheduled date.

5. The Pacific Ocean was so named because it is relatively _____ compared to the Atlantic.

6. When the wealthy man refused to give the beggar a dollar, a passerby commented that the sum was a mere _____.

7. Da Vinci painted the Mona Lisa to _____ Lisa Gherardini, who was known for her enigmatic smile.

8. When his employer praised the project he had just completed, it seemed to be an _____ moment to ask for a raise.

9. The sheriff was a strong _____ of making handguns illegal.

10. The desperate man went to a witch doctor seeking a love _____, in hopes it would make Anna Maria desire him.

11. His rage was _____: He had no way to avenge himself on the prosecutor, judge, and jury who had convicted him and sentenced him to life in prison.

12. Some of the appliances are _____; the movers can easily disconnect and transport them to your new home.

13. The authorities went to the Japanese airport to _____ Bobby Fisher on charges of violating sanctions against Yugoslavia in 1993.

14. We hope that a less conservative _____ in Rome will be more attuned to our contemporary spiritual needs.

15. When the real estate broker showed the house to _____ buyers, she highlighted its best features.

16. They gathered signatures for a _____ to stop clear-cutting in the national forest.

17. His _____ build and slow gait belied his light wit and lively speech.

18. When Barbara went to the casino to redeem her $5,000 prize, she was greatly surprised to discover that an _____ had already been there and claimed her winning.

19. _____ is required of those who would join a Christian monastic order.

20. Jack's _____ was satisfied when he ate a Quarter Pounder with Biggie Fries.

Exercise D

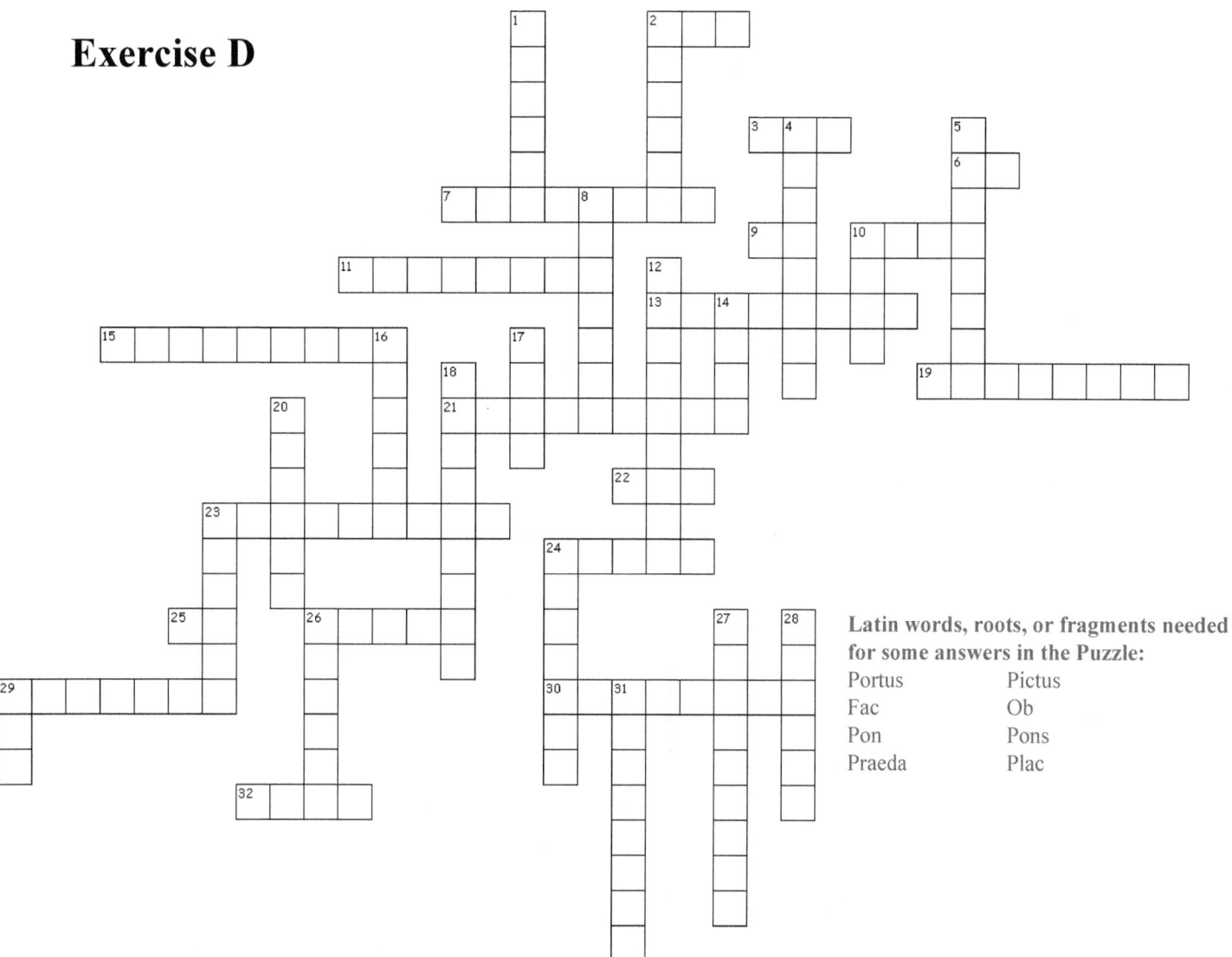

Across
2. to put (l)
3. to do, to make (l)
6. over, towards, very (l)
7. to put off until later
9. down, from (l)
10. to carry (l)
11. helpless; powerless
13. an act of retaliation
15. to arrest for a crime; to perceive
19. a formal request
21. weighty; heavy
22. to seek (l)
23. preying on others
24. reverence; devotion to God
25. to, toward
26. powerful (l)
29. to catch (l)
30. someone using a false identity
32. after (l)

Down
1. painted (l)
2. a liquid mixture with magical, healing, or poisonous properties
4. an instinctive physical desire, especially hunger
5. easily carried or moved
8. drinkable
10. to appease (l)
12. an advocate
14. religiously devoted (l)
16. to show through an art form
17. bridge (l)
18. especially convenient or appropriate
20. spoils of war (l)
23. calm; peaceful
24. the Pope
26. weight (l)
27. capacity to develop for the future
28. harbor (l)
29. to drink (l)
31. a very small amount of money

Latin words, roots, or fragments needed for some answers in the Puzzle:
Portus   Pictus
Fac   Ob
Pon   Pons
Praeda   Plac

Lesson XIX

Oppress

Fr. Opprimer
It. Opprimere
Port. Oprimir
Sp. Oprimir

PRESS-
to press

Definition:	**v.** to keep down by unjust authority
Sentence:	Slaves were oppressed by demanding masters and backbreaking work.

Pungent

Fr. Âcre
It. Pungente
Port. Pungente
Sp. Pungente

PUNG-
to puncture

Definition:	**adj.** biting or caustic to the taste or smell
Sentence:	'A Modest Proposal' was Swift's pungent satire of English attitudes toward Ireland.

Punish

Fr. Punir
It. Punire
Port. Punir
Sp. Punir

PUNI-
to punish

Definition:	**v.** to inflict a penalty on as retribution for an offense
Sentence:	Psychologists claim that to punish by spanking is to invite more aggressive behavior.

Amputate	Fr. Amputer It. Amputare Port. Amputar Sp. Amputar	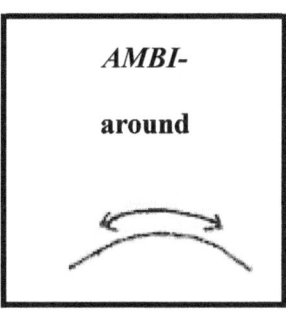	

Definition: **v.** to cut off a part of the body, usually a limb or digit

Sentence: The onset of gangrene in his leg required amputation below the knee.

Compute	Fr. Calculer It. Calcolare Port. Computar Sp. Computar		

Definition: **v.** to determine by mathematics; to determine by arithmetic or mathematical reasoning

Sentence: One computes on an abacus by pushing beads along wires stretched in a rigid frame.

Rapture	Fr. Ravissement, Extase It. Rapimento, Estasi Port. Rapto Sp. Rapto	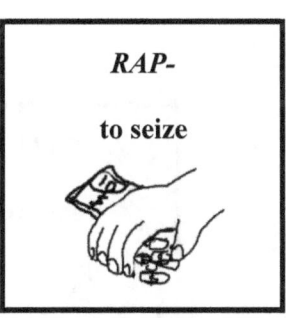	

Definition: **n.** a feeling of intense pleasure or joy; the state of being carried away

Sentence: At first news of the award, a Nobel prize winner must feel utter rapture.

Ratio

Fr. Ratio, Rapport
It. Rapporto
Port. Razão
Sp. Ratio

Definition: **n.** the quantitative relation between two amounts, showing the number of times one value contains or is contained within the other

Sentence: The Golden Ratio of 1.618, symbolized as Φ, underlies the graceful proportions of Greek architecture.

Rational

Fr. Rationnel
It. Ragionevole
Port. Racional
Sp. Racional

Definition: **adj.** based on or in accordance with reason or logic

Sentence: To an economist, 'rational action' may be either sensible or efficient, or both.

Rationale

Fr. Raisons
It. Ragione
Port. Raciocínio
Sp. Razón

Definition: **n.** a set of reasons or a logical basis for a course of action or a belief

Sentence: The rationale for the Panama Canal was economy of time and money in shipping.

Rectify

Fr. Rectifier
It. Rettificare
Port. Retificar
Sp. Rectificar

REX-, REGIS-

to rule

FAC-

to do, to make

Definition: **v.** to put right; to correct

Sentence: The situation was a lost cause and therefore impossible to rectify.

Rector

Fr. Recteur, Pasteur
It. Pastore
Port. Reitor
Sp. Rectir

REX-, REGIS-

to rule

Definition: **n.** a priest or member of the clergy in charge of a church

Sentence: A rector, or leader of a church or parish, lives in a rectory.

Regular

Fr. Régulier
It. Regolare
Port. Regular
Sp. Regular

REX-, REGIS-

to rule

Definition: **adj.** arranged in a consistent or definite pattern; recurring at short intervals; conforming to or governed by an accepted standard of procedure or convention

Sentence: The Redcoats were regular soldiers, while the Colonials were an irregular militia.

Ridicule

Fr. Ridicule
It. Ridicolo
Port. Ridículo
Sp. Ridículo

RID-
to laugh at

Definition: **n.** mockery or derision
v. subject to mockery

Sentence: Puritans with their feet locked in wooden stocks called pillories were objects of public ridicule.
When Jenny walked in the classroom with a polka dotted vest and trousers, she was immediately ridiculed by her friends.

Deride

Fr. Tourner en dérision
It. Deridere
Port. Ridicularizar
Sp. Ridiculizar

DE-
down, from

RID-
to laugh at

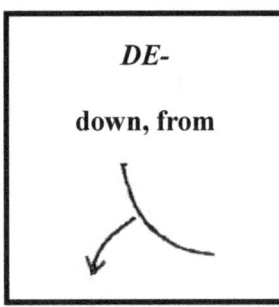

Definition: **v.** to express contempt for; to ridicule; to speak scornfully or scoff at (someone)

Sentence: Elizabethan audiences derided unpopular actors with boos and nasty epithets.

Arrogant

Fr. Arrogant
It. Arrogante
Port. Arrogante
Sp. Arrogante

AC-, AD-
to, toward

ROG-
to ask

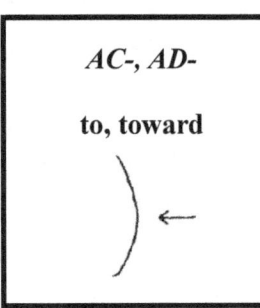

Definition: **adj.** having an exaggerated sense of one's own importance or abilities

Sentence: The US is viewed by many as an arrogant, vain, and boastful nation.

		DE-	**ROG-**
Derogatory	Fr. Dénigrant It. Dispregiativo Port. Depreciativo Sp. Despreciativo	down, from	to ask

Definition: **adj.** showing a critical or disrespectful attitude toward; disparaging

Sentence: Many gourmets make derogatory remarks about the quality of fast food, but some secretly indulge.

		INTER-	**ROG-**
Interrogate	Fr. Interroger It. Interrogare Port. Interrogar Sp. Interrogar	between	to ask

Definition: **v.** to ask questions aggressively

Sentence: The Inquisition was notorious for interrogating prisoners on pain of torture.

		INTER-	**ROG-**
Interrogative	Fr. Interrogateur It. Interrogativo Port. Interrogativo Sp. Interrogativo	between	to ask

Definition: **adj.** having the force of a question; questioning

Sentence: The interrogative arch of his eyebrows showed his disbelief.

Rotate	**Fr.** Tourner **It.** Ruotare **Port.** Rotar **Sp.** Rotar	*ROT-* **to turn**

Definition: **v.** to move in a circle around an axis; to move regularly in and out of (something)

Sentence: Before becoming hotel manager, she rotated through several menial jobs to understand the challenges faced by the employees she would supervise.

Interrupt	**Fr.** Interrompre **It.** Interrompere **Port.** Interromper **Sp.** Interrumpir	*INTER-* **between**	*RUPT-* **to break**

Definition: **v.** to stop the continuous progress of; to break the continuity of

Sentence: Morse code was sent by interrupted pulses of electricity through telegraph wires.

Rupture	**Fr.** v. Rompre, n. Rupture **It.** v. Rompere, n. Rottura **Port.** Ruptura **Sp.** Ruptura	*RUPT-* **broken** 

Definition: **v.** to break or burst suddenly; to breach or disturb
n. an instance of bursting

Sentence: Spherical bombs bouncing off the water's surface hit and ruptured the Ruhr dams.
A rupture of the Achilles tendon can keep an athlete out for an entire season.

Exercise A

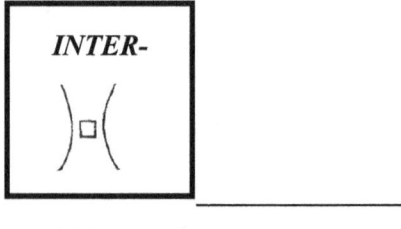 _____

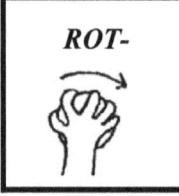 _____

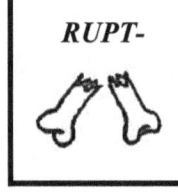 _____

 _____

Exercise B

Match the word with the letter of its definition:

1. ____ amputate
2. ____ arrogant
3. ____ compute
4. ____ derogatory
5. ____ interrogate
6. ____ interrogative
7. ____ interrupt
8. ____ oppress
9. ____ pungent
10. ____ punish
11. ____ rapture
12. ____ ratio
13. ____ rational
14. ____ rationale
15. ____ rectify
16. ____ rector
17. ____ regular
18. ____ ridicule
19. ____ rotate
20. ____ rupture
21. ____ deride

a) to put right
b) sensible; logical
c) to inflict a penalty for a wrong
d) the priest in charge of a church
e) to question aggressively
f) a quantitative relationship between two amounts
g) to cut off a limb or digit
h) questioning
i) to determine by mathematics
j) critical and disrespectful
k) to move in a circle around an axis
l) strong and unpleasant to the smell or taste
m) to disturb; to halt something
n) a logical basis for a belief or course of action
o) to keep down unjustly
p) having an exaggerated sense of one's importance
q) to mock
r) intense joy
s) arranged in a consistent pattern; occurring at consistent intervals
t) to speak of someone with scorn
u) to burst suddenly

Exercise C

1. On the mathematics test, I was not sure whether to express the answer as a percentage or a _____.

2. When he walked out of the prison and was embraced by his wife, he felt complete _____.

3. The demonstrators tried to _____ Wall Street by blocking traffic.

4. A _____ polygon is one whose sides are all of equal length.

5. After centuries of being _____, first as slaves and then through Jim Crow laws and lynchings, black Americans organized boycotts and demonstrations to win full legal equality.

6. Bill O'Reilly acts _____ and self-serving when interviewing guests on his show.

7. The dealer recommended that the new owner should _____ the tires every 5,000 miles.

8. When you bump into something, some capillaries will _____, resulting in a bruise.

9. The professor explained his _____ for requiring three papers in one week.

10. Whether by hand or machine, he was required to _____ the store's receipts and expenses daily.

11. Even though the surgeon was able to spare the patient's life, she was forced to _____ his arm.

12. In English grammar, an _____ sentence should not be confused with either an affirmative or negative one.

13. Little children have a tendency to tease and _____ those who are different.

14. He felt badly that he had gotten his co-worker in trouble, and tried to _____ the situation by taking the blame himself.

15. The hoarder's house was filled with the _____ odor of cat and dog feces.

16. If you could explain the problem in a logical, _____ way, I think I could help you solve it.

17. The police began to _____ the suspect by asking where he was when the crime occurred.

18. To _____ drunken drivers, judges can suspend their licenses or put them in jail for repeat offenses.

19. To feel better about themselves, sometimes people make _____ remarks about others.

20. The _____ greeted the members of the congregation as they exited the church.

21. He was respectful to his boss's face, but liked to _____ him behind his back, calling him an incompetent idiot.

Exercise D

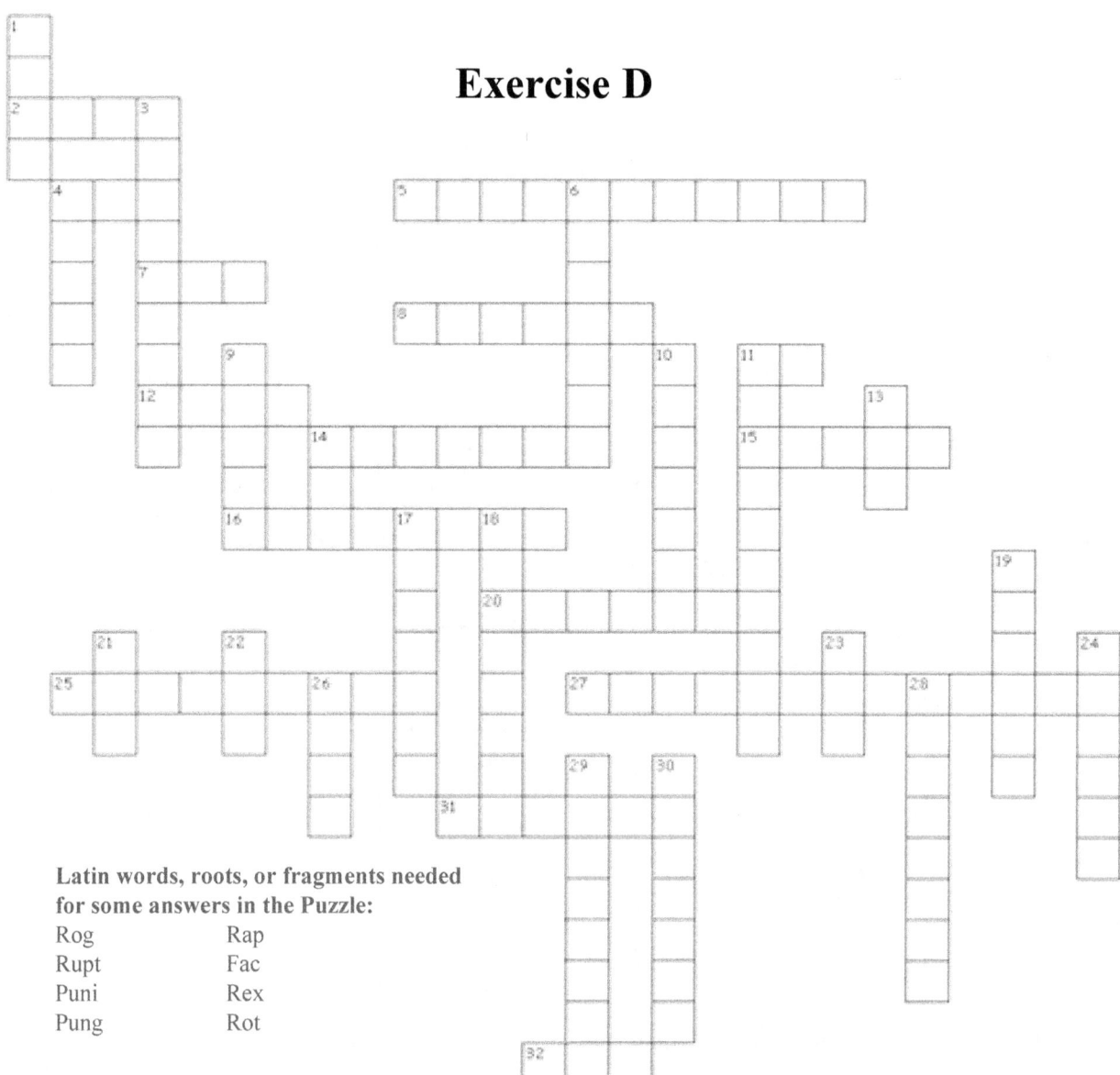

Latin words, roots, or fragments needed for some answers in the Puzzle:

Rog   Rap
Rupt Fac
Puni Rex
Pung Rot

Across
2. to punish (l)
4. to think (l)
5. to question aggressively
7. to seize (l)
8. to move in a circle around an axis
11. down, from (l)
12. to puncture (l)
14. to burst suddenly
15. a quantitative relationship between two amounts
16. sensible; logical
20. strong and unpleasant to the smell or taste
25. a logical basis for a belief or course of action
27. questioning
31. to speak of someone with scorn
32. to rule (l)

Down
1. to break (l)
3. to disturb; to halt something
4. to press (l)
6. intense joy
9. between (l)
10. to determine by mathematics
11. critical and disrespectful
13. to laugh at (l)
14. to turn (l)
17. to keep down unjustly
18. to cut off a limb or digit
19. to inflict a penalty for a wrong
21. to do, to make (l)
22. to ask (l)
23. together (l)
24. the priest in charge of a church
26. around (l)
28. having an exaggerated sense of one's importance
29. to mock
30. to put right

229

Lesson XX

Sacrament

Fr. Sacrement
It. Sacramento
Port. Sacramento
Sp. Sacramento

SACR- holy

MENTIS- mind

Definition: **n.** a religious ceremony or ritual regarded as imparting divine grace, such as baptism, communion, or marriage

Sentence: Seven sacraments or holy rites as instituted by Catholics are described in the New Testament.

Sacred

Fr. Sacré
It. Sacro
Port. Sagrado
Sp. Sagrado

SACR- holy

Definition: **adj.** connected with a deity and so deserving veneration; holy

Sentence: The Holy Grail is the legendary sacred cup used by Christ and his disciples at the Last Supper.

Assail

Fr. Assaillir
It. Assalire
Port. Assaltar
Sp. Asaltar

SALT- to jump

Definition: **v.** to make a concerted or violent attack on; to attack verbally

Sentence: Armor-piercing English longbow arrows assailed the French knights at Agincourt.

Assault	Fr. Assaut It. Assalto Port. Assalto Sp. Asalto	*SALT-* **to jump** 

Definition: **n.** a violent attack or threat of harm; an aggressive attempt to do something demanding
v. to make an attack on; to threaten

Sentence: The bank robber could not be charged with assault since the teller did not feel threatened.
The missiles assaulted the aircraft carrier.

Saline	Fr. Salin It. Salino Port. Salino Sp. Salino	*SALIS-* **salt** 

Definition: **adj.** containing or impregnated with salt

Sentence: Seawater and blood are both saline fluids.

Sanguine	Fr. Optimist, Sanguine It. Ottimista Port. Animado, Sanguíneo Sp. Optimista, Sanguíneo	*SANGUIS-* **blood** 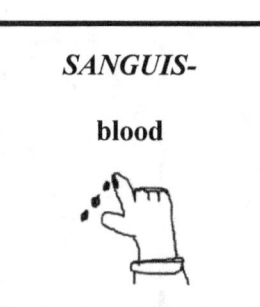

Definition: **adj.** cheerfully optimistic or hopeful; blood-red; bloody

Sentence: An optimist by nature, the recent graduate was sanguine about his job prospects, despite the recession.

Satiate	Fr. Rassasier It. Saziare Port. Saciar Sp. Saciar	 *SATIS-* enough

Definition: **v.** to satisfy fully

Sentence: The tea and hors d'oeuvres served at the garden party failed to satiate his hunger.

Prescribe	Fr. Prescrire It. Prescrivere Port. Prescrever Sp. Prescribir	 *PRE-, PRAE-* before	SCRIB- to write

Definition: **v.** to advise and to authorize the use of, especially in writing; to state authoritatively that something should be done in a particular way

Sentence: The conductor prescribed which pieces the orchestra would perform that night.

Manuscript	Fr. Manuscrit It. Manoscritto Port. Manuscrito Sp. Manuscrito	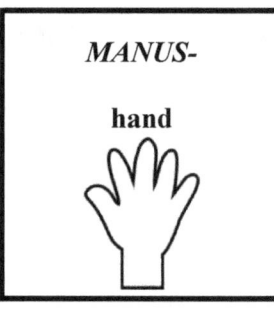 *MANUS-* hand	 SCRIB- to write

Definition: **n.** a handwritten document or piece of music; the original of a document

Sentence: Once, novelists sent a penned manuscript to their publishers; now they e-mail Word documents.

Dissect

Fr. Disséquer
It. Dissezionare
Port. Dissecar
Sp. Disecar

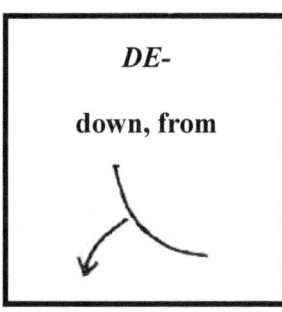

DE-
down, from

SECT-
to cut

Definition: **v.** to methodically cut up in order to study its internal parts; to analyze in minute detail

Sentence: *The Decline and Fall of the Roman Empire* dissects the causes of Rome's demise.

Segment

Fr. Segment
It. Segmento
Port. Segmento
Sp. Segmento

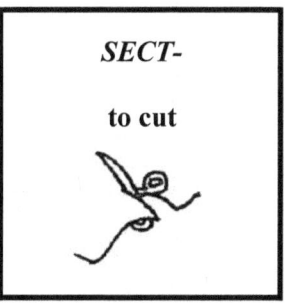

SECT-
to cut

Definition: **n.** each of the parts into which something is or may be divided
v. to divide into parts

Sentence: The presentation was divided into segments concerning the three major topics.
Sunday newspapers often carry inserts segmented to geographical areas.

Consecutive

Fr. Consécutif
It. Consecutivo
Port. Consecutivo
Sp. Consecutivo

CON-
together

SEQUI-
to follow

Definition: **adj.** following continuously or in order

Sentence: Happily, the stock market rose for several consecutive weeks.

Consequence

Fr. Conséquence
It. Conseguenza
Port. Consequência
Sp. Consecuencia

CON-
together

SEQUI-
to follow

Definition: **n.** a result or effect

Sentence: As a consequence of his hard work and loyalty, Dirk Nowitzki won the NBA finals Most Valuable Player award in 2011.

Sequel

Fr. Suite
It. Seguito, Sequel
Port. Sequela
Sp. Secuela

SEQUI-
to follow

Definition: **n.** a published broadcast or recorded work that continues the story or develops the theme of an earlier one; an event that follows another

Sentence: A thunderclap is a frequent sequel to a lightning bolt.

Sequence

Fr. Séquence
It. Sequenza
Port. Sequência
Sp. Secuencia

SEQUI-
to follow

Definition: **n.** a particular order in which related events, movements, etc. follow each other; a series of related events or movements in a particular order

Sentence: The sequence of episodes in Joyce's *Ulysses* mirrors Homer's *Odyssey*.

Session

Fr. Séssion
It. Sessione
Port. Sessão
Sp. Sesión

SID-, SED-, SESS-

to sit

Definition: **n.** a period devoted to a particular activity; a meeting of a deliberative or judicial body to conduct its business; the part of a year or a day during which teaching takes place in a school

Sentence: Cabinet meetings are conducted in sessions closed to the media.

Senile

Fr. Sénile
It. Senile
Port. Senil
Sp. Senil

SENILIS-

old

Definition: **adj.** having the weakness or diseases of old age; mentally incapacitated by reason of agedness

Sentence: One sign that she was becoming senile was that she sometimes sent birthday cards to her grandchildren at Christmas, and vice versa.

Consensus

Fr. Consensus
It. Consenso
Port. Consenso
Sp. Consenso

CON-

together

SENT-, SENS-

to think, to feel

Definition: **n.** general agreement of a group, with no major dissent

Sentence: The subcommittee reached a positive consensus and forwarded the nomination.

Resent

Fr. Éprouver du ressentiment
It. Risentirsi (per)
Port. Ressentir
Sp. Resentirse

RE-
back, again

SENT-, SENS-
to think, to feel

Definition:	**v.** to feel bitterness or indignation at
Sentence:	Those who resented Alexander's power may have tried to poison him.

Sensory

Fr. Sensoriel
It. Sensoriale
Port. Sensorial
Sp. Sensorial

SENT-, SENS-
to think, to feel

Definition:	**adj.** relating to sensation or the senses
Sentence:	Bank vaults have sensory devices to detect heat, motion, pressure, and sound."

Exercise A

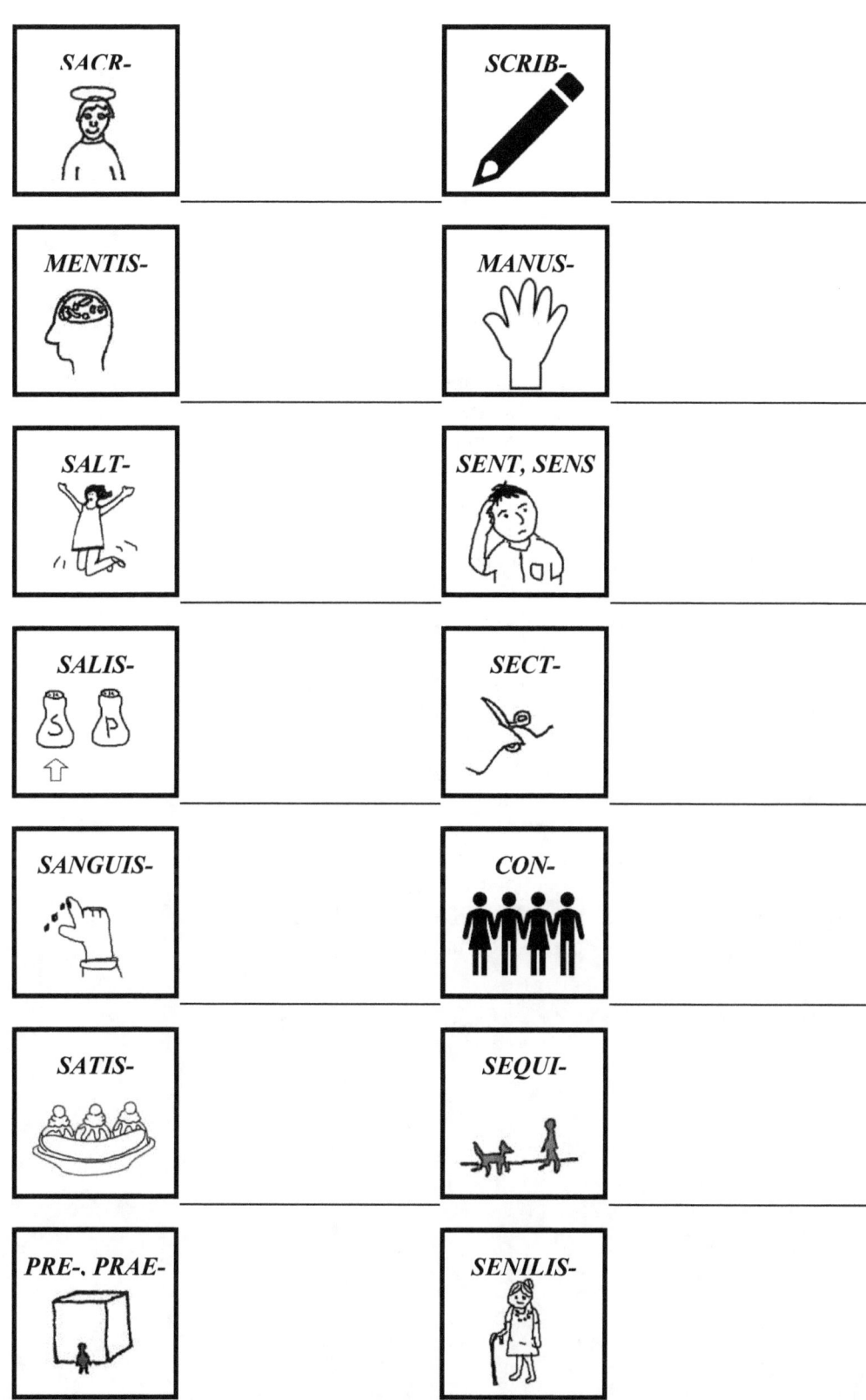

Exercise B
Match the word with the letter of its definition:

1. ____ assail
2. ____ assault
3. ____ consensus
4. ____ consecutive
5. ____ consequence
6. ____ dissect
7. ____ manuscript
8. ____ prescribe
9. ____ resent
10. ____ sacrament
11. ____ sacred
12. ____ saline
13. ____ sanguine
14. ____ satiate
15. ____ segment
16. ____ senile
17. ____ sensory
18. ____ sequel
19. ____ sequence
20. ____ session

a) cheerfully optimistic
b) a handwritten book, document, or piece of music
c) a follow-up in a series
d) to write a prescription; to advise
e) a physical attack or threat of harm
f) to divide into separate parts; a piece
g) salty in nature
h) to analyze in minute detail
i) a religious ceremony invoking divine grace
j) to attack
k) relating to sensation or the physical senses
l) a general agreement
m) religious; holy
n) to hold a grudge
o) a meeting
p) a particular order
q) successive; following immediately after
r) to satisfy to the full
s) mentally feeble due to old age
t) the result of an action

Exercise C

1. Typically, a high school biology class involves having to _____ a frog.

2. The detective arrested her abusive husband for _____ and battery.

3. When writing a descriptive essay on your environment, make full use of your _____ perception for better prose.

4. During emergencies, paramedics may maintain blood pressure by pumping _____ solution into the patient's blood supply line.

5. In India, the cow is a _____ animal and may not be killed or eaten.

6. Doctors _____ medications that they think will benefit their patients.

7. After much discussion, the tribe reached a _____ on how to punish him: banishment.

8. The President of the United States may serve only two _____ four-year terms in office.

9. An elderly man warned of an alien invasion in Utah, but his words of caution were dismissed as _____ ramblings.

10. The prosecutor laid out the _____ of events minute by minute.

11. Literary scholars love to study the original _____ of their favorite poems, books, and essays, complete with crossings out and marginal notes.

12. Christians may receive the _____ of baptism, usually when they are quite young.

13. After the training _____, they adjourned to a restaurant for dinner.

14. Some Americans _____ having to pay income taxes to the federal government.

15. After their honeymoon, the couple was _____ about their future together.

16. In "Parent Effectiveness Training," children should be given natural or logical _____ for their mistakes and mischief, such as cleaning up when they spill milk.

17. The success of the movie *Rocky* was never equaled by any of its _____.

18. Many people don't realize that bananas, like oranges, can be split into roughly equal _____.

19. Mitt Romney _____ his chief rival for the Republican presidential nomination, Rick Perry, in speeches and a series of television ads.

20. In European folklore, vampires attack humans with their preternaturally long incisors in order to _____ their thirst for blood.

Exercise D

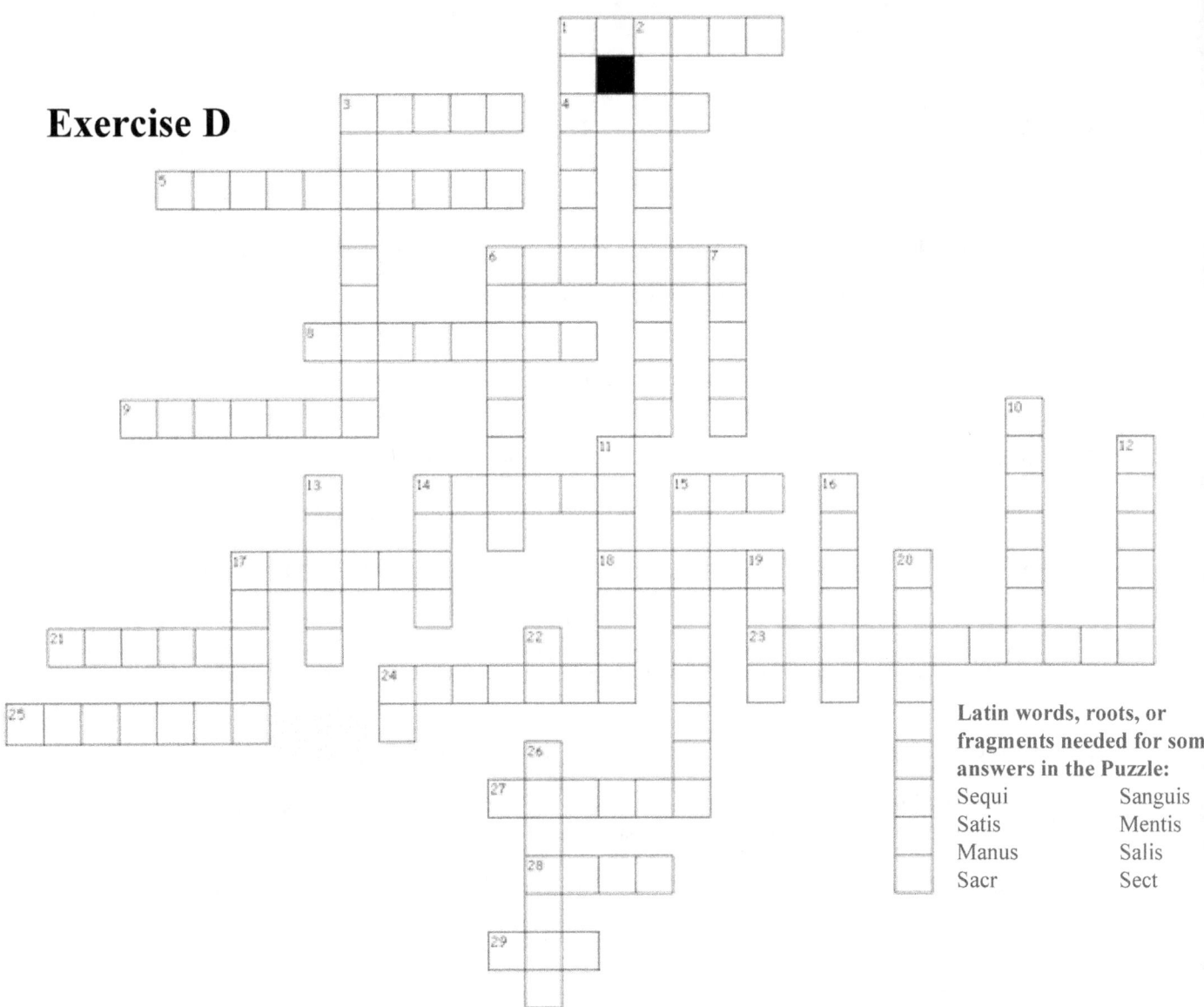

Latin words, roots, or fragments needed for some answers in the Puzzle:
Sequi   Sanguis
Satis   Mentis
Manus   Salis
Sacr   Sect

Across
1. religious; holy
3. enough (l)
4. to think, to feel (l)
5. a handwritten book, document, or piece of music
6. blood (l)
8. a particular order
9. a physical attack or threat of harm
14. mentally feeble due to old age
15. together (l)
17. a follow up in a series
18. hand (l)
21. to attack
23. the result of an action
24. to analyze in minute detail
25. old (l)
27. mind (l)
28. to cut (l)
29. before (l)

Down
1. a meeting
2. successive; following immediately after
3. a religious ceremony invoking divine grace
6. cheerfully optimistic
7. to write (l)
10. to satisfy to the full
11. to divide into separate pieces; a piece
12. salty in nature
13. to follow (l)
14. to jump (l)
15. a general agreement
16. to hold a grudge
17. salt (l)
19. holy (l)
20. to write a prescription; to advise
22. back, again (l)
24. down, from (l)
26. relating to sensation or the physical senses

240

Quiz 4

Quiz answers begin on page 318

> *mountain, opportune, interrupt, punish, proponent, sacraments, amputate, impeccable, derogatory, placid, muster, sacred, annihilate, oppress, sanguine, ridicule, consensus, resent, potential, consequence, consecutive*

1. I _____ all my energy and strength to climb the steep _____.

2. The first atomic bomb used in World War II _____ Hiroshima; the second decimated Nagasaki.

3. A _____ of nonviolent action, Gandhi led massive protest actions that helped India win independence from Great Britain.

4. The diplomat's joke did not come at an _____ time; the peace conference participants were too angry to laugh.

5. "Your summits are clear; the sky and lake are blue and _____." – *Frankenstein,* by Mary Shelley.

6. The young law school graduate demonstrated great _____, and she also had an _____ academic record.

7. After a shark mauled his foot and calf beyond repair, the doctors decided to _____ his leg below the knee.

8. Sheriffs and judges throughout the South colluded to _____ African-Americans and _____ them if they stepped out of line.

9. The student was _____ when she arrived at the formal dance in a home-sewn dress.

10. The comment was not only offensive and _____; it _____ the speaker's presentation, causing her to lose her train of thought.

11. The Seven _____ are _____ to Catholics around the world.

12. Despite two _____ years of losses, the CEO had a _____ feeling that the company's performance would turn around.

13. The _____ among the top executives was to expand by adding more stores.

14. He was spanked for the least misbehavior, a _____ so severe that he _____ his mother all his life.

Lesson XXI

Simile

Fr. Comparaison
It. Similitudine
Port. Símile
Sp. Símil

SIMIL-

similar

Definition: **n.** a figure of speech involving the comparison of one thing with another thing of a different kind

Sentence: 'Her smile dawned like a summer's morn' is a simile.

Simulate

Fr. Simuler
It. Simulare
Port. Simular
Sp. Simular

SIMUL-

to copy

Definition: **v.** to imitate or to reproduce the appearance, character, or conditions of

Sentence: Heartburn can simulate a heart attack, so a medical consultation is warranted.

Simultaneous

Fr. Simultané
It. Simultaneo
Port. Simultâneo
Sp. Simultáneo

SIMUL-

similar

Definition: **adj.** occurring, operating, or done at the same time

Sentence: Thomas Jefferson and John Adams died almost simultaneously on July 4, 1826.

Solitude

Fr. Solitude
It. Solitudine
Port. Solidão
Sp. Soledad

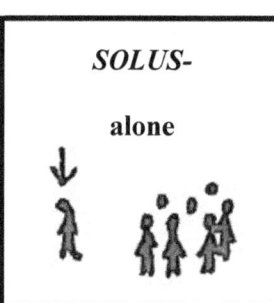

Definition: **n.** the state of being alone

Sentence: A hermit or recluse prefers a life of solitude.

Solo

Fr. Solo
It. Assolo
Port. Solo
Sp. Solo

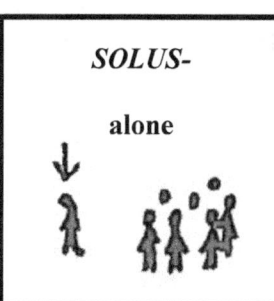

Definition: **n.** a piece of music, song, or dance for a single performer; an unaccompanied flight by a pilot
adj./adv. for or done by one person

Sentence: 'O sole mio!' is a well-known operatic solo popularized by Enrico Caruso.
He soloed only after passing the written exam for a pilot's license.

Absolute

Fr. Absolu
It. Assoluto
Port. Absoluto
Sp. Absoluto

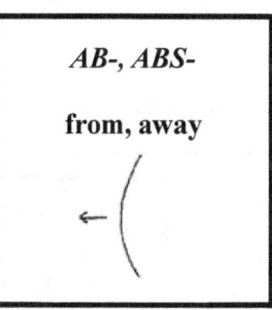 

Definition: **adj.** complete or total; complete in nature, not relative or comparative
n. a value or principle regarded as universally valid or able to be viewed without relation to other things

Sentence: At a temperature of absolute zero, molecules cease movement.
One philosophy insists on absolutes; its counterpart holds that all things are relative.

Dissolve	Fr. (Se) Dissoudre It. Dissolversi Port. Dissolver Sp. Disolver	DIS- apart	SOLV- to loosen

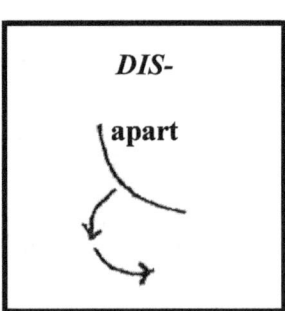

Definition: **v.** to become or to cause to become incorporated into a liquid so as to form a solution; to formally end an assembly or annul a marriage
n. an instance of dissolving from one image or scene in a film to another

Sentence: Annulment is the Catholic alternative to divorce as a means to dissolve a marriage
The fight scene slowly dissolved into a scene of the family at home together.

Resolve	Fr. Résoudre It. Risolvere Port. Resolver Sp. Resolver	RE- back, again	SOLV- to loosen

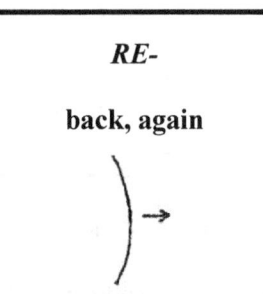 

Definition: **v.** to settle or find a solution to; to decide firmly on a course of action; to gain clarity (as in a photographic negative)
n. a firm determination

Sentence: A detective's task is to follow clues and evidence to resolve a crime.
Michael Jordan had the resolve to win the game, despite having the flu.

Resolution	Fr. Résolution It. Risoluzione Port. Resolução Sp. Resolución	RE- back, again	SOLV- to loosen

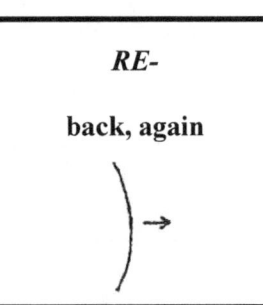 

Definition: **n.** the formal quality of being decided or determined; a firm decision; the settling of a problem or dispute

Sentence: Many New Year's resolutions to change habits or behavior are quickly broken.

Insomnia	Fr. Insomnie It. Insonnia Port. Insônia Sp. Insomnio	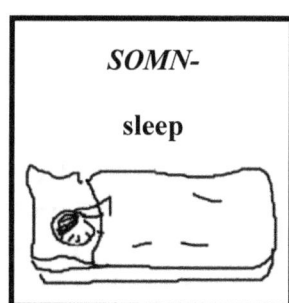 *SOMN-* sleep

Definition: **n.** habitual sleeplessness

Sentence: Insomnia is rarely a problem for cats, who sleep about 18 hours daily.

Resonate	Fr. Résonner It. Risuonare Port. Ressoar Sp. Resonar	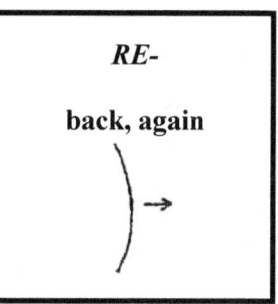 *RE-* back, again	 *SON-* to sound

Definition: **adj.** continuing to sound, ring, or reverberate; having the ability to evoke enduring images, memories or emotions

Sentence: A yodel resonates in the Alps.

Sonar	Fr. Sonar It. Sonar Port. Sonar Sp. Sonar	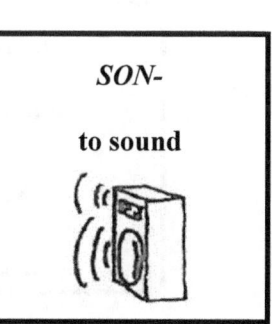 *SON-* to sound

Definition: **n.** a system for the detection of objects under water, based on the emission and measured reflection of sound pulses; the method of echolocation used in air or water by animals such as bats and whales

Sentence: A car equipped with sonar automatically stays a safe distance behind a forward car.

		SUPER- over	SON- to sound
Supersonic	Fr. Supersonique It. Supersonico Port. Supersônico Sp. Supersónico		

Definition: **adj.** involving or denoting a speed greater than the speed of sound

Sentence: Traveling faster than sound, the Concorde was an SST, or supersonic transport.

		SPARG- to scatter
Aspersion	Fr. Calomnie It. Calunnia, Diffamazione Port. Difamação Sp. Difamación	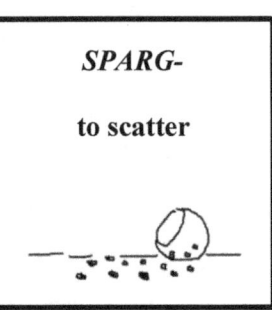

Definition: **n.** a withering attack on someone's or something's character or reputation

Sentence: The prosecuting attorney cast aspersions on the witness's character and credibility.

		DIS- apart	SPARG- to scatter
Disperse	Fr. (Se) Disperser It. Disperdersi Port. Dispersar Sp. Dispersar	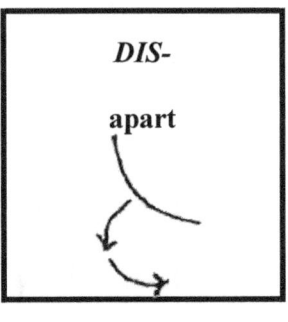	

Definition: **v.** to scatter in different directions or over a wide area

Sentence: At Lexington, a Redcoat officer cried out to the militiamen: "Disperse, ye rebels!"

Despicable	Fr. Méprisable It. Disprezzabile Port. Desprezível Sp. Despreciable	*DE-* **down, from** 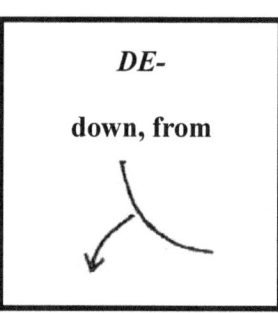	*SPECT-, SPIC-* **to look**

Definition: **adj.** deserving hatred and contempt

Sentence: In wartime, a traitor is perhaps the most despicable of men.

Perspective	Fr. Perspective It. Prospettiva Port. Perspectiva Sp. Perspectiva	*PER-* **completely, through** 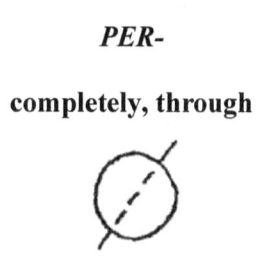	*SPECT-, SPIC-* **to look** 

Definition: **n.** (1) the art of portraying three-dimensional objects on a two-dimensional surface to indicate their height, width, depth, and position in relation to each other when viewed from a particular point of view
n. (2) point of view

Sentence: Renaissance painters used perspective to create more realistic art.
The story would look quite different from the villain's perspective.

Spectacle	Fr. Spectacle It. Spettacolo Port. Espectáculo Sp. Espectáculo	*SPECT-, SPIC-* **to look** 

Definition: **n.** a visually striking performance or display

Sentence: Nero's Coliseum was an arena for spectacles including gladiatorial contests and wild animals.

Spectator

Fr. Spectateur
It. Spettatore
Port. Espectador
Sp. Espectador

SPECT-, SPIC-

to look at

Definition: **n.** a person who watches at a show, game, or other event

Sentence: At some soccer fields, players are protected from the spectators by a moat.

Spectrum

Fr. Spectre
It. Spettro
Port. Especro
Sp. Espectro

SPECT-, SPIC-

to look

Definition: **n.** a band of colors produced by a separation of the components of light by their different degrees of refraction according to wavelength (as in a rainbow); a scale extending between two points; a range

Sentence: The spectrum of European political opinion ranges from communist to neo-Nazi.

Exercise A

Exercise B
Match the word with the letter of its definition:

1. ____ absolute
2. ____ aspersion
3. ____ despicable
4. ____ dissolve
5. ____ disperse
6. ____ insomnia
7. ____ perspective
8. ____ resolution
9. ____ resolve
10. ____ resonate
11. ____ simile
12. ____ simulate
13. ____ simultaneous
14. ____ solitude
15. ____ solo
16. ____ sonar
17. ____ spectacle
18. ____ spectator
19. ____ spectrum
20. ____ supersonic

a) at the same time
b) contemptible
c) to settle; to decide
d) a figure of speech comparing one thing to another
e) faster than the speed of sound
f) complete and total
g) point of view
h) an echolocation system
i) to distribute or spread over a wide area
j) to disappear, deteriorate, or degenerate; to disperse in a liquid
k) an attack on one's reputation
l) an audience member; a bystander
m) inability to sleep
n) the state of being alone
o) to imitate an appearance or action
p) a firm decision
q) to reverberate with sound
r) done by one person alone
s) a fantastic visual display or exhibition
t) a range

Exercise C

1. The Cubists upended the rules of _____ in painting by portraying the same object from several points of view simultaneously.

2. "Power tends to corrupt; _____ power corrupts absolutely": so said Lord Acton, a British historian.

3. If you cast unjustified _____ on my character, I will sue you for libel.

4. I hope the sun will _____ the fog.

5. Teenage students sometimes benefit from _____ right-brain and left-brain stimulation, such as listening to music while doing their homework.

6. The United Nations _____ had no legal force, but expressed the world's overwhelming condemnation of the ongoing genocide.

7. NASA space camp has computers that _____ space flight, so campers can experience the challenges and sensations of space travel without leaving Earth.

8. His crimes were so heinous and _____ that even the other prisoners looked down on him.

9. Baking soda _____ in water is an easy home remedy for mild acid indigestion.

10. He fell asleep during the day, but lay awake most of the night, so the doctor prescribed _____ medication.

11. You can be in the midst of a crowd of people and experience loneliness, but not _____.

12. The largest bells of the carillon may _____ for a full minute after they are played.

13. A _____ is a very useful device in poetry and descriptive prose.

14. Military planes were the first to use _____ technology, but some passenger aircraft now do so as well.

15. The circus came to town and provided one tremendous _____ after another, from death-defying acrobats to prancing elephants.

16. A card game that is played _____ is called solitaire.

17. You cannot _____ this dispute matter overnight.

18. Every _____ was entertained by the Sondheim musical, which included television comedian Stephen Colbert in the cast.

19. _____ is used by humans to detect objects under water and by whales to locate each other.

20. A broad _____ of colors made the paint color decision even harder.

Exercise D

Latin words, roots, or fragments needed for some answers in the Puzzle:
Solv   Simul
Spect Somn
Simil Sparg

Across
3. an echolocation system
6. apart (l)
8. a firm decision
10. back, again (l)
12. over (l)
13. to copy (l)
14. completely, through (l)
16. an audience member; a bystander
18. faster than the speed of sound
20. down, from (l)
24. to disappear, deteriorate, or degenerate; to disperse in a liquid
25. to loosen (l)
26. the state of being alone
27. from, away (l)
28. inability to sleep
29. done by one person alone

Down
1. an attack on one's reputation
2. to distribute or spread over a wide area
4. complete and total
5. a figure of speech comparing one thing to another
7. to imitate an appearance or action
9. to sound (l)
10. to reverberate with sound
11. a range
14. point of view
15. a fantastic visual display or exhibition
16. similar (l)
17. to scatter (l)
18. at the same time
19. sleep (l)
21. contemptible
22. to settle; to decide
23. alone (l)
26. to look (l)

251

Lesson XXII

Aspire

Fr. Aspirer (à)
It. Aspirare
Port. Aspirar
Sp. Aspirar

AC-, AD-
to, toward

SPIR-
to breathe

Definition: **v.** to direct one's hopes or ambitions toward achieving something

Sentence: In 2008 Hillary Clinton aspired to be the first female American president.

Conspiracy

Fr. Conspiration
It. Cospirazione
Port. Conspiração
Sp. Conspiración

CON-
together

SPIR-
to breathe

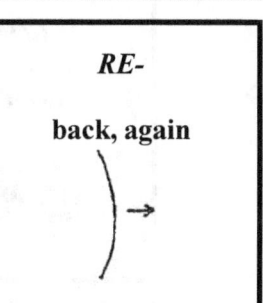

Definition: **n.** a secret plan by a group to do something harmful or unlawful

Sentence: Conspiracy theorists contend that Lee Harvey Oswald did not act alone in the assassination of President Kennedy.

Respiratory

Fr. Respiratoire
It. Respiratorio
Port. Respiratório
Sp. Respiratorio

RE-
back, again

SPIR-
to breathe

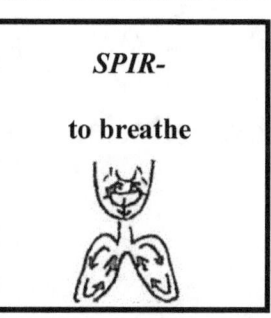

Definition: **adj.** relating to or affecting breathing

Sentence: Leaves are the main respiratory organ of plants, taking in carbon dioxide and returning oxygen to the atmosphere.

Spiritual

Fr. Spirituel
It. Spirituale
Port. Espiritual
Sp. Espiritual

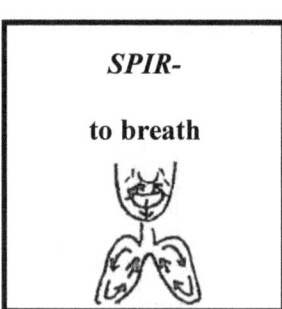

Definition:	**adj.** relating to or affecting the human spirit, as opposed to material or physical things; relating to religion or religious beliefs
Sentence:	A priest must tend to the spiritual needs of his parishioners.

Constant

Fr. Constant
It. Costante
Port. Constante
Sp. Constante

Definition:	**adj.** occurring continuously; faithful **n.** an unchanging situation
Sentence:	A lover is said to be 'constant' if he or she remains faithful to the beloved. The pain in his lower back was a constant, so he learned to ignore it.

Constellation

Fr. Constellation
It. Costellazione
Port. Constelação
Sp. Constelación

Definition:	**n.** a group of stars forming a recognized pattern and typically named after a mythological or other figure; a similar cluster of related people or objects
Sentence:	Psychologists treat dysfunctions of the individual within the family constellation.

Stellar	Fr. Stellaire It. Stellare Port. Estelar Sp. Estelar	*STELLA-* **back, again** 

Definition: **adj.** featuring or having the qualities of a star performer; relating to a star or stars

Sentence: Nadia Comaneci's performance on the balance beam was stellar, earning her a perfect 10 from the Olympic judges.

Constrict	Fr. Comprimer It. Comprimere Port. Constringir Sp. Constreñir	*CON-* **together** / *STRICT-* **to bind** 

Definition: **v.** to make or become narrower, especially by encircling pressure

Sentence: The girdle is no longer in vogue as a means to constrict the waistline.

Construct	Fr. Construire It. Costruire Port. Construir Sp. Construir	*CON-* **together**  / *STRUCT-* **to build** 

Definition: **v.** to build or erect; to form from various conceptual elements; to form according to grammatical rules
n. an idea or theory; a group of words forming a phrase

Sentence: The builders began to construct the main span of the bridge.
A passive verb construct is used in this very sentence.

Instruct

Fr. Instruire
It. Istruire
Port. Instruir
Sp. Instruir

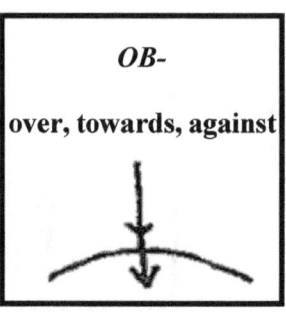

IL-, IM-, IN-
in, not

STRUCT-
to build

Definition: **v.** to direct or command; to teach; to give information to

Sentence: The commander instructed his aide to fetch maps of the terrain.

Obstruct

Fr. Obstruer
It. Ostruire
Port. Obstruir
Sp. Obstruir

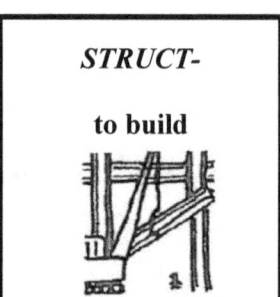

OB-
over, towards, against

STRUCT-
to build

Definition: **v.** to be in the way of; to prevent or hinder

Sentence: After a hurricane, downed trees frequently obstruct the roadways.

Suave

Fr. Charmant
It. Soave
Port. Suave
Sp. Suave

SUAVIS-
delightful

Definition: **adj.** charming, confident, and elegant

Sentence: James Bond is portrayed as a suave, sophisticated man with lightning reflexes.

Presume	Fr. Présumer It. Presumere Port. Presumir Sp. Presumir	*PRE-, PRAE-* before	*SUM-* to take

Definition: **v.** to suppose that something is the case on the basis of probability

Sentence: 'Dr. Livingstone, I presume?' were *New York Herald* reporter D. M. Stanley's words upon meeting the famed explorer in a village on Lake Tanganyika.

Tangent	Fr. Tangent (à) It. Tangente (a) Port. Tangente Sp. Tangente	*TANG-* to touch

Definition: **n.** a straight line or plane that touches a curve or curved surface at a single point or along a line; an irrelevant topic of conversation
adj. touching but not intersecting

Sentence: To 'go off on a tangent' is to digress wildly from the topic at hand.
That line is tangent to the circle.

Tangible	Fr. Tangible It. Tangibile Port. Tangível Sp. Tangible	*TANG-* to touch

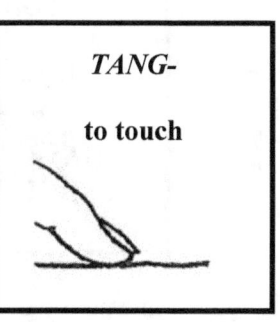

Definition: **adj.** discernible by touch; palpable; possible to be treated as fact; possible to understand or realize

Sentence: Material evidence refers to tangible clues.

Temper

Fr. n. Tempérament, v. Tempérer
It. n. Temperamento, v. Temperare
Port. Temperar
Sp. Temperar

TEMPER- to mix

Definition:	**n.** a person's state of mind or emotions; disposition; a tendency to become easily angry or irritable; an outbreak of anger **v.** to moderate; to bring to a desired consistency, texture or hardness; to harden or strengthen by application of heat or by heating and cooling; to strengthen through experience or hardship; to toughen
Sentence:	The foreman was known for his temper, so his team worked hard and kept their heads down. His enthusiasm for shark fishing was tempered by an appreciation of its dangers.

Temperament

Fr. Tempérament
It. Temperamento
Port. Temperamento
Sp. Temperamento

TEMPER- to mix

Definition:	**n.** the manner of thinking, behaving, or reacting typical of a specific person; excessive irritability or sensitivity
Sentence:	He had an easy temperament, but his brother was an impatient man.

Contemporary

Fr. Contemporain
It. Contemporaneo
Port. Contemporâneo
Sp. Contemporáneo

CON- together

TEMPOR- time

Definition:	**adj.** (1) belonging to the same period of time; about the same age **adj.** (2) current; modern **n.** a person of similar age
Sentence:	The *Mona Lisa* is contemporary to the paintings on the ceiling of the Sistine Chapel. The Metropolitan Museum features both historical and contemporary art. Abraham Lincoln was a contemporary of Charles Darwin; in fact, they were born on the same day.

Temporal

Fr. Temporal
It. Temporale
Port. Temporal
Sp. Temporal

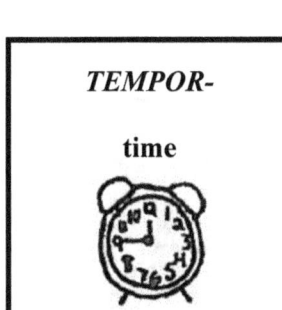

TEMPOR-

time

Definition: **adj.** (1) limited by time; worldly; lasting only for a time; not eternal; secular or lay

Sentence: Christians believe one's temporal life is followed by an eternal one.

Exercise A

Exercise B
Match the word with the letter of its definition:

1. ____ **aspire**
2. ____ **conspiracy**
3. ____ **constant**
4. ____ **constellation**
5. ____ **constrict**
6. ____ **construct**
7. ____ **contemporary**
8. ____ **instruct**
9. ____ **obstruct**
10. ____ **presume**
11. ____ **respiratory**
12. ____ **spiritual**
13. ____ **stellar**
14. ____ **suave**
15. ____ **tangent**
16. ____ **tangible**
17. ____ **temper**
18. ____ **temperament**
19. ____ **temporal**

a) involving the stars
b) to suppose
c) nonmaterial; religious
d) touchable
e) to build; to erect
f) a group of stars
g) to hope to accomplish
h) a line that touches a curve at one point
i) secular; material
j) to block
k) a secret plot involving more than one person
l) to teach
m) unchanging
n) disposition
o) to make narrower
p) modern
q) affecting breathing or respiration
r) charming and elegant
s) a fit of rage

Exercise C

1. Ideals are abstract, but actions are a _____ measure of someone's true values.

2. They were quite disappointed when they realized the new house across the street would _____ their ocean view.

3. The real estate agent was searching for a large _____ house, as his clients had an extensive modern art collection they wanted to display in suitable surroundings.

4. Many young boys _____ to become professional athletes, but few realize their dreams.

5. Girlfriends may come and go, but my dog, Tara, is my _____ companion.

6. I did not wish to _____ the outcome, so I waited patiently until the movie ended.

7. The cat tried to claw off her collar, which was so tight that it _____ her breathing.

8. The mosque is my _____ home.

9. Golden and Labrador retrievers are especially known for their calm _____.

10. Audra McDonald gave a _____ performance as Bess in Gershwin's beloved musical, "Porgy and Bess."

11. A _____ disease would cause breathing difficulties.

12. To the disappointment of the spectators and the rest of the team, the pitcher walked off the mound in fit of _____.

13. The architect drew up a basic colonial house design the builder could _____ in less than six months and easily adapt to different families' needs.

14. _____ affairs relate to the secular side of things, as opposed to the religious side.

15. There was a _____ to manipulate the results of the election.

16. She went off on a _____, but it was so fascinating that no one tried to steer the discussion back to the original topic.

17. Your costume should show what a _____ man your character is.

18. There are 88 named _____, according to modern astronomers.

19. They were waiting for the teacher to _____ them on proper CPR procedure.

Exercise D

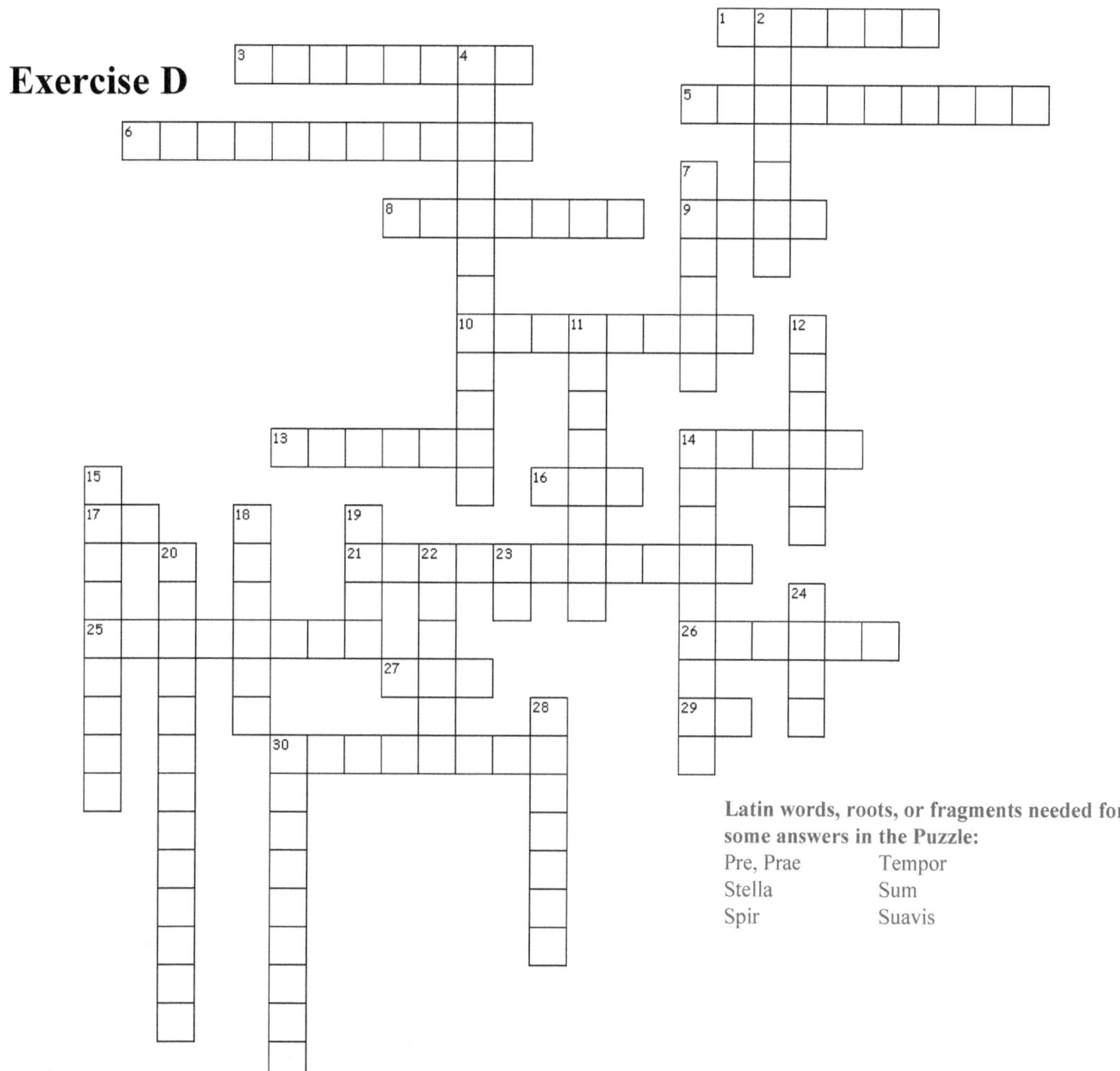

Latin words, roots, or fragments needed for some answers in the Puzzle:
Pre, Prae   Tempor
Stella   Sum
Spir   Suavis

Across
1. star (l)
3. to teach
5. a secret plot involving more than one person
6. disposition
8. to suppose
9. to touch (l)
10. to block
13. a fit of rage
14. charming and elegant
16. together
17. over, towards, against (l)
21. affecting breathing or respiration
25. touchable
26. time (l)
27. to take (l)
29. to, toward (l)
30. unchanging

Down
2. a line that touches a curve at one point
4. modern
7. to bind (l)
11. secular; material
12. delightful (l)
14. nonmaterial; religious
15. to make narrower
18. to hope to accomplish
19. before (l)
20. a group of stars
22. to build (l)
23. in, not (l)
24. to breathe (l)
28. involving the stars
30. to build; to erect

Lesson XXIII

Pertain

Fr. Concerner
It. Concernere
Port. Pertencer
Sp. Pertenecer

PER- completely, through

TEN- to hold

Definition: **v.** to have reference to; to relate; to belong as an adjunct part, holding or quality; to be fitting or suitable

Sentence: Rules and laws do not pertain to a dictator who is above the law.

Pertinent

Fr. Pertinent
It. Pertinente
Port. Pertinente
Sp. Pertinente

PER- completely, through

TEN- to hold

Definition: **adj.** having precise logical relevance to the matter at hand

Sentence: A court permits only arguments and evidence pertinent to the guilt or innocence of the accused.

Terminate

Fr. Terminer
It. Terminare
Port. Terminar
Sp. Terminar

TERM- end

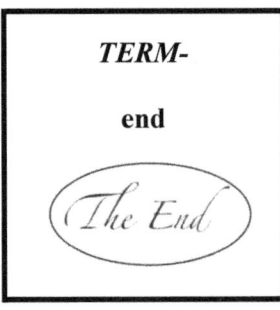

Definition: **v.** to bring to an end or to halt; to occur at or form the end of; to conclude or finish to discontinue the employment of

Sentence: The insubordinate employee was promptly terminated.

		 *EXTRA-* outside	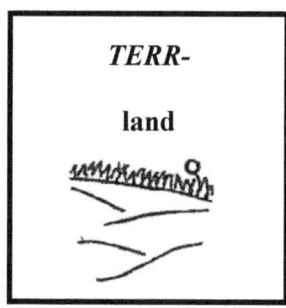 *TERR-* land
Extraterrestrial	Fr. Extraterrestre It. Extraterrestre Port. Extraterrestre Sp. Extraterrestre		

Definition: **adj.** originating, located, or occurring outside Earth or its atmosphere
n. an extraterrestrial life form

Sentence: Meteors are extraterrestrial objects that usually burn up in Earth's atmosphere.
In Steven Spielberg's classic movie, E.T. was an extraterrestrial who accidentally landed on Earth.

		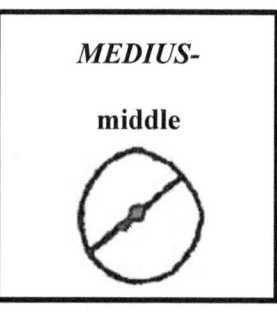 *MEDIUS-* middle	*TERR-* land
Mediterranean	Fr. Méditerranée It. Mediterraneo Port. Mediterrâneo Sp. Mediterraneo		

Definition: **adj.** surrounded nearly or completely by dry land
n. (capital M) of or relating to the Mediterranean Sea and the countries along it

Sentence: The Caspian Sea is in fact a mediterranean lake.
Greece's is surrounded on three sides by the Mediterranean Sea.

		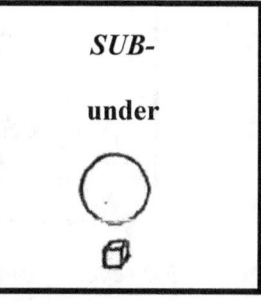 *SUB-* under	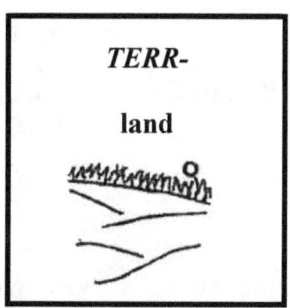 *TERR-* land
Subterranean	Fr. Souterrain It. Sotteraneo Port. Subterrâneo Sp. Subterráneo		

Definition: **adj.** situated or operating beneath the earth's surface; underground; hidden; secret

Sentence: The gold sarcophagus of Tutankhamen was discovered in a subterranean tomb.

Terrain	Fr. Terrain It. Terreno Port. Terreno Sp. Terreno	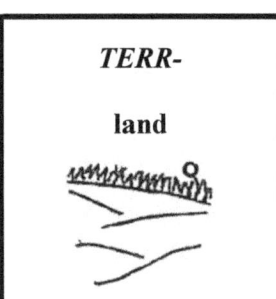

Definition: **adj.** an area of land; ground; a particular geographic area; a region; the surface features of an area of land; topography

Sentence: Topographical maps show the various elevations in a given terrain.

Context	Fr. Contexte It. Contesto Port. Contexto Sp. Contexto	

Definition: **n.** the part of a text or statement that surrounds a particular word or passage and determines its meaning; a setting

Sentence: Sometimes you can determine the meaning of an unfamiliar word from its context.

Contort	Fr. Tordre It. Contorcere Port. Contorcer Sp. Contorsionar	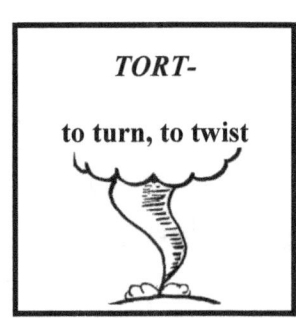

Definition: **v.** to twist, wrench, or bend severely out of shape; to become twisted into a strained shape or expression

Sentence: The pretzel is a contorted piece of dough that is salted and baked.

Distort	Fr. Distordre It. Distorcere Port. Distorcer Sp. Distorsionar	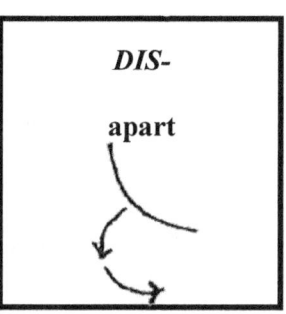 DIS- apart	 TORT- to turn, to twist
Definition:	**v.** to twist out of a proper or natural relation of parts; to misshape; to misrepresent; to pervert		
Sentence:	The claim that slavery alone led to the Civil War distorts a more complex truth.		

Totalitarian	Fr. Totalitaire It. Totalitario Port. Totalitarista Sp. Totalitario	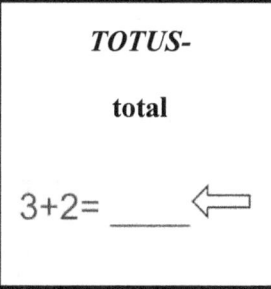 TOTUS- total
Definition:	**adj.** a form of government in which the political authority exercises absolute and centralized control over all aspects of life	
Sentence:	Communist China is governed by a totalitarian regime, although some aspects of central control have eased in recent years.	

Detract	Fr. Réduire It. Ridurre Port. Detrair Sp. Detraer	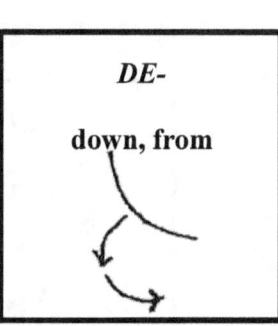 DE- down, from	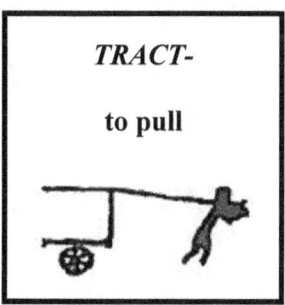 TRACT- to pull
Definition:	**v.** to draw or take away from; to reduce the value, importance, or quality of something		
Sentence:	The offshore wind farm detracted from the view of an unobstructed seascape.		

Extract	Fr. v. Extraire, n. Extrait It. v. Estrarre, n. Estratto Port. Extrair Sp. Extraer	*EX-* out 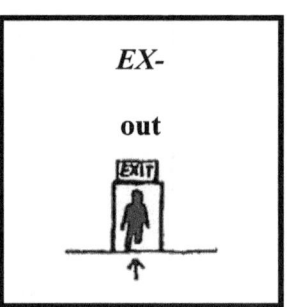	*TRACT-* to pull 

Definition: **v.** to draw or pull out; to obtain despite resistance; to remove from separate consideration or publication; to excerpt; to derive or obtain from a source; to derive from an experience
n. an excerpt or concentrated essence of a substance

Sentence: The neurosurgeon carefully extracted a bullet from the patient's brain.
Peppermint extract is used to flavor gum, ice cream, and candy.

Intrude	Fr. S'infiltrer It. Intrufolarsi Port. Intrometer Sp. Entrometer	*IL-, IM-, IN-* in, not 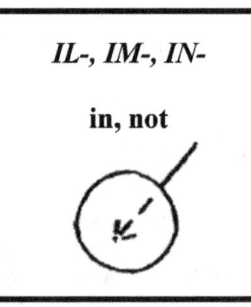	*TRUD-, TRUS-* to thrust 

Definition: **v.** to put or force in inappropriately, especially without invitation or permission; to enter as an improper or unwanted element

Sentence: The sound of her son's rock band practicing intruded on the reader's concentration.

Turbid	Fr. Troublé It. Torbido Port. Túrbido Sp. Turbio/Túrbido	*TURB-* to disturb 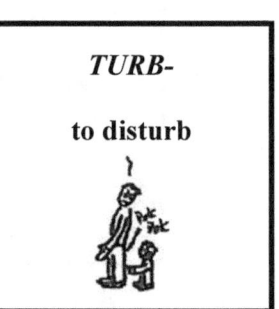

Definition: **adj.** having sediment or foreign particles stirred up or suspended; muddy; in a state of turmoil; muddled

Sentence: The motorboat left a turbid wake in the shallow pond.

Ultimate	Fr. Ultime It. Ultimo Port. Último Sp. Último	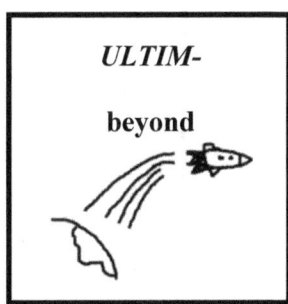

Definition: **adj.** being or happening at the end of a process; being the best or most extreme example of its kind

Sentence: The Medal of Honor is the ultimate decoration awarded in the American military.

Ultimatum	Fr. Ultimatum It. Ultimatum Port. Ultimato Sp. Ultimátum	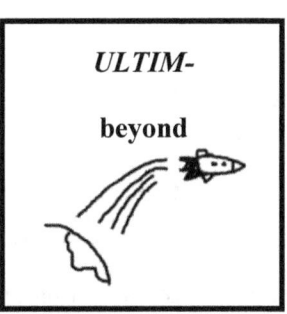

Definition: **n.** a final offer or statement of terms made by one party to another

Sentence: Attila's ultimatum to the Roman town defenders was to surrender or be slaughtered.

Corrupt	Fr. Corrompu It. Corrotto Port. Corrupto Sp. Corrupto	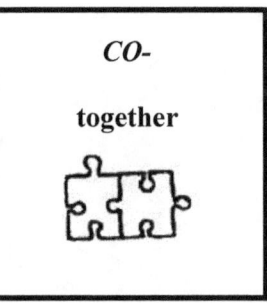	

Definition: **adj.** marked by immorality and perversion; depraved; dishonest; containing errors or alterations
v. to debase; to bribe someone or otherwise compromise their ethics

Sentence: Not long ago, elections in West Virginia were highly corrupt: In many towns, a man's vote could be bought for a bottle of liquor.
Juvenile offenders should never be housed with adult criminals, who will only corrupt them further.

Abundant

Fr. Abbondant
It. Abbondante
Port. Abundante
Sp. Abundante

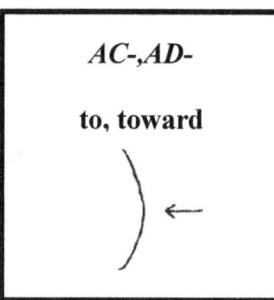

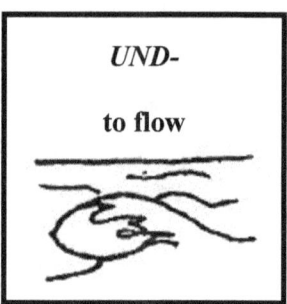

Definition:	**adj.** plentiful; rich
Sentence:	A bumper crop is an abundant harvest.

Redundant

Fr. Redondant
It. Ridondante
Port. Redundante
Sp. Redundante

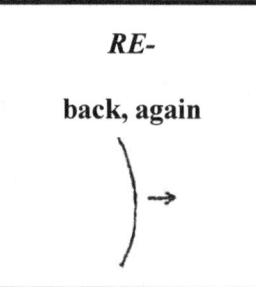

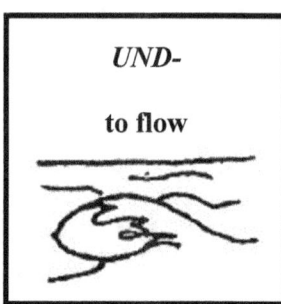

Definition:	**adj.** exceeding what is necessary or natural; needlessly repetitive or verbose; superfluous
Sentence:	The radio talk show caller's comments were redundant; every point he made had already been discussed by someone else.

Exercise A

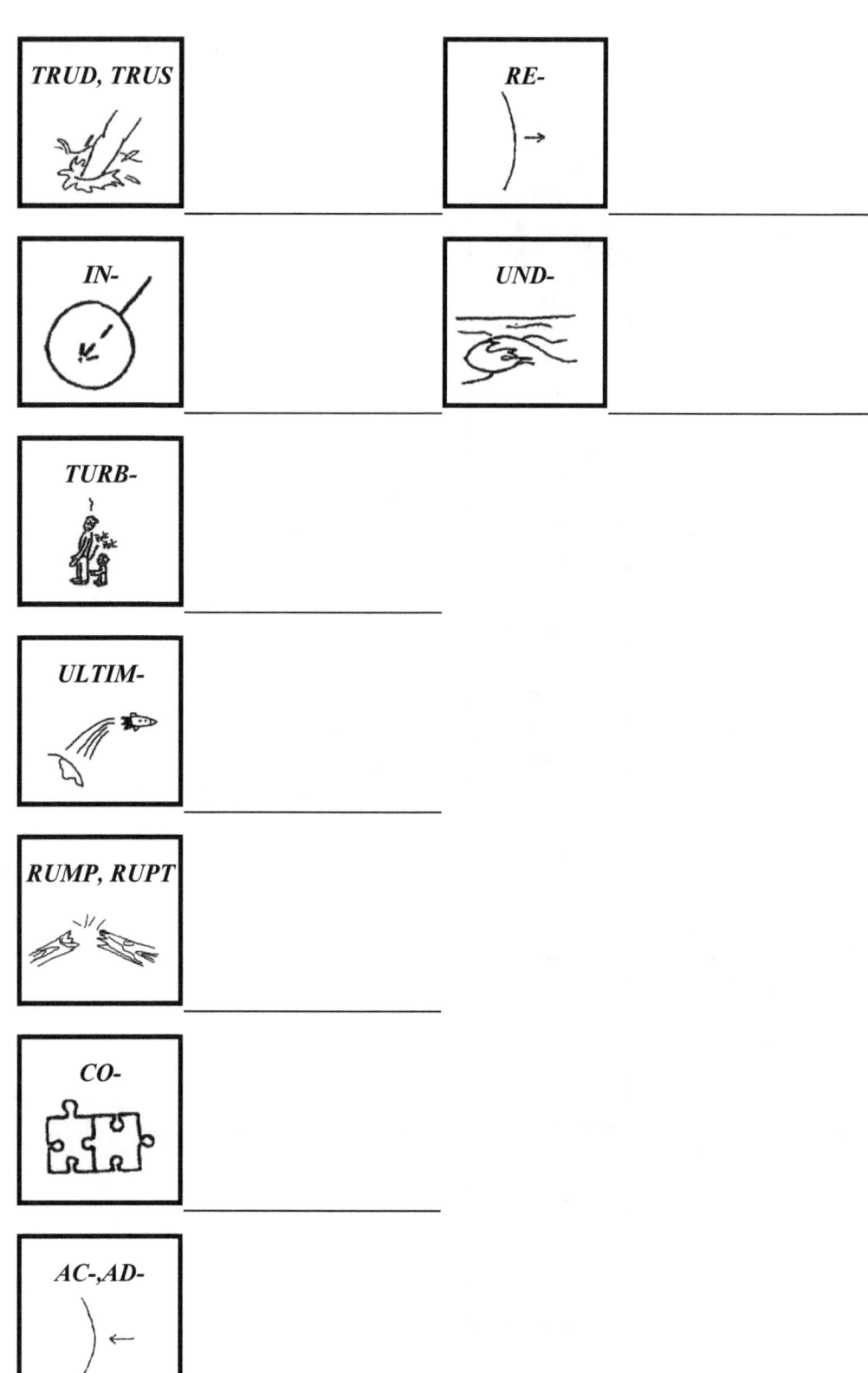

Exercise B

Match the word with the letter of its definition:

1. ____ abundant
2. ____ context
3. ____ contort
4. ____ corrupt
5. ____ detract
6. ____ distort
7. ____ extract
8. ____ extraterrestrial
9. ____ intrude
10. ____ Mediterranean
11. ____ pertain
12. ____ pertinent
13. ____ redundant
14. ____ subterranean
15. ____ terminate
16. ____ terrain
17. ____ totalitarian
18. ____ turbid
19. ____ ultimate
20. ____ ultimatum

a) characteristic of the Mediterranean Sea
b) to pull out; to remove
c) a final statement of terms
d) relevant
e) to twist
f) plentiful
g) to bring to an end
h) a stretch of land; surface characteristics of the land
i) to belittle
j) frame of reference
k) to enter without permission
l) autocratic
m) dishonest; unethical
n) to pull out of shape
o) alien; originating outside the earth and its atmosphere
p) to relate to
q) unnecessary; repetitive
r) eventual; final
s) murky
t) below the earth's surface

Exercise C

1. The _____ Diet is very healthy because it emphasizes fresh fruits and vegetables, fish and olive oil.

2. The kidnappers gave the man's employer an _____: pay the $1 million ransom or he would die.

3. Taking a calcium supplement within 48 hours of a bone density test can _____ the results.

4. An alarming number of Americans believe they have been abducted by UFOs and studied by _____.

5. The professor appreciated that the students asked only questions _____ to the topic at hand.

6. Politicians who are caught saying something embarrassing frequently blame the newspaper reporters cover them, saying, "I was quoted out of _____!"

7. Their _____ aim was to force the resignation of the unpopular university president.

8. A _____ regime seeks to dominate its citizens through a combination of terror and thought control.

9. Spelunking in _____ caves is an interesting but sometimes dangerous hobby.

10. We have an _____ supply of fish, lobsters, and shrimp, thanks to strict fishing regulations.

11. All _____ vehicles, or ATV's, are gaining in popularity, even as hiking and camping decline.

12. The entertainment media _____ on the private lives of rock stars and celebrities to a disturbing degree.

13. The contractor threatened to _____ the project if they did not pay their first bill immediately.

14. His crass remarks _____ from an otherwise genteel dinner party.

15. William Shockley's racist theories about genetics were widely disparaged because they did not _____ to the research that won him the Nobel Prize in Physics.

16. He did not want his 16-year-old daughter to date the 19-year-old high school dropout, because he feared the young man would _____ her.

17. In the United Kingdom, they refer to a person who is laid off as being "_____," because their skills or tasks are no longer needed.

18. The accomplished yoga teacher could _____ her limbs into extraordinary poses, leading her students to nickname her "The Human Pretzel."

19. The dentist would only _____ a tooth as a last resort.

20. The _____ waters of Pomp's Pond are not translucent.

Exercise D

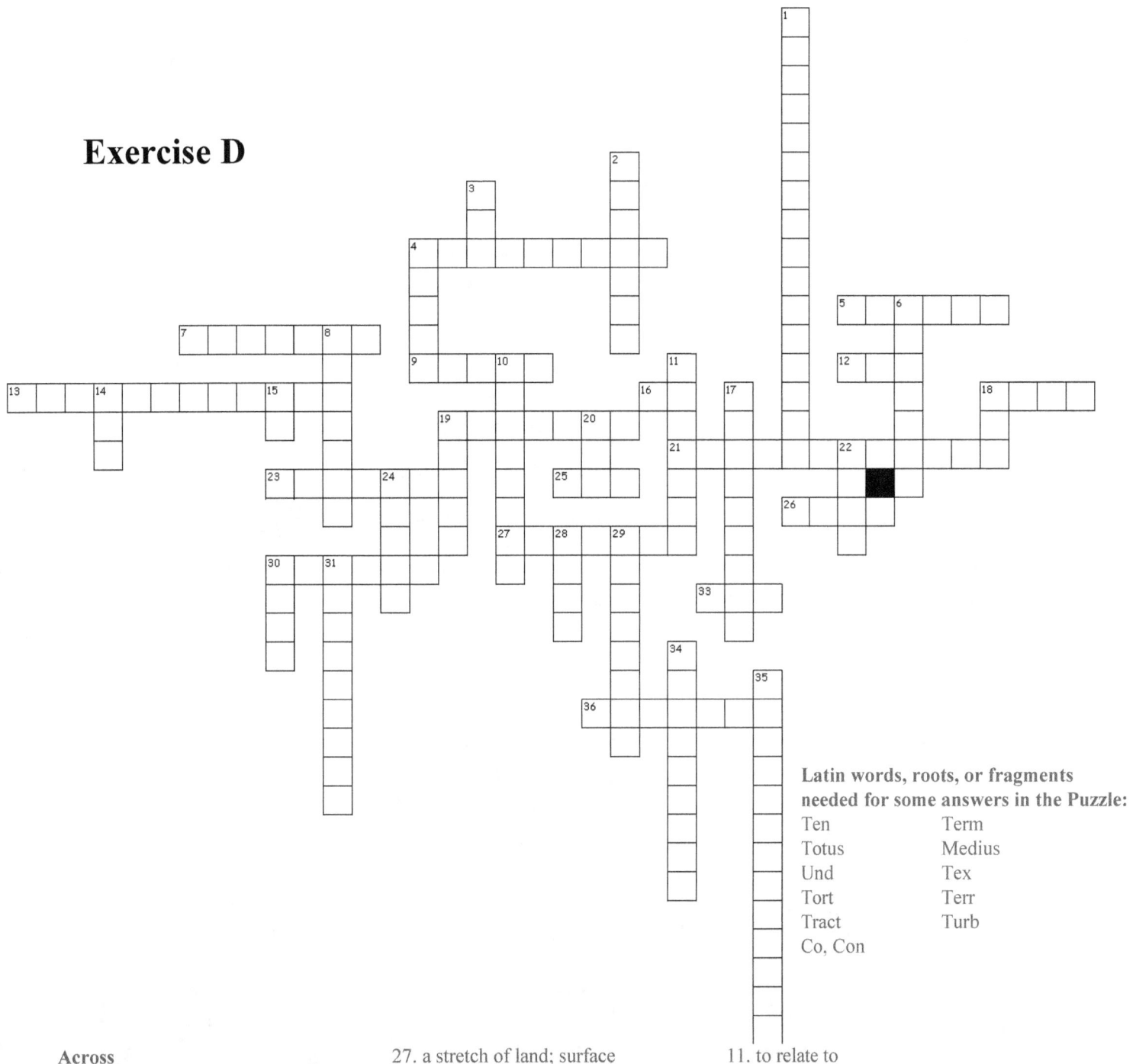

Latin words, roots, or fragments needed for some answers in the Puzzle:

Ten
Totus
Und
Tort
Tract
Co, Con
Term
Medius
Tex
Terr
Turb

Across
4. to bring to an end
5. middle (l)
7. to belittle
9. total (l)
12. apart (l)
13. below the earth's surface
16. down, from (l)
18. land (l)
19. to pull out; to remove
21. autocratic
23. dishonest; unethical
25. to flow (l)
26. end (l)
27. a stretch of land; surface characteristics of the land
30. murky
33. under (l)
36. to enter without permission

Down
1. alien; originating outside the earth and its atmosphere
2. frame of reference
3. completely, through (l)
4. to pull (l)
6. to pull out of shape
8. to twist
10. eventual; final
11. to relate to
14. to weave (l)
15. out (l)
17. a final statement of terms
18. to hold (l)
19. outside (l)
20. together (l)
22. to twist, to turn (l)
24. beyond (l)
28. to break (l)
29. plentiful
30. to disturb (l)
31. unnecessary; repetitive
34. relevant
35. characteristic of the Mediterranean Sea

Lesson XXIV

Urban

Fr. Urbain
It. Urbano
Port. Urbano
Sp. Urbano

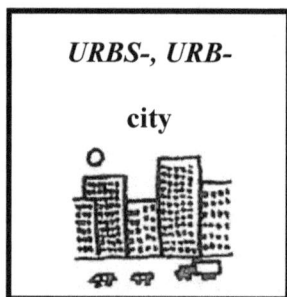

Definition: **adj.** of or located in a city; characteristic of the city or city life

Sentence: Urban dwellers forgo the fresh air and broad lawns of the outlying suburbs in exchange for convenience and culture.

Urbane

Fr. Raffiné, Urbain
It. Raffinato
Port. Urbano
Sp. Urbano

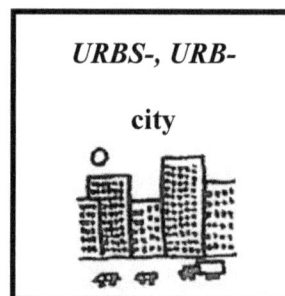

Definition: **adj.** polite, refined, and sophisticated

Sentence: The Ivy League ideal is a gentleman or woman of culture, etiquette, wit, and an urbane manner.

Evacuate

Fr. Évacuer
It. Evacuare
Port. Evacuar
Sp. Evacuar

 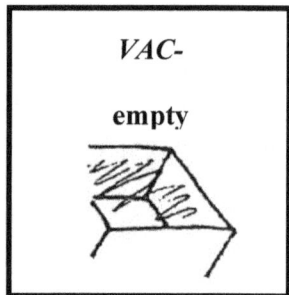

Definition: **v.** to remove from a place or area (to a safer place); to leave a place; to excrete waste matter from the body

Sentence: An air pump is employed to evacuate a bell jar and create a vacuum.

Vacant	Fr. Vacant It. Vacante Port. Vacante Sp. Vacante	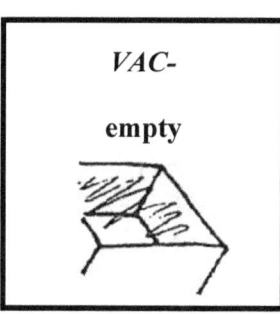 VAC- empty

Definition: **adj.** containing nothing; empty; unfilled; unoccupied; without activity

Sentence: The movers left behind a house vacant of furnishings.

Evasive	Fr. Évasif It. Evasivo Port. Evasivo Sp. Evasivo	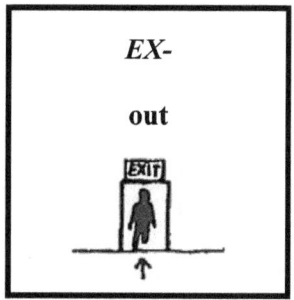 EX- out	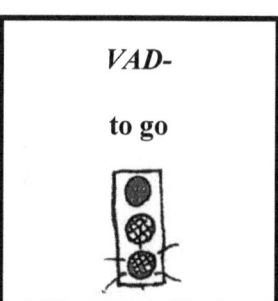 VAD- to go

Definition: **adj.** inclined or intended to evade; intentionally vague or ambiguous

Sentence: To avoid the oncoming truck, the driver swerved in an evasive maneuver.

Invasion	Fr. Invasion It. Invasione Port. Invasão Sp. Invasión	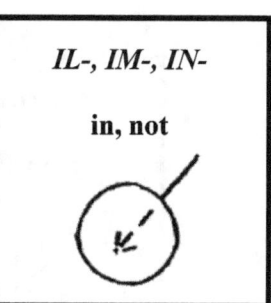 IL-, IM-, IN- in, not	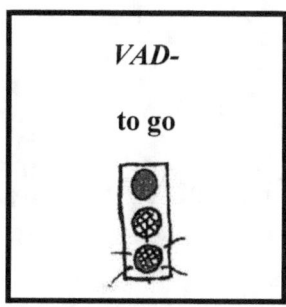 VAD- to go

Definition: **n.** an instance of invading a country or region; an intrusion or encroachment

Sentence: An invasion of locusts coupled with drought has led to widespread famine in Niger.

Prevail

Fr. Prévaloir
It. Prevalere
Port. Prevalecer
Sp. Prevalecer

PRE-, PRAE-
before

VAL-
to be strong

Definition: **v.** to be greater in strength or influence; to triumph, win out, or predominate

Sentence: After whining and pleading, he prevailed on his dad to buy him an ice cream.

Vindicate

Fr. Innocenter
It. Rivendicare
Port. Vindicar
Sp. Vindicar

VINDIC-
to avenge

Definition: **v.** to clear of accusation, blame, suspicion or doubt with supporting evidence or proof; to provide justification or support for; to defend, maintain, or insist on the recognition of one's rights; to avenge

Sentence: Galileo's astronomical observations vindicated Copernicus's controversial theory.

Vindictive

Fr. Vindicatif
It. Vendicativo
Port. Vindicativo
Sp. Vindicativo

VINDIC-
to avenge

Definition: **adj.** disposed to seek revenge; spiteful

Sentence: The desire to get even is a vindictive response.

Advent	Fr. Avent, Avènement It. Avvento Port. Advento Sp. Adviento	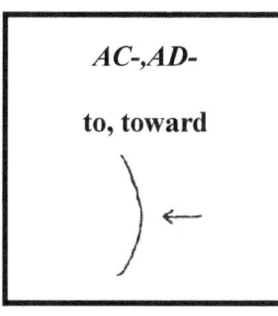 *AC-, AD-* to, toward	 *VENI-* to come

Definition: **n.** a coming or arrival; the liturgical period preceding Christmas

Sentence: The advent of a reliable chronometer allowed navigators to determine a ship's longitude.

Event	Fr. Èvènement It. Evento Port. Evento Sp. Evento	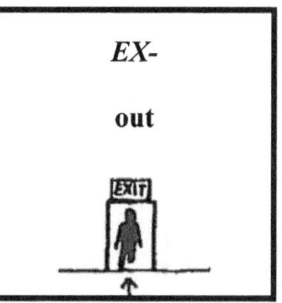 *EX-* out	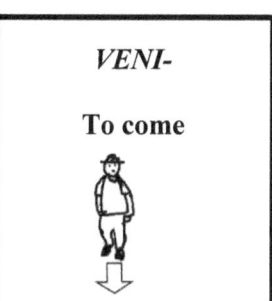 *VENI-* To come

Definition: **n.** something that takes place; a social gathering or activity; the final result or outcome; a contest or item in a sports program

Sentence: The outcomes of the roll of two dice comprise 36 possible random events.

Vent	Fr. v. Se défouler It. v. Sfogare, n. Sfogo Port. Ventilação Sp. Ventilación	 *VENTUS-* wind

Definition: **v.** 1) to express one's thoughts or feelings
v. 2) to release or discharge through an opening
n. a means of escape or release from confinement; an opening or outlet permitting the escape of fumes, a liquid, a gas, or steam

Sentence: When she got home from work, she vented to her husband about her incompetent boss.
The steam was vented through the pipe to avoid overheating.
In winter, you can see steam coming out of the dryer vent on the side of the house.

		VERUS-	**FAC-**
Verify	Fr. Vérifier It. Verificare Port. Verificar Sp. Verificar	true	to do, to make

Definition: **v.** to prove the truth of something with evidence or testimony; to substantiate; to determine or test the truth or accuracy of by comparison or investigation; to affirm formally under oath

Sentence: The predicted deflection of light during a solar eclipse verified Einstein's General Theory of Relativity.

		VERUS-	**FAC-**
Verity	Fr. Vérité It. Verità Port. Verdade Sp. Verdad	true	to do, to make

Definition: **n.** the quality or state of being true, factual, or real; a true principal or belief

Sentence: Ponce de Leon's quest for the Fountain of Youth showed he did not doubt its verity.

		VERBUM-
Verbal	Fr. Verbal It. Verbale Port. Verbal Sp. Verbal	word 

Definition: **adj.** of, relating to, or associated with words; consisting of only words without action; spoken rather than written; oral

Sentence: Gestures, body language, and facial expressions are non-verbal forms of communication.

Verbose

Fr. Verbeux
It. Verboso
Port. Verboso
Sp. Verboso

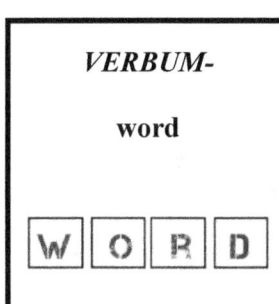

Definition: **adj.** containing a great and usually an excessive number of words; wordy

Sentence: 'Verbose', 'prolix,' and 'windy' are all synonyms descriptive of wordiness.

Adversity

Fr. Adversité
It. Avversità
Port. Adversidade
Sp. Adversidad

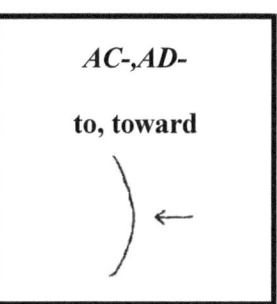 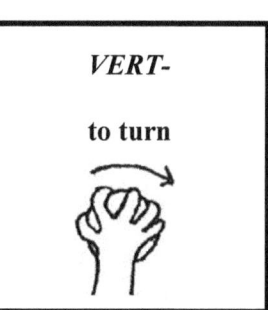

Definition: **n.** a state of hardship or affliction

Sentence: Hannibal's elephants faced adversity in the form of snow and steep terrain when they crossed the Alps.

Controversy

Fr. Controverse
It. Controversia
Port. Controvérsia
Sp. Controversia

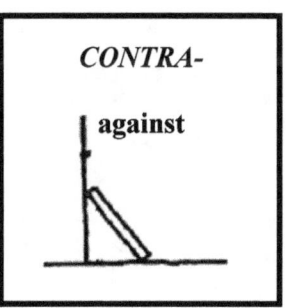 

Definition: **n.** prolonged public disagreement or heated debate

Sentence: To postpone further controversy, the proposal to impose a dress code on the students was tabled.

Diversion

Fr. Diversion
It. Diversione
Port. Desvio
Sp. Desvío

DIS-
aside

VERT-
to turn

Definition: **n.** the act or instance of diverting or turning aside; a distraction or deviation; something that distracts the mind and relaxes or entertains

Sentence: After a demanding day of work or school, many people find diversion in watching television.

Exercise A

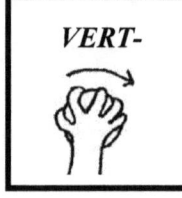 _____

Exercise B

Match the word with the letter of its definition:

1. ___ advent
2. ___ adversity
3. ___ controversy
4. ___ diversion
5. ___ evacuate
6. ___ evasive
7. ___ event
8. ___ invasion
9. ___ prevail
10. ___ urban
11. ___ urbane
12. ___ vacant
13. ___ vent
14. ___ verify
15. ___ verity
16. ___ verbal
17. ___ verbose
18. ___ vindicate
19. ___ vindictive

a) vague or elusive
b) to win
c) polite and sophisticated
d) prolonged or widespread disagreement
e) to remove; to clear out
f) empty; blank
g) wordy
h) arrival
i) vengeful
j) an influx
k) to confirm the truth of
l) oral
m) an occurrence; a competition
n) misfortune; difficulty
o) to acquit; to absolve
p) of a city
q) a duct allowing the passage of air or fumes
r) a distraction; a detour
s) truth

Exercise C

1. At the NASCAR _____, we cheered until we were hoarse.

2. The _____ of the personal computer revolutionized science, education, the workplace, and personal communication.

3. Academic language has a reputation for being _____.

4. Now that our children have all graduated from college, we're looking to move from our suburban home to an _____ condominium.

5. Each year when school gets out, we expect an _____ of tourists on Cape Cod.

6. Alex created a _____ to keep his mother occupied while Andrew stole the cookies from the cookie jar.

7. Our _____ agreement would not hold up in court: We need a written contract as well.

8. Even after we chatted for a while, he was _____ about sharing his investment strategy.

9. A _____ person usually harbors a grudge.

10. A congressional bill that would allow the FBI and CIA to tap American citizens' telephones without a warrant aroused a storm of _____.

11. The doctor expected the nurse to be _____ of the accusation that she administered an overdose.

12. She doubted the _____ of the story that the lion had befriended a lamb.

13. In the classic adventure story, the hero overcomes great _____ to reach his goal.

14. The environmental group mounted a protest when it learned the chemical plant was _____ toxic fumes.

15. The old _____ lot will become a community garden.

16. We hope to _____ on our members to contribute generously to our fund raising campaign.

17. To _____ his gold claim, he left his partner in charge and rode into the city to the assayer's office.

18. Whenever a hurricane is predicted, plans to _____ flood-prone areas are announced on the media.

19. The _____ English actor was noted for his elegant dinners at his winter retreat in the south of France.

Exercise D

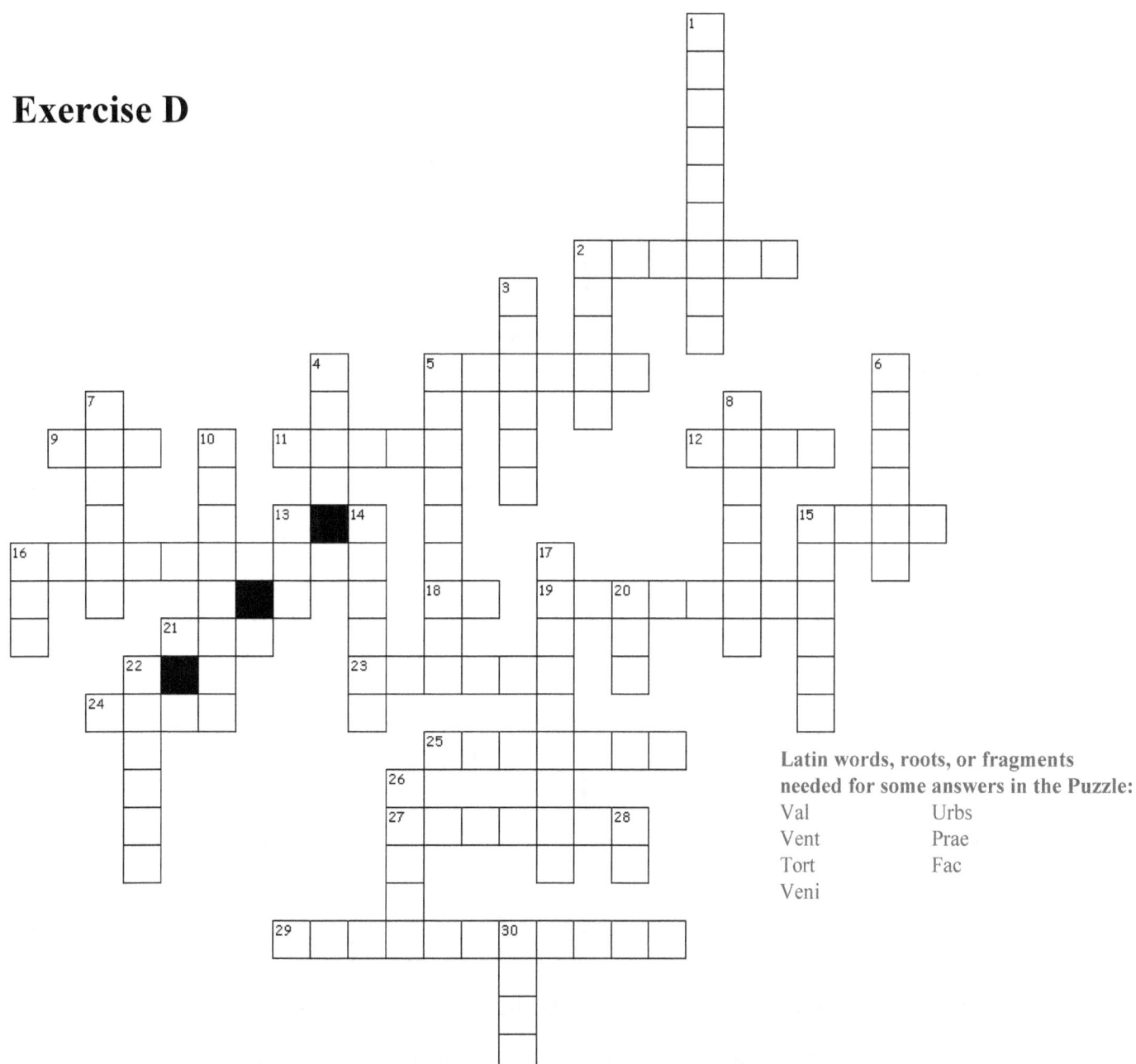

Latin words, roots, or fragments needed for some answers in the Puzzle:
Val   Urbs
Vent   Prae
Tort   Fac
Veni

Across
2. to confirm the truth of
5. word (l)
9. to do, to make (l)
11. of a city
12. city (l)
15. to come (l)
16. vengeful
18. to, toward (l)
19. an influx
21. to be strong
23. English definition of Latin root VINDIC-
24. before (l)
25. vague or elusive
27. wordy
29. prolonged or widespread disagreement

Down
1. misfortune; difficulty
2. true
3. truth
4. to turn, to twist (l)
5. to acquit; to absolve
6. arrival
7. empty; blank
8. to win
10. to remove; to clear out
13. aside (l)
14. oral
15. wind (l)
16. to go (l)
17. a distraction; a detour
20. empty (l)
22. polite and sophisticated
26. an occurrence; a competition
28. out (l)
30. a duct allowing the passage of air or fumes

Lesson XXV

Deviate

Fr. Dévier
It. Deviare
Port. Desviar
Sp. Desviar

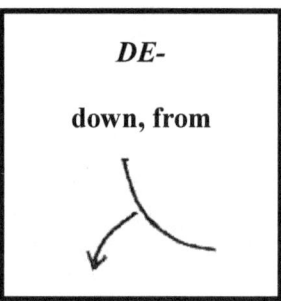

Definition: **v.** to turn aside or cause to turn aside from a course or way; to depart from a norm; to stray

Sentence: A car that repeatedly deviates from its lane signals an impaired or distracted driver.

Devious

Fr. Sournois
It. Subdolo
Port. Desonesto
Sp. Deshonesto

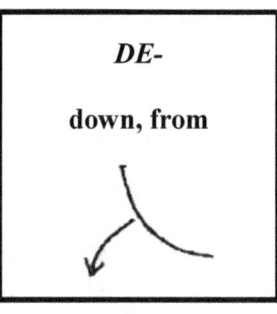 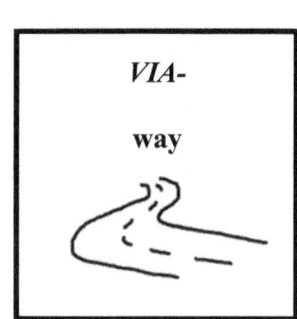

Definition: **adj.** not straightforward; shifty; departing from a correct or accepted way

Sentence: The devious wolf donned grandmother's clothes to hoodwink Red Riding Hood.

Evidence

Fr. Indice
It. Prova
Port. Evidência
Sp. Evidencia

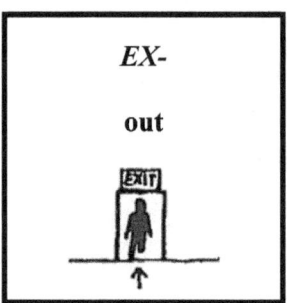 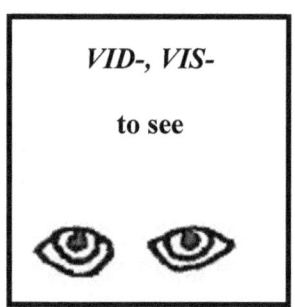

Definition: **n.** a thing or things that are helpful in forming a conclusion or judgment; an outward sign; facts used for proof

Sentence: Defense attorneys often try to get judges to exclude evidence by arguing that it was obtained through an unconstitutional search.

Evident

Fr. Évident
It. Evidente
Port. Evidente
Sp. Evidente

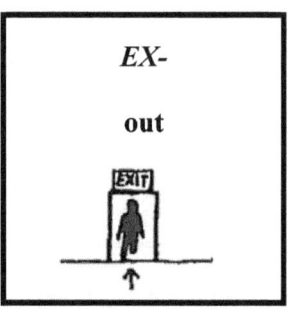

Definition:	**adj.** easily seen or understood; plain or obvious; clear
Sentence:	Something patently obvious and requiring no explanation is self-evident.

Improvise

Fr. Improviser
It. Improvvisare
Port. Improvisar
Sp. Improvisar

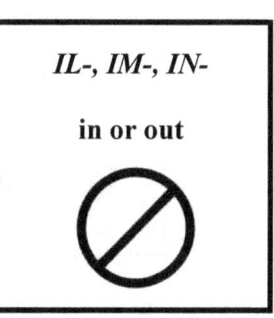

Definition:	**v.** to invent, compose, or perform with little or no preparation; to do something extemporaneously; to make do without regular tools, materials, or income
Sentence:	A prisoner improvised a rope from torn bed sheets to drop himself down the wall.

Invisible

Fr. Invisible
It. Invisibile
Port. Invisível
Sp. Invisible

 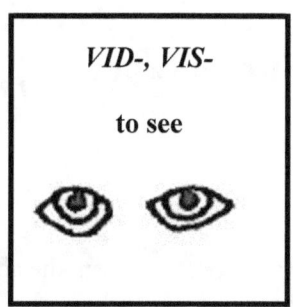

Definition:	**adj.** impossible to see; not accessible to view; hidden
Sentence:	The highway signs and lane markings rapidly became invisible as the fog rolled in.

Supervise	Fr. Superviser It. Sovrintendere (a) Port. Supervisionar Sp. Supervisar	*SUPER-* over 	*VID-, VIS-* to see

Definition: **v.** to observe and direct the execution of

Sentence: Eisenhower planned and supervised the D-Day invasion.

Visualize	Fr. Visualiser It. Visualizzare Port. Visualizar Sp. Visualizar	*VID-, VIS-* to see

Definition: **v.** to form a mental image; to make visible

Sentence: Daydreaming in his office cubicle, he visualized a romantic evening.

Surveillance	Fr. Surveillance It. Sorveglianza Port. Vigilância Sp. Vigilancia	*VIGIL-* to watch 

Definition: **n.** the act of observing a person or group under suspicion

Sentence: Surveillance cameras are mounted in stores to detect and discourage shoplifters.

Vigil

Fr. Veille
It. Veglia
Port. Vigília
Sp. Vigilia

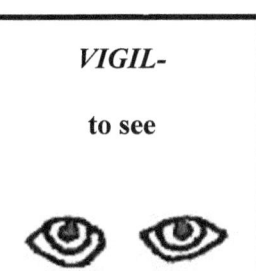

Definition: **n.** a period of staying awake during the time usually spent asleep, especially to watch or pray; a peaceful demonstration in support of a cause

Sentence: Prior to the burial, mourners conducted a reverential vigil around the casket.

Evict

Fr. Expulser
It. Sfrattare
Port. Expulsar, Desalojar
Sp. Desahuciar (a), Desalojar

Definition: **v.** to expel someone from a property

Sentence: The Pied Piper was hired by the town of Hamelin to evict the rats.

Invincible

Fr. Invincible
It. Invincibile
Port. Invencível
Sp. Invencible

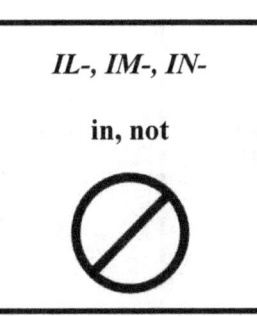 

Definition: **adj.** incapable of being overcome or defeated; unconquerable

Sentence: The supposedly invincible Maginot Line proved little deterrent to the invading Nazis.

Victory

Fr. Victoire
It. Vittoria
Port. Vitória
Sp. Victoria

VINC-, VICT-

to conquer

Definition: **n.** the defeat of an enemy or opponent; success in a struggle against difficulties or an obstacle.

Sentence: A Phyrric victory is one so costly that it is ruinous.

Survival

Fr. Survie
It. Sopravvivenza
Port. Sobrevivência
Sp. Supervivencia

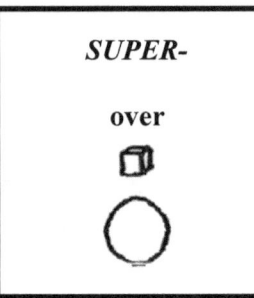

SUPER-

over

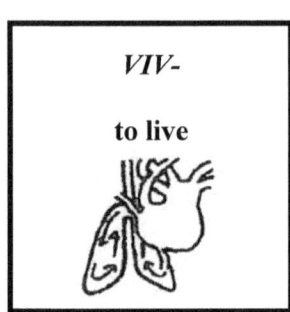

VIV-

to live

Definition: **n.** the act or process of remaining alive; the fact of having endured

Sentence: *Robinson Crusoe* is a work of fiction based on the true story of Alexander Selkirk's survival as an island castaway.

Advocate

Fr. n. Advocat, v. Recommander
It. n. Sostenitore, v. Sostenere
Port. Advogar
Sp. Advocar

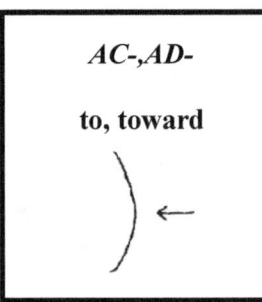

AC-, AD-

to, toward

VOC-

to call

Definition: **n.** a person who publicly supports or recommends a particular cause or policy; a person who pleads a case on someone else's behalf; a lawyer
v. to recommend publicly or to support

Sentence: A defense lawyer serves as advocate for the accused.

Vocation	Fr. Vocation It. Vocazione Port. Vocação Sp. Vocación	 *VOC-* to call

Definition: **n.** a person's employment or main occupation; a strong feeling of suitability for a particular career or occupation; a calling (especially religious)

Sentence: Ben Franklin was a printer by vocation; invention was merely his avocation.

Voluntary	Fr. Voluntaire It. Volontario Port. Voluntário Sp. Voluntario	 *VOL-* wish

Definition: **adj.** done, given, or acting of one's own free will; working without payment

Sentence: His work as head of the soccer association is completely voluntary.

Volition	Fr. Volonté It. Volontà Port. Volição Sp. Volición	 *VOL-* wish

Definition: **n.** the faculty or power of using one's own will

Sentence: Depression often expresses itself in low energy and lack of volition.

Evolve	Fr. Évolver It. Evolvere Port. Evoluir Sp. Evolucionar	*EX-* **out** 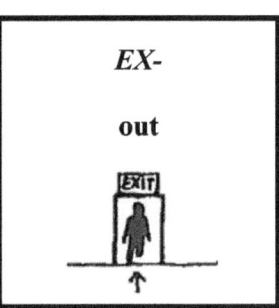	*VOLV-* **to roll** 
Definition:	**v.** to develop or achieve gradually; the process of evolution (of species)		
Sentence:	A worm evolves into a chrysalis from which a butterfly emerges.		

Revolve	Fr. Tourner It. Ruotare Port. Rotar Sp. Rotar	*RE-* **back, again** 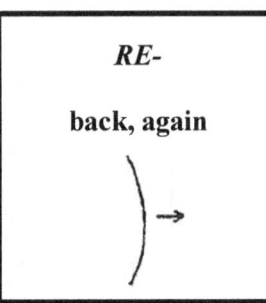	*VOLV-* **to roll** 
Definition:	**v.** (1) to orbit a central point; to turn on an axis; to rotate; to recur in cycles or periodically; to be centered **v.** (2) to treat as the center or most important element of		
Sentence:	Over the course of a night, the visible stars seem to revolve around the North Star.		

Exercise A

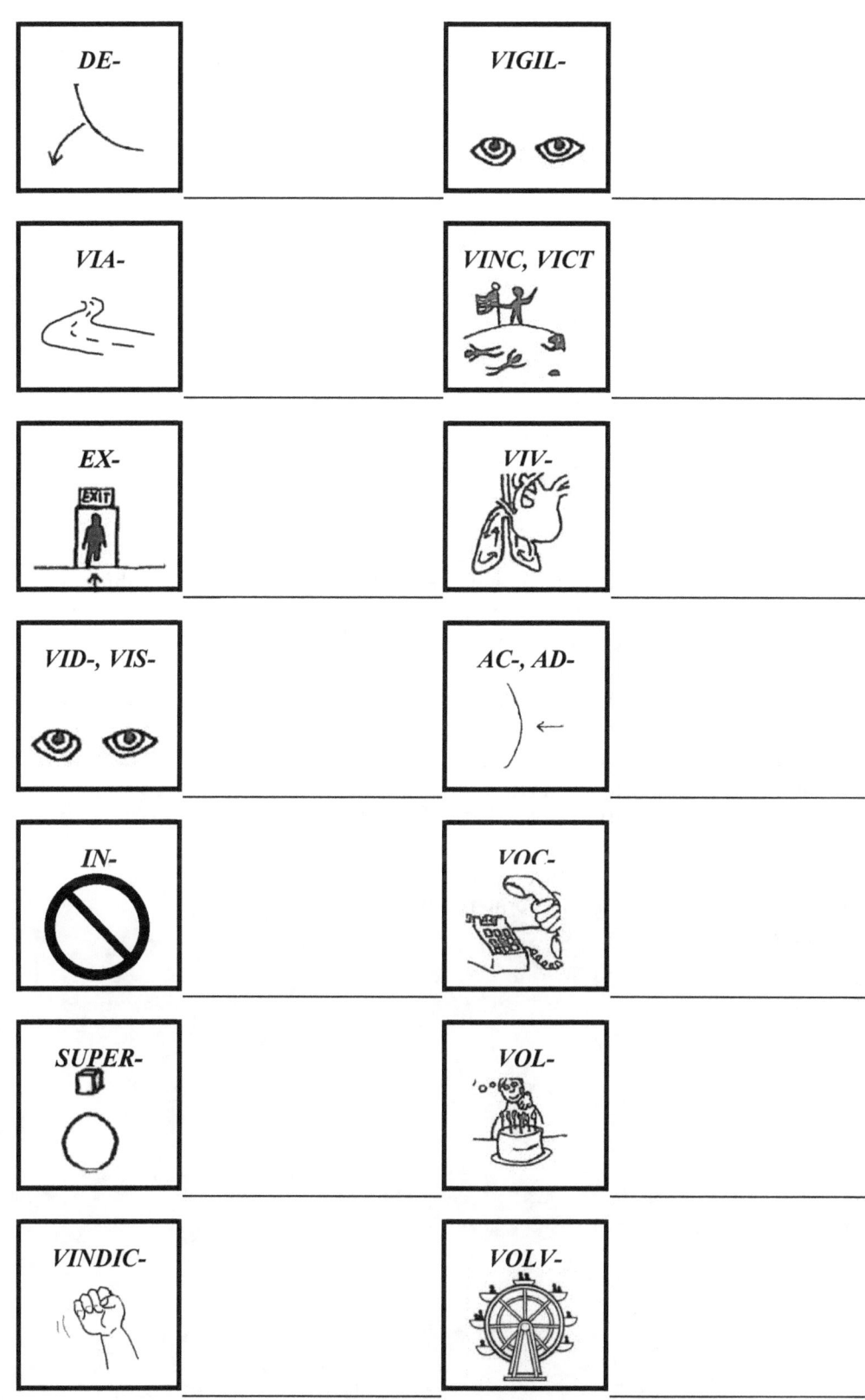

Exercise B
Match the word with the letter of its definition:

1. ___ advocate
2. ___ deviate
3. ___ devious
4. ___ evict
5. ___ evidence
6. ___ evident
7. ___ evolve
8. ___ improvise
9. ___ invincible
10. ___ invisible
11. ___ revolve
12. ___ supervise
13. ___ surveillance
14. ___ survival
15. ___ victory
16. ___ vigil
17. ___ visualize
18. ___ vocation
19. ___ volition
20. ___ voluntary

a) an occupation; a calling
b) obvious
c) to oust
d) a supporter or promoter
e) free will
f) to ad lib
g) invulnerable
h) the continued existence of (someone or something)
i) unable to be seen
j) to diverge from
k) a night watch
l) to develop slowly
m) sneaky; not straight
n) to oversee
o) optional
p) to rotate around a center
q) to envisage; to imagine
r) observation
s) facts or items of proof
t) success

Exercise C

1. What sets jazz musicians apart from their peers in other musical genres is their ability to _____.

2. Please, do not _____ from the architect's blueprint.

3. In graduate school, I continued to study philosophy of my own _____.

4. In the Christian Church, a _____ may be held the night before a festival or holy day.

5. The foreman's job is to _____ the line workers and make sure the machines are kept in good repair.

6. It is _____ that he is skilled at both analyzing and writing code; he quickly fixed several bugs that had bedeviled the other software engineers for weeks.

7. In the children's mystery story, the _____ ink on the back of the map could be made visible with a mild solution of lemon juice and water.

8. The hackers' _____ methods matched their unethical aims: to blackmail corporations into paying them to prevent denial-of-service attacks.

9. His _____ was dependent on his ability to evade the Mafia assassins.

10. We had a hard time _____ the wrinkled old lady as a once-famous beauty – until we saw her wedding photos.

11. In 2007, we celebrate the 100th anniversary of Rachel Carson, an early _____ for the environment who wrote about the devastating effects of DDT on the entire food chain.

12. Your attendance at the lecture is mandatory, but the T.A.'s discussion session is _____.

13. Our _____ at the homecoming game this year was even sweeter after last year's losing streak.

14. Charles Darwin scandalized the religious establishment with his claim that humans _____ from the great apes.

15. At the end of the month, the landlord always threatened to _____ any tenants who did not pay their rent on time.

16. Swordfishing on George's Bank is my _____.

17. When the weather is warm and humid, the fans over our beds _____ and keep us cool.

18. The prosecutor presented ample circumstantial _____ that he had committed the crime, so the jury convicted him.

19. Government _____ of our citizenry has greatly increased since the terrorist attacks of Sept. 11, 2001.

20. Children love superheroes because they are _____.

Exercise D

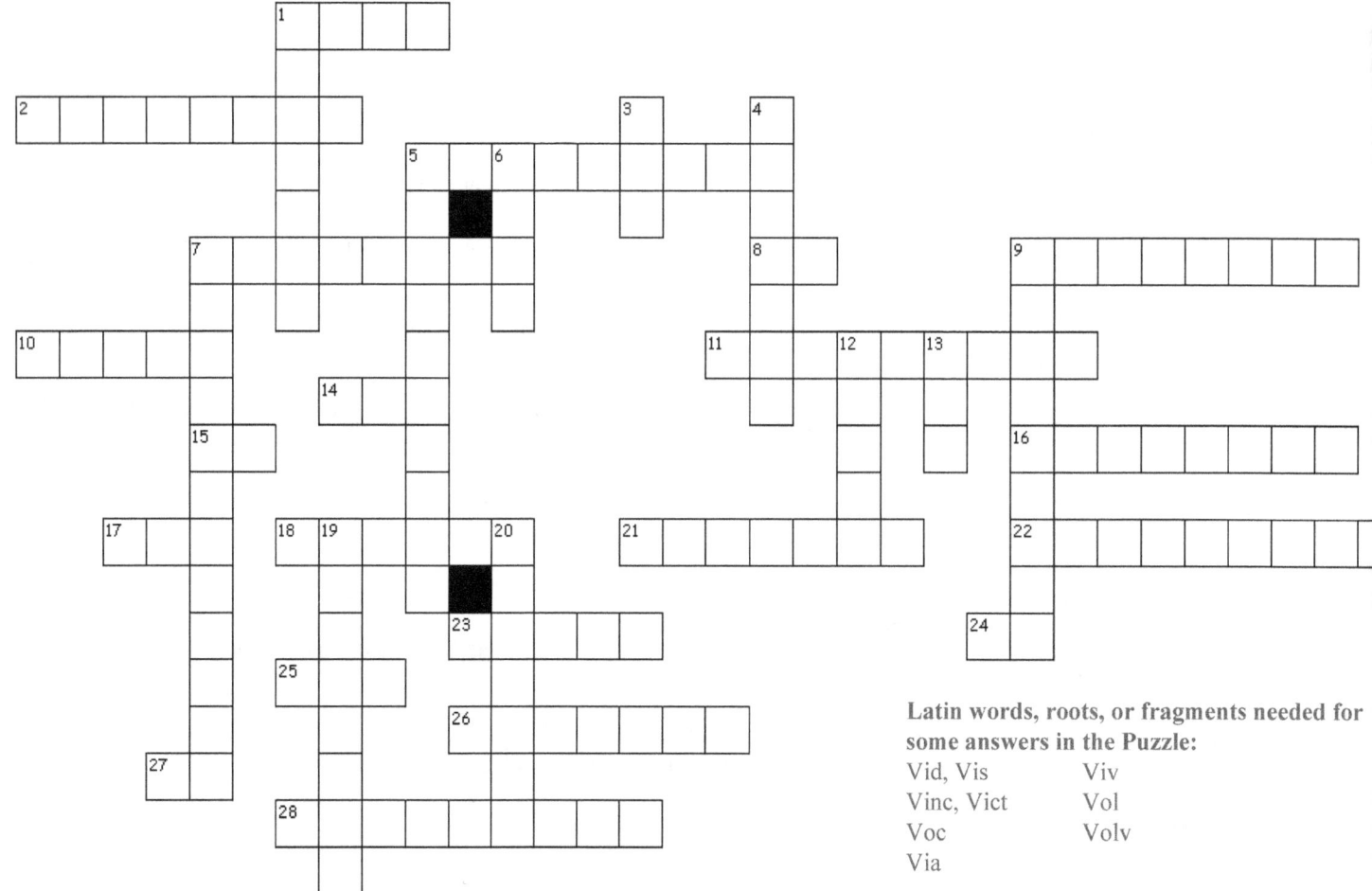

Latin words, roots, or fragments needed for some answers in the Puzzle:
Vid, Vis   Viv
Vinc, Vict   Vol
Voc   Volv
Via

Across
1. to conquer (l)
2. facts or items of proof
5. unable to be seen
7. the continued existence of (someone or something)
8. in or not (l)
9. an occupation; a calling
10. over (l)
11. to oversee
14. to call (l)
15. out (l)
16. a supporter or promoter
17. wish (l)
18. to develop slowly
21. to diverge from
22. to ad lib
23. a night watch
24. back, again (l)
25. to live (l)
26. to rotate around a center
27. down, from (l)
28. optional

Down
1. success
3. to see (l)
4. sneaky; not straight
5. invulnerable
6. to roll (l)
7. observation
9. to envisage; to imagine
12. to oust
13. way (l)
19. free will
20. obvious

Quiz 5

Quiz answers begin on page 318

> *evacuate, controversy, stellar, vacant, invincible, victory, pertain, surveillance, constant, context, instruction, evident, event, turbid, improvise, devious, survival, aspire, spectators, dissolve, abundant, invisible, evolve*

1. In the _____ of an emergency, citizens must _____ their homes immediately.

2. The _____ over allowing gay men and lesbians to serve openly in the military has not ended, even with the repeal of "Don't ask, don't tell."

3. It was immediately _____ that the Driver's Education student was not ready to get behind the wheel, so the instructor had him practice on the simulator first.

4. After the team won its tenth straight _____ and moved into first place, the players' confidence and winning attitude made their team _____.

5. The sign outside the run-down motel always said "_____."

6. The Ukraine, once known as the "bread basket" of the Soviet Union for its _____ crops, was decimated: first by collective farming, and later by the Chernobyl nuclear disaster.

7. Although his contribution was interesting, it did not _____ to the topic.

8. Foreign language students often must rely on the _____ of a sentence or paragraph to decide which of several dictionary definitions applies to a particular use of a word.

9. His SAT scores were _____, helping earn him admission to Yale.

10. Cruise control keeps a driver's car at a _____ speed.

11. He _____ to play in the NBA, but his coaches gave him little formal _____.

12. Because of the widespread deployment of _____ cameras, even the most _____ robbers can no longer sneak around as though they were _____.

13. The ability to walk on two legs must have given the earliest humans a _____ advantage; therefore, we _____ to be exclusively bipedal.

14. The red clay partially _____ in the water, giving it a _____ appearance.

15. The _____ cheered after the saxophone player _____ a soul-stirring solo.

Answer Key

(Answers to Exercise B further down)

Lesson I

EXERCISE C

1. abduct
2. abhor
3. abrupt
4. absorb
5. abrasion
6. accord
7. adversary
8. adhered
9. adjacent
10. adaptable
11. ambiguous
12. ambidextrous
13. ante meridian
14. anticipate
15. benediction
16. bicuspid
17. bisected
18. bilateral
19. benefactor
20. bilingual

EXERCISE A

1. AB-, ABS- from, away
2. DUC- to lead
3. HOR- to shudder
4. RAD- to scrape, shave
5. RUMP-, RUPT- to break
6. SORB- to soak in
7. CORD- heart, mind, spirit
8. HER, HES- to stick
9. JAC, JEC- to throw, lay down
10. VERT- to turn
11. DEXTER- right (hand)
12. AG- to drive, to act
13. MERIDIES- noon
14. CAP- to take
15. DICT- to say
16. FAC-, FIC- to do, to make
17. CUSPIS- sharp point
18. LATUS- side
19. BI- two
20. BENE- good
21. ANTE- before
22. AMBI- both
23. AC-, AD- to, toward
24. LINGUA- language
25. SECT- cut

EXERCISE D

Across
2. fac 4. meridies 9. bi 12. antemeridian 13. cord 14. benediction 18. ambiguous 20. anticipate 22. ab 23. lingua 24. adaptable 27. ac or ad 28. sect 31. rad 32. abhor 34. cap 35. dexter 36. jac 37. bicuspid 38. hor

Down
1. bisect 3. abrasion 5. adjacent 6. rump 7. absorb 8. dict 10. ante 11. ambi 12. ambidextrous 13. cuspis 15. ag 16. sorb 17. latus 18. adversary 19. Bilateral 21. duc 24. adhere 25. accord 26. benefactor 29. abduct 30. vert 32. abrupt 33. her 37. bilingual

Lesson II

EXERCISE C

1. contrast
2. contraband
3. circumscribed
4. contradicting
5. circulated
6. circumstantial
7. condone
8. collision
9. commiserate
10. collaborated
11. devoured
12. demented
13. demoted
14. deterred
15. decadence
16. dedicated
17. distinct
18. duplicate
19. distortion
20. duet
21. distract

EXERCISE A

1. CIRCUM- around
2. CIRCULUS- circle
3. SCRIB- to write
4. STARE- to stand
5. CO- together
6. LABOR- to work
7. LAED- to strike
8. MISERARI- to pity, to lament
9. DON- to give
10. CONTRA- against
11. BANNUS- ban
12. DICT- to say, to devote
13. DE- down, from
14. CAD- to fall
15. DIC- to say, to devote
16. MENTIS- mind
17. MOT-, MOV- to move
18. TERR- to scare
19. VOR- to eat
20. STINGU- mark off, seperate
21. TORT- to turn, to twist
22. TRACT- to pull
23. DUO- two
24. PLIC- to fold
25. DIS- apart

298

EXERCISE D

Across

2. demented 5. dict 9. devour 11. collision 14. contradict 16. dict 20. mentis 22. circumstantial 26. labor 27. contrast 28. duo 29. decadence 31. miserari 33. tort 34. de 36. dedicate 38. commiserate 39. distract

Down

1. bannus 3. mot 4. duet 6. circum 7. dis 8. contra 10. don 12. laed 13. circulus 14. circulate 15. vor 17. collaborate 18. deter 19. cad 22. co 23. contraband 24. terr 25. plic 27. condone 30. distinct 32. stare 35. demote 37. scrib

Lesson III

EXERCISE C

1. equivalent
2. emigrated
3. eradicated
4. evoke
5. equities
6. extroverts
7. illuminate
8. implicating
9. inclusive
10. inscription
11. illegible
12. irrelevant
13. illiterate
14. incessant
15. intersect
16. interlude
17. intravenous
18. introvert
19. intervene
20. interjection

EXERCISE A

1. EQUI- equal
2. VAL- strong
3. EX- out
4. MIGR- to move
5. RADIC- to take root
6. EXTRA- outside
7. VERT- to turn
8. IL- in, not
9. LUMIN- to light up
10. IM- in, not
11. PLIC- to fold
12. CLAUS- to close, to shut
13. IN- in, not
14. SCRIB- to write
15. LEG- to read
16. LITTERA- letter, books
17. CESS- to cease
18. IR- in, not
19. RELEV- to raise up, to elevate
20. INTER- between
21. JAC-, JEC- to throw, lay down
22. LUD-, LUS- to play, game
23. SECT- to cut
24. VENI- to come
25. VENA- vein
26. INTRA- within
27. INTRO- inside

EXERCISE D

Across

3. lumin 5. 7. inter, intra, or intro 9. equivalent 11. illegible 16. littera 17. extrovert 18. intervene 21. migr 23. ex 24. intravenous 25. illuminate 26. equi 29. sect 30. inclusive 32. emigrate 35. jac or jec 37. incessant 41. irrelevant 42. interjection 43. vert

Down

1. val 2. illiterate 4. interlude 6. implicate 7. im, in, or il 8. intra 10. intersect 11. intra or intro 12. im, in, or il 13. extra 14. plic 15. veni 19. relev 20. equity 22. introvert 24. im, in, or il 27. inscription 28. 29. scrib 31. vena 33. im, in, or il 34. evoke 36. leg 38. claus 39. eradicate 40. cess

Lesson IV

EXERCISE C

1. magnificent
2. multilateral
3. major
4. malicious
5. magnitude
6. majority
7. multitude
8. obliterate
9. obsessing
10. obligation
11. persevere
12. perforated
13. perspective
14. omnivorous
15. postpone
16. prediction
17. precluded
18. presume
19. postscript
20. posterity

EXERCISE A

1. MAGNUS- big, great
2. FAC-, FIC- to do, to make
3. MALIGNUS- evil
4. MULTI- many
5. LATERAL- side

6. OB- over, towards, against
7. LIG- to bind
8. LITTERA- letter, books
9. SID- sit, stay, besiege
10. OMNI- all
11. VOR- to eat
12. PER- completely, through
13. FOR- to pierce
14. SEVERUS- severe
15. SPECT-, SPIC- to look
16. POST- after, behind
17. PON- to place
18. SCRIB- to write
19. PRE-, PRAE- before
20. CLAUS- to close, to shut
21. DIC- to say
22. SUM- to take

EXERCISE D

Across

3. major 4. multilateral 6. sum 8. for 10. magnificent 11. postpone 14. posterity 15. malicious 18. obligation 19. presume 20. dic 21. post 22. multi 23. vor 24. per 25. lateral 26. pon 28. preclude 29. perforate 31. scrib 32. severus 33. perspective

Down

1. claus 2. obliterate 3. majority 4. magnitude 5. littera 6. spic 7. magnus 9. omni 10. malignus 12. lig 13. multitude 14. prae 16. sid 17. fac 18. ob 21. persevere 27. obsess 30. omnivorous

Lesson V

EXERCISE C

1. primary
2. primate
3. proceed
4. procession
5. provoked
6. profit
7. recite
8. reiterated
9. retrospect
10. recline
11. secluded
12. secure
13. supervised
14. suggested
15. suffocate
16. subscribe
17. unanimous
18. translucent
19. unity
20. transparent

EXERCISE A

1. PRIM- first
2. PRO- forward
3. CED-, CESS- to yield
4. FAC-, FIC- to do, to make
5. VOC- to call
6. RE- back, again
7. CIT- read out, summon
8. CLIN- to lean
9. ITERARE- to repeat
10. SPECT-, SPIC- to look
11. RETRO- backward
12. SE- apart
13. CLAUS- to close, to shut
14. CURA- care, concern
15. SUB- under
16. FAUCES- throat
17. SCRIB- to write
18. GER- to supply, to prompt
19. SUPER- over
20. VID-, VIS- to see
21. TRANS- across
22. LUC- to shine
23. PARERE- to show
24. UNI- one
25. ANIM- spirit, mind, life

EXERCISE D

Across

1. se 6. reiterate 7. uni 8. fic 11. re 12. pro 14. super 15. recline 17. voc 20. fauces 22. profit 23. transparent 25. proceed 26. suggest 27. anim 28. ger 29. procession 31. provoke 32. unanimous 34. clin 35. unity 36. subscribe 38. retrospect 39. cit

Down

1. suffocate 2. retro 3. primary 4. trans 5. luc 9. iterare 10. primate 13. secure 15. recite 16. ced 18. claus 19. vis 21. supervise 24. translucent 26. spect 30. seclude 31. prim 33. sub 37. scrib

Lesson VI

EXERCISE C

1. acrid
2. alias
3. agility
4. altitude
5. acute
6. agitate
7. alienate
8. alter
9. aliens
10. agriculture
11. annual
12. inept
13. animosity
14. animate
15. amateur
16. aptitude
17. aperture
18. annuity

19. amiable
20. ambulatory

EXERCISE A

1. AC- sharp, pungent
2. AG- to drive, to urge
3. AGRI- field
4. CULTURA- growing
5. ALI- another
6. ALT- other
7. APT- fit
8. ALTI- high
9. AM- to love
10. AMBUL- to walk
11. ANIM- spirit, mind, life
12. IN- on or not
13. APER- to open
14. ANNUS- year

EXERCISE D

Across

1. agri 4. am 5. annual 6. ag 7. alias 8. agriculture 10. animosity 12. acrid 13. alt 16. annuity 18. agility 19. aperture 20. altitude

Down

1. amiable 2. im, in, or il 3. alti 4. ambul 5. annus 6. aptitude 7. aper 8. apt 9. ambulatory 10. anim 11. animate 12. ali 14. inept 15. alienate 16. alter 17. cultura 18. alien

Lesson VII

1. beatitude
2. battery
3. audible
4. army
5. audience
6. artifacts
7. artificial
8. avuncular
9. auditorium
10. casualty
11. abbreviation
12. candid
13. rebellious
14. brevity
15. candidate
16. incantation
17. imbibe
18. recalcitrant
19. capture
20. participated

EXERCISE A

1. ARM- weapon
2. ART- skill, craft
3. BELLUM- war
4. FAC-, FIC- to do, to make
5. ALI- another
6. AUD- to hear
7. AVUNCULUS- uncle
8. BATTU- to strike, to beat
9. BEATUS- blessed
10. PARS-, PART- part
11. BIB- to drink
12. BREVE- brief, short
13. CAS- to fall
14. CALCITR- to kick, resist
15. CANDIDUS- transparent, white, glow
16. IM- in, not
17. RE- back, again
18. CANT- to sing
19. CAP- to take

EXERCISE D

Across

3. fac or fic 5. abbreviation 9. avunculus 10. aud 11. artificial 14. battu 15. artifact 16. beatitude 17. bib 18. candid 21. breve 23. re 24. capture 25. recalcitrant 28. army 32. calcitr 33. cas 35. beatus

Down

1. incantation 2. auditorium 4. audience 5. avuncular 6. audible 7. candidate 8. battery 12. imbibe 14. brevity 19. art 20. bellum 22. arm 26. cant 27. casualty 29. participate 34. rebellious

Lesson VIII

EXERCISE C

1. carnivorous
2. discernment
3. decapitate
4. castigated
5. cerebral
6. access
7. census
8. accessories
9. decelerates
10. censor
11. accelerate
12. incision
13. century
14. incited
15. civilian
16. concise
17. centennial
18. civilization
19. excite
20. civil

EXERCISE A

1. DE- down, from
2. CAPUT- head
3. CARN- flesh, meat
4. VOR- to eat
5. CIVIS- citizen
6. CASTIG- to punish
7. CEREBRUM- brain
8. DIS- apart
9. CERN- to seperate

10. AC-, AD- to, toward
11. CED-, CESS- to yield
12. CELER- fast
13. CENS- to assess
14. CENT- one hundred
15. CON- against
16. CAED-, CIS- to cut, to kill
17. IN- in, not
18. EX- out
19. CIT- to start, call

EXERCISE D

Across

4. accessory 6. de 10. censor 11. ac 13. concise 14. cerebrum 15. cens 19. discernment 21. decapitate 23. castig 27. im, in, or il 29. excite 30. carnivorous 31. ex 32. access 34. decelerate 35. incision

Down

1. century 2. cern 3. carn 5. castigate 7. civilian 8. accelerate 9. census 12. cerebral 14. cit 16. civis 17. caput 18. cent 20. civil 22. civilization 24. celer 25. centennial 26. vor 28. dis 30. caed 33. ced

Lesson IX

EXERCISE C

1. cloister
2. clarify
3. clarity
4. acclaim
5. closure
6. enclosure
7. inclined
8. decline
9. comply
10. copious
11. accolades
12. complement
13. cognition
14. incognito
15. cordial
16. incorporate
17. creed
18. corpses
19. credible
20. recluse

EXERCISE A

1. AC-, AD- to, toward
2. CLAM- to shout
3. CLAR- clear
4. CLAUS- to close, to shut
5. RE- back, again
6. DE- down, from
7. CLIN- to lean
8. CRED- to believe
9. COGNIT- to learn
10. COLLUM- neck
11. COMPL- to fill
12. COPLA- plenty
13. CORD- heart, mind, spirit
14. CORPUS- body

EXERCISE D

Across

1. clin 3. clar 4. re 7. ac 9. closure 10. copious 11. inclined 12. decline 13. clarity 16. acclaim 17. cord 18. corpse 21. cognit 22. complement 23. accolade 24. claus, clau 25. enclosure 27. cloister

Down

1. clam 2. incognito 3. corpus 4. recluse 5. cognition 6. de 8. compl 10. cordial 13. credible 14. incorporate 15. comply 19. copia 20. cred 22. clarify 26. creed

Lesson X

EXERCISE C

1. crescendo
2. succumb
3. culpable
4. cruciform
5. incumbent
6. cupidity
7. accrue
8. docile
9. mandate
10. curriculum
11. trident
12. data
13. concur
14. indentation
15. domestic
16. domain
17. dominant
18. diction
19. verdict
20. dictator

EXERCISE A

1. CRESC- to grow
2. AC-, AD- to, toward
3. CRUC- cross
4. FORMA- shape
5. CUMB- to lie down
6. SUB- under
7. CULPA- fault, guilt
8. CUPI- to desire
9. CURR- to run
10. DO-, DA-, DAT- to give
11. MANUS- hand
12. DENT- tooth
13. TRI- three
14. DICT- to say
15. VERUS- true
16. DOC- to teach
17. DOMUS- house
18. DOMIN- to rule
19. IN- in, not
20. CON- together

EXERCISE D

Across

1. dictator 7. indentation 9. cruc 11. domin 13. domestic 14. forma 17. domus 18. crescendo 20. da or do 22. ac or ad 23. succumb 24. dict 28. incumbent 29. culpable 31. accrue 32. docile 33. cruciform 34. mandate

Down

2. cupidity 3. con 4. tri 5. manus 6. verdict 8. data 10. cresc 11. diction 12. trident 13. dominant 15. curr 16. domain 18. cumb 19. cupi 20. doc 21. culpa 23. sub 25. curriculum 26. in 27. verus 29. concur 30. dent

Lesson XI

EXERCISE C

1. egocentric
2. equal
3. dormant
4. erratic
5. erroneous
6. endorsed
7. façade
8. fervor
9. facsimile
10. deface
11. infallible
12. fiction
13. falsify
14. affinity
15. fidelity
16. conferred
17. finite
18. fertile
19. figurative
20. configuration

EXERCISE A

1. DORMI- to sleep
2. IN- in, not
3. DORSUM- back
4. EGO- I
5. EQU- equal
6. ERR- to wander
7. FAC-, FIC- to do, to make
8. SIMIL- same
9. FIGUR-, FING- to shape
10. DE- down, from
11. FACIES- face
12. FALSUS- false
13. FALL- to deceive, fail
14. CON- together
15. FER- to bring, to carry
16. FERV- to boil
17. FIDES- faith
18. FINIS- end
19. AC-, AD- to, toward
20. FIGURATIVUS- symbolic

EXERCISE D

Across

2. fervor 3. dormant 5. fall 6. fing 7. ac 9. fac or fic 11. im, in, or il 13. endorse 16. de 18. ego 19. fertile 21. figurative 22. com or con 24. figurativus 25. simil 26. dormi 28. infallible 29. deface 31.

Down

1. confer 2. fidelity 4. affinity 5. facsimile 6. facade 8. configuration 9. fer 10. falsify 12. erroneous 13. egocentric 14. err 15. erratic 17. equal 19. fiction 20. equ 21. fides 23. finite 24. facies 27. ferv 29. dorsum 30. falsus

Lesson XII

EXERCISE C

1. fluid
2. floral
3. confirmed
4. deflect
5. infirmary
6. fragile
7. forum
8. inflection
9. fugitive
10. fortunate
11. fraternal
12. fragments
13. confronted
14. diffuse
15. fusion
16. gorge
17. genre
18. generous
19. genuine
20. generate

EXERCISE A

1. CON- together
2. FIRMUS- strong
3. GEN- birth, family
4. GURG- throat
5. FLECT- to bend
6. FLORIS- flower
7. FLU- to flow
8. FORTIS- luck
9. FORUM- public place
10. FRAG-, FRACT- to break
11. FRATER- brother
12. FRONS-, FRONT- front
13. FUG- to flee
14. FUS- to pour

EXERCISE D

Across

1. frag 2. floral 5. fluid 8. gorge 9. fus 10. confirm 14. genuine 16. infirmary

303

20. gen 22. confront
26. generous 27. con
28. deflect 30. generate
31. frater

Down

1. firmus 3. fug 4. forum
5. flect 6. il, im, or in
7. floris 9. fragment
11. inflection 12. fortis
13. gurg 15. frons or front
17. fraternal 18. fragile
19. diffuse 21. fortunate
23. flu 24. fugitive 25. genre
29. de 31. fusion

Lesson XIII

EXERCISE C

1. congregation
2. junction
3. inherent
4. gratitude
5. prejudice
6. itinerary
7. graduation
8. ingredient
9. inject
10. juncture
11. irate
12. incense
13. graduated
14. projectile
15. impelled
16. transition
17. transit
18. jocular
19. gradual
20. congratulation

EXERCISE A

1. GRAD- step, advance
2. IN- in, not
3. PRO- forward
4. CON- together
5. GRAT- favor, please
6. GREG- flock, herd
7. HER- to stick
8. IMPEL- drive, persuade
9. INCEND- to set fire
10. IRA- anger
11. ITER- journey, road
12. TRANS- across
13. ITUM- moved
14. JAC-, JEC- to throw, lay down
15. JOCUS- joke
16. JUDIC- to judge
17. PRE, PRAE- before
18. JUNCT- to join

EXERCISE D

Across

3. her 4. juncture
8. ingredient 9. transit
12. inject 13. jocus
14. inherent 17. gratitude
18. progress 19. impel
20. grad 21. junct 22. pre
24. incend 25. itum
26. congratulation 27. ira
28. gradual 29. projectile
30. transition

Down

1. trans 2. irate 4. judic
5. con 6. graduate 7. jac
10. itinerary 15. junction
16. pro 17. greg 19. iter
21. jocular 22. prejudice
23. congregation

Lesson XIV

EXERCISE C

1. eloquent
2. League
3. deluge
4. liberal
5. legitimate
6. locality
7. delegate
8. legacy
9. collateral
10. colloquial
11. levity
12. liberty
13. delusions
14. lingual
15. literal
16. illuminate
17. laborious
18. elusive
19. license
20. lucid

EXERCISE A

1. LABOR- to work
2. CON- together
3. LATERAL- side
4. DE- down, from
5. LEGIS- law
6. LAV- wash away
7. LEVIS- to rise
8. LIBER- free
9. LICENCIA- freedom
10. LIG- to bind
11. LINGUA- language
12. LITTERA- letter
13. LOCUS- place
14. LOQU- to talk
15. LUMIN- to light up
16. LUCIS- light
17. LUD-, LUS- to play, game
18. EX- out

EXERCISE D

Across

2. lumin 3. locus 5. labor 6. colloquial 9. legitimate 12. league 13. literal 17. liberal 18. lateral 20. eloquent 24. licencia 25. illuminate 26. lucid 28. license 30. laborious 31. lav 32. lingua

Down

1. lingual 2. locality 4. loqu
5. legacy 7. lig 8. collateral 9.
liberty 10. ex 11. lud or lus
14. liber 17. littera 19. levis
21. lucis 22. deluge 23.
delusion 27. de 28. legis 29.
elusive 30. levity

Lesson XV

EXERCISE C

1. manufacture
2. immersion
3. mediocre
4. minimal
5. medieval
6. motion
7. promise
8. manipulate
9. memorabilia
10. matrimony
11. memory
12. merge
13. maternal
14. missile
15. moment
16. mandatory
17. maritime
18. mend
19. momentum
20. minimize

EXERCISE A

1. MANUS- hand
2. DO-, DA-, DAT- to give
3. FAC-, FIC- to do, to make
4. MAR-, MOR- sea
5. MATER- mother
6. PRO- forward
7. MEDIUS- middle
8. MEM- to remember
9. MENDUM- defect, fault
10. IN- in, not
11. MERG- to plunge
12. MINUS- small

13. MISSUS- thrown
14. PRO- forward
15. MITT-, MISS- to send forth
16. MOT-, MOV- to move

EXERCISE D

Across

2. moment 4. in 5.
memorabilia 6. maritime 8.
mem 9. missus 10. mendum
12. merg 13. da 15.
momentum 18. mot 20.
minimize 21. immersion 23.
mandatory 24. mend 25. mar
or mor 26. minus 27. manus

Down

1. matrimony 2. minimal 3.
fac 5. mediocre 7. missile
8. manufacture 11. minimal
12. maternal 14. promise
15. mater 16. medieval
17. motion 19. mitt or miss
20. merge 22. memory
23. manipulate 25. medius

Lesson XVI

EXERCISE C

1. native
2. immortal
3. mountain
4. innovation
5. mortify
6. commute
7. navigated
8. nocturnal
9. novelty
10. announce
11. mutates
12. mustered
13. negate
14. annihilate
15. monitor

16. Naval
17. nominal
18. negative
19. morality
20. novice

EXERCISE A

1. MON- to warn, advise
2. MONS- mountain
3. MOR- custom
4. MORT- to die
5. COM- together
6. MUT- to change
7. NAT- born
8. NAVIS- ship
9. AG- to drive, to urg
10. NEG- to deny
11. NIHIL- nothing
12. NOMEN- name
13. IN- in, not
14. NOV- to make new
15. NOCT- night
16. NUNCI- to announce
17. AC-, AD- to, toward
18. FAC-, FIC- to do, to work

EXERCISE D

Lesson 16

Across

2. navigate 4. neg 6. nunci 7.
mut 8. fac 10. mort 11.
innovation 14. commute 15.
com or con 16. mon 17. il,
im, or in 18. nocturnal 19.
noct 22. nominal 24. muster
25. monitor 27. nihil 28.
announce 29. mutate

Down

1. nat 2. negate 3. immortal 5.
native 6. navis 7. morality 9.
novice 10. mountain 12.
negative 13. nomen 18.

305

novelty 20. nov 21. annihilate 23. mortify 25. mons 26. naval 29. mor 30. ag

Lesson XVII

EXERCISE C

1. patron
2. operate
3. pacify
4. ostentatious
5. repast
6. passionate
7. ordain
8. impeccable
9. pedestrian
10. olfactory
11. pedal
12. oculist
13. orbit
14. odious
15. patriotism
16. orator
17. pendant
18. ornate
19. propeller
20. pecuniary

EXERCISE A

1. OCULUS- eye
2. ODI- to hate
3. OLE- smell
4. OPER- to work
5. ORA- to speak, to pray
6. ORBIS- circle, orbit
7. ORDO- rank
8. ORN- to adorn
9. OSTEND- to exhibit
10. PASC- to feed
11. PASS- to suffer
12. PATER- father
13. PAX- peace
14. RE- back, again
15. PEC- to sin
16. PECUNIA- money
17. PELL- to drive
18. PEND- to hang
19. PED- foot
20. IM- in, not

EXERCISE D

Across

1. ordain 4. pacify 7. ostentatious 8. pedestrian 10. orbit 11. pend 12. pecunia 15. patron 18. pater 19. orator 20. pro 22. odi 23. repast 25. orbis 26. ped 29. oculus 30. ostend 31. pell 32. pedal 33. pass

Down

1. olfactory 2. operate 3. passionate 5. impeccable 6. ornate 9. re 10. oculist 11. pendant 13. patriotism 14. ora 16. propeller 17. orn 19. odious 21. ordo 24. pecuniary 26. pax 27. pec 28. in 29. ole 30. oper 32. pasc

Lesson XVIII

EXERCISE C

1. potable
2. predatory
3. reprisal
4. postpone
5. placid
6. pittance
7. depict
8. opportune
9. proponent
10. potion
11. impotent
12. portable
13. apprehend
14. pontiff
15. potential
16. petition
17. ponderous
18. imposter
19. piety
20. appetite

EXERCISE A

1. AC-, AD- to, toward
2. PET- to seek
3. DE- down, from
4. PICTUS- painted
5. PLAC- to appease
6. PIUS- religiously devoted
7. IN- in, not
8. PON- to put
9. POST- after
10. PRO- forward
11. PONDUS- weight
12. PONS- bridge
13. FAC-, FIC- to do, to make
14. PORT- to carry
15. OB- over, towards, against
16. PORTUS- harbor
17. POTEN- powerful
18. POT- to drink
19. PRAEDA- spoils of war
20. PREHEND- to catch
21. RE- back, again

EXERCISE D

Across

2. pon 3. fac 6. ob 7. postpone 9. de 10. port 11. impotent 13. reprisal 15. apprehend 19. petition 21. ponderous 22. pet 23. predatory 24. piety 25. ac 26. poten 29. prehend 30. imposter 32. post

Down

1. pictus 2. potion 4. appetite 5. portable 8. potable 10. plac 12. proponent 14. pius 16. depict 17. pons 18. opportune 20. praeda 23. placid 24.

pontiff 26. pondus 27. potential 28. portus 29. pot 31. pittance

Lesson XIX

EXERCISE C

1. ratio
2. rapture
3. interrupt
4. regular
5. oppressed
6. arrogant
7. rotate
8. rupture
9. rationale
10. compute
11. amputate
12. interrogative
13. ridicule
14. rectify
15. pungent
16. rational
17. interrogate
18. punish
19. derogatory
20. rector
21. derided

EXERCISE A

1. AC-, AD- to, toward
2. PRESS- to press
3. PUNG- to puncture
4. PUNI- to punish
5. AMBI- around
6. PUT- to think
7. COM- together
8. RAP- to seize
9. RATIO- reasoning
10. RID- to laugh at
11. REX- to rule
12. DE- down, from
13. FAC-, FIC- to do, to make
14. ROG- to ask
15. INTER- between
16. ROT- to turn
17. RUPT- to break

EXERCISE D

Across

2. puni 4. put 5. interrogate 7. rap 8. rotate 11. de 12. pung 14. rupture 15. ratio 16. rational 20. pungent 25. rationale 27. interrogative 31. deride 32. rex

Down

1. rupt 3. interrupt 4. press 6. rapture 9. inter 10. compute 11. derogatory 13. rid 14. rot 17. oppress 18. amputate 19. punish 21. fac 22. rog 23. con or com 24. rector 26. ambi 28. arrogant 29. ridicule 30. rectify

Lesson XX

EXERCISE C

1. dissect
2. assault
3. sensory
4. saline
5. sacred
6. prescribe
7. consensus
8. consecutive
9. senile
10. sequence
11. manuscript
12. sacrament
13. session
14. resent
15. sanguine
16. consequences
17. sequel
18. segment
19. assailed
20. satiate

EXERCISE A

1. SACR- holy
2. MENTIS- mind
3. SALT- to jump
4. SALIS- salt
5. SANGUIS- blood
6. SATIS- enough
7. PRAE- before
8. SCRIB- to write
9. MANUS- hand
10. SENT-, SENS- to think, to feel
11. SECT- to cut
12. CON- together
13. SEQUI- to follow
14. SENILIS- old

EXERCISE D

Across

1. sacred 3. satis 4. sens or sent 5. manuscript 6. sanguis 8. sequence 9. assault 14. senile 15. con or com 17. sequel 18. manus 21. assail 23. consequence 24. dissect 25. senilis 27. mentis 28. sect 29. pre

Down

1. session 2. consecutive 3. sacrament 6. sanguine 7. scrib 10. satiate 11. segment 12. saline 13. sequi 14. salt 15. consensus 16. resent 17. salis 19. sacr 20. prescribe 22. re 24. de 26. sensory

Lesson XXI

EXERCISE C

1. perspective
2. absolute
3. aspersions
4. disperse

5. simultaneous
6. resolution
7. simulate
8. despicable
9. dissolve
10. insomnia
11. solitude
12. resonate
13. simile
14. supersonic
15. spectacle
16. solo
17. resolve
18. spectator
19. Sonar
20. spectrum

EXERCISE A

1. SIMIL- similar
2. SIMUL- to copy
3. SOLUS- alone
4. PER- completely, through
5. AB-, ABS- from, away
6. SOLV- to loosen
7. DIS- apart
8. RE- back, again
9. SOMN- sleep
10. SON- to sound
11. SUPER- over
12. SPARG- to scatter
13. SPECT-, SPIC- to look

EXERCISE D

Across

3. sonar 6. dis 8. resolution 10. re 12. super 13. simul 14. per 16. spectator 18. supersonic 20. de 24. dissolve 25. solv 26. solitude 27. ab 28. insomnia 29. solo

Down

1. aspersion 2. disperse 4. absolute 5. simile 7. simulate 9. son 10. resonate 11. spectrum 14. perspective 15. spectacle 16. simil 17. sparg 18. simultaneous 19. somn 21. despicable 22. resolve 23. solus 26. spect

Lesson XXII

EXERCISE C

1. tangible
2. obstruct
3. contemporary
4. aspire
5. constant
6. presume
7. constricted
8. spiritual
9. temperaments
10. stellar
11. respiratory
12. temper
13. construct
14. Temporal
15. conspiracy
16. tangent
17. suave
18. constellations
19. instruct

EXERCISE A

1. AC-, AD- to, toward
2. SPIR- to breathe
3. CON- together
4. RE- back, again
5. PRE-, PRAE- before
6. STELLA- star
7. STRICT- to bind
8. STRUCT- to build
9. OB- over, towards, against
10. SUAVIS- delightful
11. SUM- to take
12. TANG- to touch
13. TEMPER- to mix
14. TEMPOR- time

EXERCISE D

Across

1. stella 3. instruct 5. conspiracy 6. temperament 8. presume 9. tang 10. obstruct 13. temper 14. suave 16. con or com 17. ob 21. respiratory 25. tangible 26. tempor 27. sum 29. ac or ad 30. constant

Down

2. tangent 4. contemporary 7. strict 11. temporal 12. suavis 14. spiritual 15. constrict 18. aspire 19. prae 20. constellation 22. struct 24. spir 28. stellar 30. construct

Lesson XXIII

EXERCISE C

1. Mediterranean
2. ultimatum
3. distort
4. extraterrestrials
5. pertinent
6. context
7. ultimate
8. totalitarian
9. subterranean
10. abundant
11. terrain
12. intrude
13. terminate
14. detracted
15. pertain
16. corrupt
17. redundant
18. contort
19. extract
20. turbid

EXERCISE A

1. PER- completely, through
2. TEN- to hold
3. TERM- end
4. EXTRA- outside
5. TERR- land
6. MENDIUS- middle
7. SUB- under
8. CON- together
9. TEX- to weave
10. TORT- to twist, to turn
11. DIS- apart
12. TOTUS- total
13. TRACT- to pull
14. EX- out
15. TRUD-, TRUS- to thrust
16. IN- in, not
17. TURB- to disturb
18. ULTIM- beyond
19. RUMP-, RUPT- to break
20. CO- together
21. AC-, AD- to, toward
22. RE- back, again
23. UND- to flow

EXERCISE D

Across

4. terminate 5. medius 7. detract 9. totus 12. dis 13. subterranean 16. de 18. terr 19. extract 21. totalitarian 23. corrupt 25. und 26. term 27. terrain 30. turbid 33. sub 36. intrude

Down

1. extraterrestrial 2. context 3. per 4. tract 6. distort 8. contort 10. ultimate 11. pertain 14. tex 15. ex 17. ultimatum 18. ten 19. extra 20. con 22. tort 23. co 24. ultim 28. rump or rupt 29. abundant 30. turb 31. redundant 34. pertinent 35. mediterranean

Lesson XXIV

EXERCISE C

1. event
2. advent
3. verbose
4. urban
5. invasion
6. diversion
7. verbal
8. evasive
9. vindictive
10. controversy
11. vindicated
12. verity
13. adversity
14. venting
15. vacant
16. prevail
17. verify
18. evacuate
19. urbane

EXERCISE A

1. URBS- city
2. EX- out
3. VAC- empty
4. VAD- to go
5. PRE, PRAE- before
6. VAL- to be strong
7. VINDIC- to avenge
8. AC- AD- to toward
9. VENI- to come
10. DIS- aside
11. VENTUS- wind
12. VERUS- true
13. FAC- to do, to make
14. VERBUM- true
15. VERT- to turn

EXERCISE D

Across

2. verify 5. verbum 9. fac 11. urban 12. urbs 15. veni 16. vindictive 18. ac or ad 19. invasion 21. val 23. avenge 24. prae 25. evasive 27. verbose 29. controversy

Down

1. adversity 2. verus 3. verity 4. tort 5. vindicate 6. advent 7. vacant 8. prevail 10. evacuate 13. dis 14. verbal 15. vent 16. 17. diversion 20. 22. urbane 26. event 28. 30. vent

Lesson XXV

EXERCISE C

1. improvise
2. deviate
3. volition
4. vigil
5. supervise
6. evident
7. invisible
8. devious
9. survival
10. visualizing
11. advocate
12. voluntary
13. victory
14. evolved
15. evict
16. vocation
17. revolve
18. evidence
19. surveillance
20. invincible

EXERCISE A

1. DE- down, from

2. VIA- way
3. EX- out
4. VID-, VIS- to see
5. IN- in, out
6. SUPER- over
7. VINDIC- to avenge
8. VIGIL- to watch
9. VINC-, VICT- to conquer
10. VIV- to live
11. AC-AD- wind
12. VOC- to call
13. VOL- wish
14. VOLV- to roll

EXERCISE D

Across

1. vinc or vict 2. evidence 5. invisible 7. survival 8. in, im, or il 9. vocation 10. super 11. supervise 14. voc 15. ex 16. advocate 17. vol 18. evolve 21. deviate 22. improvise 23. vigil 24. re 25. viv 26. revolve 27. de 28. voluntary

Down

1. victory 3. vid or vis 4. devious 5. invincible 6. volv 7. surveillance 9. visualize 12. evict 13. via 19. volition 20. evident

Lesson I

EXERCISE B

1. abduct — f. to carry off unlawfully
2. abhor — d. to detest
3. abrasion — c. the result of wearing away
4. abrupt — e. a sudden change in action or manner
5. absorb — b. to soak up
6. accord — g. an agreement
7. adaptable — j. able to adjust to new situations
8. adhere — h. to attach
9. adjacent — i. bordering
10. adversary — a. an opponent
11. ambidextrous — n. ability to use left and right hands equally
12. ambiguous — l. having more than one interpretation
13. ante meridian — r. before noon
14. anticipate — m. to expect
15. benediction — o. a blessing
16. benefactor — t. a person who offers financial support
17. bicuspid — p. a double pointed tooth
18. bilateral — q. having two sides
19. bilingual — k. the ability to speak two languages
20. bisect — s. to divide into two equal parts

Lesson II

EXERCISE B

1. circulate — e. to move continuously or freely
2. circumscribe — f. to restrict
3. circumstantial — d. incidental; dependent on circumstances
4. collaborate — h. to work together on a project
5. collision — j. a crash
6. commiserate — i. to sympathize with the sorrow of another
7. condone — g. to excuse or forgive; to overlook
8. contraband — c. illegally imported or smuggled goods
9. contradict — a. to say the opposite of
10. contrast — b. striking difference in comparison
11. decadence — o. the process of moral or cultural decline
12. dedicate — p. to devote a creative work to a person
13. demented — m. mentally ill; wild and irrational
14. demote — l. to lower in rank or grade
15. deter — k. to discourage or prevent from occurring
16. devour — n. to consume voraciously
17. distortion — q. the action of twisting something out of shape
18. distract — s. to draw attention away from
19. duet — t. a performance by two entertainers
20. duplicate — r. to make an exact copy
21. distinct — u. different from something else

Lesson III

EXERCISE B

1. equity — f. value of property after debts
2. equivalent — b. equal in all respects
3. emigrate — d. to leave one's country for another
4. eradicate — a. to get rid of entirely
5. evoke — c. to call forth
6. extrovert — e. an outgoing person
7. illuminate — h. to light up; to shed light on
8. implicate — g. to show to be involved in a crime
9. inclusive — i. including the limits specified
10. inscription — j. words written on a monument
11. illegible — m. difficult or impossible to read
12. illiterate — o. unable to read or write
13. incessant — n. continuing without interruption
14. irrelevant — p. off the subject
15. interjection — q. an exclamation
16. interlude — k. the time between two events
17. intersect — l. to cut across or through
18. intervene — s. to come between
19. intravenous — t. into vein(s)
20. introvert — r. a shy person

Lesson IV

EXERCISE B

1. magnificent — e. spectacular; exceptional
2. magnitude — f. scope or importance
3. major — b. a rank in the army
4. majority — d. more than half of a group
5. malicious — g. intending to do harm
6. multilateral — c. involving three or more parties
7. multitude — a. a great throng of people or things
8. obligation — h. a duty
9. obliterate — i. to utterly destroy
10. obsess — j. to think about constantly
11. omnivorous — n. feeding on both plants and animals
12. perforate — l. to make a hole in; to pierce
13. persevere — k. to remain devoted to a difficult task
14. perspective — m. a point of view
15. posterity — p. future generations
16. postpone — o. to put off to a later time
17. postscript — t. an added note at the end of a letter
18. preclude — s. to make impossible; to prevent
19. prediction — r. a claim about future events
20. presume — q. to make an assumption

Lesson V

EXERCISE B

1. primary — d. first in rank or importance
2. primate — a. humans, gorillas, and monkeys
3. proceed — e. to begin a course of action
4. procession — b. a parade
5. profit — c. to benefit financially
6. provoke — f. to deliberately annoy or anger
7. recite — i. to repeat by memory
8. recline — j. to lean back or lie down
9. reiterate — g. to say again
10. retrospect — h. a review of past events
11. seclude — n. to remove from social interaction; to isolate
12. secure — k. to protect against threats
13. supervise — m. to oversee
14. subscribe — p. to arrange to receive periodically
15. suffocate — o. to make unable to breathe
16. suggest — l. to put forward for consideration
17. translucent — r. allowing light to pass through partially
18. transparent — s. see-through
19. unanimous — t. completely in agreement
20. unity — q. oneness

Lesson VII

EXERCISE B

1. abbreviation — g. a shortened form of a word
2. army — m. an organized military force
3. artifact — a. a man-made object
4. artificial — t. unnatural
5. audible — i. able to be heard
6. audience — o. spectators
7. auditorium — c. a theater or hall
8. avuncular — q. kindly, like an uncle
9. battery — e. injury purposely inflicted on someone else
10. beatitude — k. supreme blessedness or happiness
11. brevity — d. the quality of being concise
12. casualty — n. a person or thing killed or injured, usually
13. candid — b. honest and frank
14. candidate — s. a job applicant or nominated official
15. capture — f. to take, seize
16. imbibe — l. to drink
17. incantation — j. a magic spell
18. participate — h. to take part in
19. rebellious — p. unmanageable
20. recalcitrant — r. obstinate

Lesson VI

EXERCISE B

1. acrid — g. pungent and bitter
2. acute — l. very perceptive
3. agility — b. nimbleness
4. agitate — n. to disturb
5. agriculture — h. farming
6. alias — o. a false label or name
7. alien — c. foreign
8. alienate — p. to estrange
9. alter — d. to change
10. altitude — e. height from the ground or sea level
11. amateur — q. a non-professional
12. amiable — t. friendly
13. ambulatory — k. able to walk; mobile
14. animate — f. to bring to life; to inspire
15. animosity — j. a strong hostility
16. annual — a. yearly
17. annuity — r. a yearly payment of money
18. aperture — m. an opening
19. aptitude — s. a natural ability
20. inept — i. incompetent

Lesson VIII

EXERCISE B

1. access — f. to approach or enter
2. accessory — j. a supplementary item
3. accelerate — p. to speed up
4. carnivorous — a. eating only meat
5. castigate — i. to reprimand severely
6. censor — b. someone who monitors and suppresses unacceptable
7. census — q. an official count of population
8. cerebral — l. of the brain; intellectual
9. centennial — c. one hundredth anniversary
10. century — m. a period of one hundred years
11. civil — d. relating to ordinary citizens (not military)
12. civilian — o. someone not in the military
13. civilization — e. an advanced system of human development
14. concise — s. expressed clearly and in few words
15. decapitate — n. to cut off the head
16. decelerate — r. to slow down
17. discernment — g. the ability to make fine distinctions
18. excite — t. to arouse; to awaken
19. incision — h. a surgical cut
20. incite — k. to stir up or cause to act

Lesson IX

EXERCISE B

1. acclaim — j. praise
2. accolade — n. a high honor
3. clarify — g. to separate out the impurities; to clear up
4. clarity — k. transparency
5. cloister — e. a covered walkway; to seclude in an abbey or monastery
6. closure — p. a feeling of resolution
7. cognition — h. the process of thinking
8. complement — l. to fit well with something else
9. comply — d. to meet specified standards
10. copious — r. abundant
11. cordial — c. warm and friendly
12. corpse — i. a dead body
13. credible — m. competent, but not outstanding
14. creed — b. articles of faith
15. decline — a. to decrease; to refuse
16. enclosure — t. something placed in an envelope with a letter
17. inclined — s. leaning toward (something)
18. incognito — f. anonymously
19. incorporate — o. to take in; to include
20. recluse — q. a hermit

Lesson XI

EXERCISE B

1. affinity — k. natural preference
2. confer — n. to consult with
3. configuration — f. an arrangement or pattern
4. deface — e. to disfigure
5. dormant — q. asleep or inactive
6. egocentric — d. self-centered
7. endorse — h. to publicly support
8. equal — p. having the same value
9. erratic — m. irregular
10. erroneous — b. incorrect
11. facade — s. an illusion
12. facsimile — g. a duplicate
13. falsify — c. to alter so as to mislead or make false
14. fervor — a. heightened passion
15. fertile — t. capable of supporting abundant life
16. fiction — i. prose literature that is not factual
17. fidelity — r. loyalty
18. figurative — l. using figures of speech
19. finite — j. having a limit
20. infallible — o. foolproof

Lesson X

EXERCISE B

1. accrue — e. to increase or add to over time
2. concur — j. to agree
3. crescendo — m. a steady increase in volume
4. cruciform — f. shaped like a cross
5. culpable — s. deserving blame
6. cupidity — p. an extreme desire for riches
7. curriculum — i. a course of study
8. data — k. information for analysis
9. dictator — q. an absolute ruler
10. diction — b. manner or clarity of speech
11. docile — o. submissive
12. domain — c. an area under control
13. domestic — g. a household servant
14. dominant — a. controlling; most powerful
15. incumbent — n. the current holder of a public office or post
16. indentation — h. the space set in from the margin of a document
17. mandate — l. to demand action
18. succumb — r. to yield; to give in to
19. trident — d. a three-pronged weapon
20. verdict — t. a jury's decision

Lesson XII

EXERCISE B

1. confirm — k. to acknowledge the truth of
2. confront — b. to face
3. diffuse — g. to spread over a wide area
4. deflect — l. to turn (something) aside
5. floral — m. consisting of or relating to flowers
6. fluid — c. a shapeless substance; a liquid or gas
7. fortunate — h. favored by good luck
8. forum — f. a place for discussion
9. fragment — a. a piece of a whole
10. fragile — o. easily breakable
11. fraternal — n. brotherly
12. fugitive — d. a person who flees from the law
13. fusion — s. a joining together
14. generate — e. to cause to exist
15. generous — j. freely giving
16. genre — t. a category
17. genuine — r. authentic
18. gorge — i. a steep valley; to eat greedily
19. inflection — p. the modulation of intonation in the voice
20. infirmary — q. a hospital within a larger institution

Lesson XIII

EXERCISE B

1. congratulation — h. acknowledgement and approval
2. congregation — m. a gathering of people; a religious flock
3. impel — b. to drive toward
4. gradual — g. taking place in stages over a period of time
5. graduate — l. to complete a diploma or degree
6. gratitude — n. thankfulness
7. ingredient — k. a component
8. inherent — p. permanent or essential (of a characteristic or attribute)
9. incense — d. to infuriate
10. inject — o. to force liquid into something
11. irate — c. extremely angry
12. itinerary — f. a planned route
13. jocular — r. humorous
14. junction — t. an intersection of two roads or rail lines
15. juncture — a. a critical point in time
16. prejudice — i. a preconceived idea or bias
17. progress — q. to move forward
18. projectile — s. a missile; something propelled with force
19. transit — j. the act of passing from one place to another
20. transition — e. the process of changing

Lesson XIV

EXERCISE B

1. collateral — k. something pledged as security for a loan
2. colloquial — d. familiar and conversational speech
3. delegate — j. to entrust to someone
4. delusion — p. an unrealistic idea or belief
5. deluge — q. to flood or inundate
6. eloquent — a. articulate and expressive
7. elusive — r. difficult to find or achieve
8. illuminate — e. to shed light on
9. laborious — i. requiring considerable time and effort
10. legitimate — n. conforming to the law
11. levity — f. lighthearted or humorous speech
12. league — s. a union of persons or countries
13. legacy — c. something bequeathed at death
14. liberal — l. having or giving freely
15. liberty — b. freedom
16. license — t. a permit or official permission
17. lingual — g. relating to the tongue
18. literal — m. straightforward; using the exact words
19. locality — h. an area or specific site
20. lucid — o. clear

Lesson XV

EXERCISE B

1. immersion — j. covering completely with liquid
2. manipulate — f. to cleverly control or influence, especially for one's own
3. mandatory — r. required
4. manufacture — m. to fabricate
5. maritime — l. relating to the sea
6. maternal — b. related through one's mother
7. matrimony — n. the rite of marriage
8. medieval — e. belonging to the Middle Ages
9. mediocre — i. of average quality
10. memorabilia — t. objects kept in association with memorable events
11. memory — d. the mental faculty of retaining information
12. mend — q. to restore to a sound condition
13. merge — h. to combine into a single entity
14. minimal — g. the least possible
15. minimize — o. to reduce to the least possible amount
16. missile — a. a projectile
17. moment — k. a very brief period of time
18. momentum — s. the impetus gained by a moving object
19. motion — c. the action or process of moving
20. promise — p. a binding statement of intent

Lesson XVI

EXERCISE B

1. annihilate — k. to destroy completely
2. announce — d. to make known publicly
3. commute — b. to travel a certain distance regularly
4. immortal — s. living forever
5. innovation — p. a new method, idea, or product
6. monitor — t. to observe over time
7. morality — e. a set of principles of conduct
8. mortify — m. to humiliate
9. mountain — h. a conical, natural elevation of the earth's s
10. muster — o. to gather together
11. mutate — f. to undergo a change or alteration
12. naval — g. relating to ships
13. native — j. original to a particular person or place
14. navigate — r. to travel on a desired course
15. negate — i. to invalidate
16. negative — n. a contradiction, denial, or refusal
17. nocturnal — a. active at night
18. nominal — q. symbolic or minimal; existing in name on
19. novelty — c. something new and/or unusual
20. novice — l. an inexperienced person

Lesson XVII

EXERCISE B

1. impeccable — j. faultless
2. oculist — n. one who treats eye diseases
3. odious — e. hateful; extremely unpleasant
4. olfactory — s. relating to the sense of smell
5. operate — b. to manage or function
6. orator — r. a proficient public speaker
7. orbit — c. the rotation of a smaller heavenly body around a larger one
8. ordain — k. to appoint officially
9. ornate — l. highly decorated
10. ostentatious — a. characterized by pretentious display
11. pacify — f. to make quiet; to bring peace
12. passionate — o. having or showing powerful emotions
13. patriotism — d. strong support for one's country
14. patron — i. a person who gives financial support
15. pecuniary — g. relating to money
16. pedal — h. a foot-operated lever or control
17. pedestrian — m. a person traveling by foot
18. pendent — p. a suspended ornament
19. propeller — t. a fan-like device that drives an aircraft or boat
20. repast — q. a meal

Lesson XIX

EXERCISE B

1. amputate — g. to cut off a limb or digit
2. arrogant — p. having an exaggerated sense of one's importance
3. compute — i. to determine by mathematics
4. derogatory — j. critical and disrespectful
5. interrogate — e. to question aggressively
6. interrogative — h. questioning
7. interrupt — m. to disturb; to halt something
8. oppress — o. to keep down unjustly
9. pungent — l. strong and unpleasant to the smell or taste
10. punish — c. to inflict a penalty for a wrong
11. rapture — r. intense joy
12. ratio — f. a quantitative relationship between two amounts
13. rational — b. sensible; logical
14. rationale — n. a logical basis for a belief or course of action
15. rectify — a. to put right
16. rector — d. the priest in charge of a church
17. regular — s. arranged in a consistent pattern; occurring at consistent intervals
18. ridicule — q. to mock
19. rotate — k. to move in a circle around an axis
20. rupture — u. to burst suddenly
21. deride — t. to speak of someone with scorn

Lesson XVIII

EXERCISE B

1. appetite — k. an instinctive physical desire, especially hunger
2. apprehend — i. to arrest for a crime; to perceive
3. depict — d. to show through an art form
4. imposter — h. someone using a false identity
5. impotent — n. helpless; powerless
6. opportune — q. especially convenient or appropriate
7. petition — b. a formal request
8. piety — j. reverence; devotion to God
9. pittance — e. a very small amount of money
10. placid — r. calm; peaceful
11. ponderous — a. weighty; heavy
12. pontiff — c. the Pope
13. portable — o. easily carried or moved
14. postpone — t. to put off until later
15. potable — s. drinkable
16. potential — p. capacity to develop for the future
17. potion — g. a liquid mixture with magical, healing, or poisonous properties
18. predatory — m. preying on others
19. proponent — f. an advocate
20. reprisal — l. an act of retaliation

Lesson XX

EXERCISE B

1. assail — j. to attack
2. assault — e. a physical attack or threat of harm
3. consensus — l. a general agreement
4. consecutive — q. successive; following immediately after
5. consequence — t. the result of an action
6. dissect — h. to analyze in minute detail
7. manuscript — b. a handwritten book, document, or piece of music
8. prescribe — d. to write a prescription; to advise
9. resent — n. to hold a grudge
10. sacrament — i. a religious ceremony invoking divine grace
11. sacred — m. religious; holy
12. saline — g. salty in nature
13. sanguine — a. cheerfully optimistic
14. satiate — r. to satisfy to the full
15. segment — f. to divide into separate pieces; a piece
16. senile — s. mentally feeble due to old age
17. sensory — k. relating to sensation or the physical senses
18. sequel — c. a follow up in a series
19. sequence — p. a particular order
20. session — o. a meeting

Lesson XXI

EXERCISE B

1. absolute — f. complete and total
2. aspersion — k. an attack on one's reputation
3. despicable — b. contemptible
4. dissolve — j. to disappear, deteriorate, or degenerate; to disperse in a liquid
5. disperse — i. to distribute or spread over a wide area
6. insomnia — m. inability to sleep
7. perspective — g. point of view
8. resolution — p. a firm decision
9. resolve — c. to settle; to decide
10. resonate — q. to reverberate with sound
11. simile — d. a figure of speech comparing one thing to another
12. simulate — o. to imitate an appearance or action
13. simultaneous — a. at the same time
14. solitude — n. the state of being alone
15. solo — r. done by one person alone
16. sonar — h. an echolocation system
17. spectacle — s. a fantastic visual display or exhibition
18. spectator — l. an audience member; a bystander
19. spectrum — t. a range
20. supersonic — e. faster than the speed of sound

Lesson XXIII

EXERCISE B

1. abundant — f. plentiful
2. context — j. frame of reference
3. contort — e. to twist
4. corrupt — m. dishonest; unethical
5. detract — i. to belittle
6. distort — n. to pull out of shape
7. extract — b. to pull out; to remove
8. extraterrestrial — o. alien; originating outside the earth and its atmosphere
9. intrude — k. to enter without permission
10. Mediterranean — a. characteristic of the Mediterranean Sea
11. pertain — p. to relate to
12. pertinent — d. relevant
13. redundant — q. unnecessary; repetitive
14. subterranean — t. below the earth's surface
15. terminate — g. to bring to an end
16. terrain — h. a stretch of land; surface characteristics of the land
17. totalitarian — l. autocratic
18. turbid — s. murky
19. ultimate — r. eventual; final
20. ultimatum — c. a final statement of terms

Lesson XXII

EXERCISE B

1. aspire — g. to hope to accomplish
2. conspiracy — k. a secret plot involving more than one person
3. constant — m. unchanging
4. constellation — f. a group of stars
5. constrict — o. to make narrower
6. construct — e. to build; to erect
7. contemporary — p. modern
8. instruct — l. to teach
9. obstruct — j. to block
10. presume — b. to suppose
11. respiratory — q. affecting breathing or respiration
12. spiritual — c. nonmaterial; religious
13. stellar — a. involving the stars
14. suave — r. charming and elegant
15. tangent — h. a line that touches a curve at one point
16. tangible — d. touchable
17. temper — s. a fit of rage
18. temperament — n. disposition
19. temporal — i. secular; material

Lesson XXIV

EXERCISE B

1. advent — h. arrival
2. adversity — n. misfortune; difficulty
3. controversy — d. prolonged or widespread disagreement
4. diversion — r. a distraction; a detour
5. evacuate — e. to remove; to clear out
6. evasive — a. vague or elusive
7. event — m. an occurrence; a competition
8. invasion — j. an influx
9. prevail — b. to win
10. urban — p. of a city
11. urbane — c. polite and sophisticated
12. vacant — f. empty; blank
13. vent — q. a duct allowing the passage of air or fu[me]
14. verify — k. to confirm the truth of
15. verity — s. truth
16. verbal — l. oral
17. verbose — g. wordy
18. vindicate — o. to acquit; to absolve
19. vindictive — i. vengeful

XXV

EXERCISE B

1. advocate — d. a supporter or promoter
2. deviate — j. to diverge from
3. devious — m. sneaky; not straight
4. evict — c. to oust
5. evidence — s. facts or items of proof
6. evident — b. obvious
7. evolve — l. to develop slowly
8. improvise — f. to ad lib
9. invincible — g. invulnerable
10. invisible — i. unable to be seen
11. revolve — p. to rotate around a center
12. supervise — n. to oversee
13. surveillance — r. observation
14. survival — h. the continued existence of (someone or something)
15. victory — t. success
16. vigil — k. a night watch
17. visualize — q. to envisage; to imagine
18. vocation — a. an occupation; a calling
19. volition — e. free will
20. voluntary — o. optional

Quizzes

Quiz 1

1. anticipated
2. retrospect
3. condone
4. multitude
5. provoke
6. obliterate, eradicate
7. unity
8. postponed, imminent
9. demote
10. evoke
11. abhor
12. magnificent, secluded
13. emigrated, bilingual
14. interjections, irrelevant
15. intersection

Quiz 2

1. civilians
2. verdict
3. copious
4. artifacts
5. alienated, amiable
6. acute, corpses, acrid
7. recluse, incorporate
8. civilization
9. amateur, agility
10. annuity
11. aptitude
12. agitate, carnivorous
13. crescendo
14. incumbent
15. inept

Quiz 3

1. transition
2. irate
3. legacy
4. fragile, fortunate
5. fertile, defaced
6. fragment
7. lucid
8. genuine, levity
9. mandatory, immersion
10. progress, elusive
11. mediocre
12. dormant
13. congregation, incense
14. liberal

Quiz 4

1. mustered, mountain
2. annihilated
3. proponent
4. opportune
5. placid
6. potential, impeccable
7. amputate
8. oppress, punish
9. ridiculed
10. derogatory, interrupted
11. Sacraments, sacred
12. consecutive, sanguine
13. consensus
14. consequence, resented

Quiz 5

1. event, evacuate
2. controversy
3. evident
4. victory, invincible
5. vacant
6. abundant
7. pertain
8. context
9. stellar
10. constant
11. aspired, instruction
12. surveillance, devious, invisible
13. survival, evolved
14. dissolved, turbid
15. spectators, improvised

Index

abbreviation, 80
abduct, 7
abhor, 7
abrasion, 7
abrupt, 8
absolute, 242
absorb, 8
abundant, 269
accelerate, 91
access, 90
accessory, 91
acclaim, 101
accolade, 104
accord, 8
accrue, 112
acrid, 66
acute, 66
adaptable, 9
adhere, 9
adjacent, 9
advent, 278
adversary, 10
adversity, 280
affinity, 129
agility, 66
agitate, 67
agriculture, 67
alias, 67
alien, 68
alienate, 68
alter, 68
altitude, 69
amateur, 69
ambidextrous 10
ambiguous, 10
ambulatory, 70
amiable, 69
amputate, 219
animate, 70
animosity, 70
annihilate, 186
announce, 188
annual, 71

annuity, 71
ante meridian, 11
anticipate, 11
aperture, 71
appetite, 206
apprehend, 212
aptitude, 72
army, 77
arrogant, 222
artifact, 77
artificial, 77
aspersion, 245
aspire, 252
assail, 230
assault, 231
audible, 78
audience, 78
auditorium, 78
avuncular, 79
battery, 79
beatitude, 79
benediction, 11
benefactor, 12
bicuspid, 12
bilateral, 12
bilingual, 13
bisect, 13
brevity, 81
candid, 82
candidate, 82
capture, 83
carnivorous, 89
castigate, 89
casualty, 81
censor, 92
census, 92
centennial, 92
century, 93
cerebral, 90
circulate, 19
circumscribe, 19
circumstantial, 19
civil, 94

civilian, 95
civilization, 95
clarify, 101
clarity, 101
cloister, 102
closure, 102
cognition, 104
collaborate, 20
collateral, 159
collision, 20
colloquial, 164
commiserate, 20
commute, 184
complement, 105
comply, 105
compute, 219
concise, 93
concur, 114
condone, 21
confer, 128
configuration, 130
confirm, 136
confront, 139
congratulation(s) 148
congregation, 149
consecutive, 233
consensus, 235
consequence, 234
conspiracy, 252
constant, 253
constellation, 253
constrict, 254
construct, 254
contemporary, 257
context, 265
contort, 265
contraband, 21
contradict, 21
contrast, 22
controversy, 280
copious, 105
cordial, 106
corpse, 106
corrupt, 268
creditable, 112
creed, 107
crescendo, 112
cruciform, 112
culpable, 113

cupidity, 114
curriculum 114
data, 115
decadence, 22
decapitate, 89
decelerate, 91
decline, 103
dedicate, 22
deface, 126
deflect, 136
delegate, 160
deluge, 159
delusion, 165
demented, 23
demote, 23
depict, 206
deride, 222
derogatory, 223
despicable, 246
deter, 23
detract, 266
deviate, 287
devious, 287
devour, 24
dictator, 116
diction, 116
diffuse, 140
discernment, 90
disperse, 245
dissect, 233
dissolve, 243
distinct, 24
distort, 266
distortion, 24
distract, 25
diversion, 281
docile, 117
domain, 118
domestic, 117
dominant, 118
dormant, 124
duet, 25
duplicate, 25
egocentric, 124
eloquent, 163
elusive, 165
emigrate, 30
enclosure, 102
endorse, 124

equal, 125
equity, 30
equivalent, 30
eradicate, 31
erratic, 125
erroneous, 125
evacuate, 275
evasive, 276
event, 278
evidence, 287
evident, 288
evoke, 31
excite, 94
extract, 267
extraterrestrial, 264
extrovert, 31
façade, 127
facsimile, 126
falsify, 127

fertile, 128
fervor, 128
fiction,
fidelity, 129
figurative, 130
finite, 129
floral, 137
fluid, 137
fortunate, 138
forum, 138
fragment, 138
fraternal, 139
fugitive, 140
fusion, 140
generate, 141
generous, 141
genre, 142
genuine, 142
gorge, 141
gradual, 147
graduate, 147
gratitude, 148
illegible, 33
illiterate, 33
illuminate, 164
imbibe, 80
immersion, 174
immortal, 183
impeccable, 199
impel, 149

implicate, 32
imposter, 208
impotent, 210
improvise, 288
incantation, 82
incense, 150
incessant, 34
incision, 93
incite, 94
inclined, 103
inclusive, 32
incognito, 104
incorporate, 106
incumbent, 113
indentation, 115
inept, 72
infallible, 127
infirmary, 136
inflection, 137
ingredient, 147
inherent, 149
inject, 151
innovation, 187
inscription, 33
insomnia, 244
instruct, 255
interjection, 34
interlude, 35
interrogate, 223
interrogative, 223
interrupt, 224
intersect, 35
intervene, 35
intravenous, 36
introvert, 36
intrude, 267
invasion, 276
invisible, 288
irate, 150
irrelevant, 34
itinerary, 150
jocular, 152
junction, 153
juncture, 153
laborious, 159
league, 162
legacy, 160
legitimate, 160
levity, 161

liberal, 161
liberty, 161
license, 162
lingual, 162
literal, 163
locality, 163
lucid, 88
magnificent, 42
magnitude, 42
major, 42
majority, 43
malicious, 43
mandate, 115
mandatory, 171
manipulate, 171
manufacture, 171
manuscript, 232
maritime, 172
maternal, 172
matrimony, 172
medieval, 173
mediocre, 173
mediterranean, 264
memorabilia, 173
memory, 174
mend, 174
merge, 175
minimal, 175
minimize, 175
missile, 176
moment, 176
momentum, 177
monitor, 182
morality, 183
mortify, 183
motion, 177
mountain, 182
multilateral, 43
multitude, 44
muster, 182
mutate, 184
native, 184
naval, 185
negate, 185
negative, 186
nocturnal, 188
nominal, 186
novelty, 187
novice, 187

obligation, 25
obliterate, 44
obsess, 45
obstruct, 255
oculist, 194
odious, 194
olfactory, 194
omnivorous, 45
operate, 195
opportune, 210
oppress, 218
orator, 195
orbit, 195
ordain, 196
ornament, 196
ornate, 196
ostentatious, 197
pacify, 198
participate, 83
passionate, 197
patriotism, 198
patron, 198
pecuniary, 199
pedal, 200
pedestrian, 200
pendant, 200
perforate, 45
persevere, 45
perspective, 46
pertain, 263
pertinent, 263
petition, 206
piety, 207
pittance, 207
placid, 207
ponderous, 209
pontiff, 209
portable, 209
posterity, 46
postpone, 47
postscript, 47
potable, 211
potential, 210
potion, 211
preclude, 47
predatory, 211
prediction, 48
prejudice, 152
prescribe, 232

presume, 48
prevail, 277
primary, 54
primate, 54
proceed, 54
procession, 54
profit, 55
progress, 148
projectile, 152
promise, 176
propeller, 199
proponent, 208
provoke, 55
pungent, 218
punish, 218
rapture, 219
ratio, 220
rational, 220
rationale, 220
rebellious, 80
recalcitrant, 81
recite, 55
recline, 56
recluse, 103
rectify, 221
rector, 221
redundant, 269
regular, 221
reiterate, 56
repast, 197
reprisal, 212
resent, 236
resolution, 243
resolve, 243
resonate, 244
respiratory, 252
retrospect, 56
ridicule, 222
rotate, 224
rupture, 224
sacrament, 230
sacred, 230
saline, 231
sanguine, 231
satiate, 232
seclude, 57
secure, 57
segment, 233
senile, 235

sensory, 236
sequel, 234
sequence, 234
session, 235
simile, 241
simulate, 241
simultaneous, 241
solitude, 242
solo, 242
sonar, 244
spectacle, 246
spectator, 247
spectrum, 247
spiritual, 253
stellar, 254
suave, 255
subscribe, 57
subterranean, 264
succumb, 113
suffocate, 58
suggest, 58
supersonic, 245
supervise, 289
tangent, 256
tangible, 256
temper, 257
temperament, 257
temporal, 258
terminate, 263
terrain, 265
totalitarian, 266
transit, 151
transition, 151
translucent, 59
transparent, 59
trident, 116
turbid, 267
ultimate, 268
ultimatum, 268
unanimous, 59
unity, 60
urban, 275
urbane, 275
vacant, 276
vent, 278
verbal, 279
verbose, 280
verdict, 117
verify, 279

verity, 279
vindicate, 277

vindictive, 277

www.ingramcontent.com/pod-product-compliance
Lightning Source LLC
Chambersburg PA
CBHW081346230426
43667CB00017B/2742